Ruby on Rails™ For Dummies®

Cheat Sheet

Ruby Keywords

alias	defined?	__FILE__	not	then
and	do	for	or	true
BEGIN	else	if	redo	undef
begin	elsif	in	rescue	unless
break	END	__LINE__	retry	until
case	end	module	return	when
class	ensure	next	self	while
def	false	nil	super	yield

Rails Naming Conventions

When you create a new application (for example, an `album` project with a `photos` database table):

- Create a Rails project named **`album`**.
- Create databases named **`album_development`**, **`album_test`**, **`album_production`**.
- Generate a **`Photo`** model. (In the RadRails Generators view, select *model* in the drop-down list, and type **`Photo`** in the text field to the right of the drop-down list.)
    - Rails creates a class named **`Photo`** in a file named **`pho`**
    - Rails creates a migration file named **`001_create_p`** b.
- Create a database table named **`photos`**.
- Generate a **`Photo`** scaffold. (In the RadRails Generators *scaffold* in the drop-down list and type **`Photo`** in the text field to the right of the dr st.)
    - Rails creates a class named **`PhotosContro`** ile named **`photos_controller.rb`**.
- Visit **`http://localhost:300x/photos/`**.

When you work with a foreign key in a one-to-many relationship (for example, one photo with many comments):

- The `comments` table has a **`photo_id`** column.
- The `Comment` model contains the statement **`belongs_to :photo`**.
- The `Photo` model contains the statement **`has_many :comments`**.

When you work with a many-to-many relationship (for example, photos and tags):

- The `Photo` model contains the statement **`has_and_belongs_to_many :tags`**.
- The `Tag` model contains the statement **`has_and_belongs_to_many :photos`**.
- The **`photos_tags`** table (so named because `photos` comes before `tags` alphabetically) has no `id` column.

For Dummies: Bestselling Book Series for Beginners

Ruby on Rails™ For Dummies®

Cheat Sheet

Rails Validation Helpers

```
validates_acceptance_of
validates_associated
validates_confirmation_of
validates_each
validates_exclusion_of
validates_format_of
validates_inclusion_of
validates_length_of
validates_numericality_of
validates_presence_of
validates_size_of
validates_uniqueness_of
```

Some Useful Iterators and Methods

```
[1, 2, 3].each { }                          => [1, 2, 3]
[1, nil, nil, 2, 3, nil].compact { }        => [1, 2, 3]
[1, 2, 3].delete_if { |x| x >= 3 }          => [1, 2]
[1, 2, 3].collect { |x| x + 1 }             => [2, 3, 4]
[1, 2, 3].find_all { |x| x % 2 == 1 }       => [1, 3]
[1, 2, 3].reject { |x| x % 2 == 1 }         => [2]
[2, 5, 1, 0, 7].sort                        => [0, 1, 2, 5, 7]
[2, 5, 1, 0, 7].max                         => 7
[1, [2, 3]].flatten                         => [1, 2, 3]
[1, 2, 3].empty?                            => false
[].empty?                                   => true
[0, 5, 9].length                            => 3
[1, 2, 3].include?(2)                       => true
[1, 2, 3].include?(16)                      => false
[1, 2, 3].reverse                           => [3, 2, 1]
```


For more information about Wiley Publishing, call 1-800-762-2974.

Ruby on Rails™ FOR DUMMIES®

by Barry Burd

Wiley Publishing, Inc.

Ruby on Rails™ For Dummies®

Published by
Wiley Publishing, Inc.
111 River Street
Hoboken, NJ 07030-5774
www.wiley.com

Published by Wiley Publishing, Inc., Indianapolis, Indiana

Published simultaneously in Canada

For general information on our other products and services, please contact our Customer Care Department within the U.S. at 800-762-2974, outside the U.S. at 317-572-3993, or fax 317-572-4002.

For technical support, please visit www.wiley.com/techsupport.

Wiley also publishes its books in a variety of electronic formats. Some content that appears in print may not be available in electronic books.

Library of Congress Control Number: 2006936826

ISBN: 978-0-470-08120-4

10 9 8 7 6 5 4 3 2 1

1O/RZ/RS/QW/IN

About the Author

Dr. Barry Burd received an M.S. degree in Computer Science at Rutgers University and a Ph.D. in Mathematics at the University of Illinois. As a teaching assistant in Champaign-Urbana, Illinois, he was elected to the university-wide "List of Teachers Ranked as Excellent by Their Students" five times.

Since 1980, Dr. Burd has been a professor in the Department of Mathematics and Computer Science at Drew University in Madison, New Jersey. When he's not lecturing at Drew University, Dr. Burd leads training courses for professional programmers in business and industry. He has lectured at conferences in the United States, Europe, Australia, and Asia. He is the author of several articles and books, including *Java For Dummies,* 4th Edition, and *JSP: JavaServer Pages,* both from Wiley Publishing, Inc.

Dr. Burd lives in Madison, New Jersey, with his wife and two children. In his spare time, he enjoys being a workaholic.

Dedication

for
Harriet, Sam and Jennie,
Sam and Ruth,
Abram and Katie, Benjamin and Jennie

Author's Acknowledgments

Many thanks to Paul Levesque who worked so closely with me on this project, and thanks to Katie Feltman who headed up the project at Wiley. And to Andy Cummings who steers the *For Dummies* series, thanks. And, yes, thanks to copy editors Mary Lagu and Virginia Sanders. Also, thanks to Laura Lewin, agent at StudioB. Thanks, and thanks again to Jay Zimmerman and the speakers in the No Fluff, Just Stuff Symposium for opening my eyes to Ruby on Rails. And to Charles Nutter and Thomas Enebo, who bridge the gap between Ruby and Java, thanks. Of course, Matt Kent, Kyle Shank, and Marc Baumbach, thanks for the use of RadRails, both inside and outside of this book. I extend thanks to Stefan Reichert with his Wicked Shell. To Francis Hwang and the members of the Ruby-NYC group, I say thanks. Thanks indeed to Frank Greco and his New York Java Special Interest Group and to Mike Redlich and the gang at the Amateur Computer Group of New Jersey because without them I wouldn't know anything about object-relational mapping. Thanks. And special thanks to Sam and Jennie, and of course, to Harriet, thanks I say thanks I will Thanks.

Publisher's Acknowledgments

We're proud of this book; please send us your comments through our online registration form located at www.dummies.com/register/.

Some of the people who helped bring this book to market include the following:

Acquisitions, Editorial, and Media Development

Senior Project Editor: Paul Levesque

Acquisitions Editor: Katie Feltman

Copy Editors: Mary Lagu, Virginia Sanders

Technical Editor: Charles Nutter

Editorial Manager: Leah Cameron

Media Development Specialists: Angela Denny, Kate Jenkins, Steven Kudirka, Kit Malone

Media Development Coordinator: Laura Atkinson

Media Project Supervisor: Laura Moss

Media Development Manager: Laura VanWinkle

Editorial Assistant: Amanda Foxworth

Sr. Editorial Assistant: Cherie Case

Cartoons: Rich Tennant (www.the5thwave.com)

Composition Services

Project Coordinator: Erin Smith

Layout and Graphics: Claudia Bell, Lavonne Cook, Denny Hager, Barbara Moore, Barry Offringa, Laura Pence, Heather Ryan

Proofreaders: Cynthia Fields, Jessica Kramer, Techbooks

Indexer: Techbooks

Anniversary Logo Design: Richard Pacifico

Publishing and Editorial for Technology Dummies

Richard Swadley, Vice President and Executive Group Publisher

Andy Cummings, Vice President and Publisher

Mary Bednarek, Executive Acquisitions Director

Mary C. Corder, Editorial Director

Publishing for Consumer Dummies

Diane Graves Steele, Vice President and Publisher

Joyce Pepple, Acquisitions Director

Composition Services

Gerry Fahey, Vice President of Production Services

Debbie Stailey, Director of Composition Services

Contents at a Glance

Table of Contents

Introduction

"Ruby on Rails? What's that?" asks my uncle. "You write about this stuff for dummies? You mean those black and yellow books that everyone buys?"

"Yes, like the one I'm quoting you in," I say. "Please check your spelling as you speak."

"I will. But what's Ruby on Rails? Is it the 6:05 train to Poughkeepsie? Is it the name of an old vaudeville act? Is it a pop singer? A rock band? Is it a rare stone from India? Is it the codename of an informer in a political scandal?"

"No."

"Is it the name of an exotic cocktail? A species of bird? An animal act in a circus? A John D. MacDonald title?"

Finally, I interrupt. "Ruby on Rails is a computer thing."

"What kind of computer thing?" he asks.

"It's a framework for creating applications with Web interfaces to databases."

"Oh, yeah?" he says. "Your nephew from Brooklyn, he read *Getting Ahead in Politics For Dummies.* He loved the book. Did you write that one?"

How to Use This Book

As a computer book author, I strive not to be full of myself. I have no illusions that you plan on reading this book from cover to cover. I read sections and chapters out of order when I buy a computer book. Why would I expect you to approach my book any differently? And even if I read something in Chapter 2, who says I remember it when I read Chapter 11?

I write each section with these thoughts in mind. In the middle of Chapter 12, I might want you to remember some nugget of knowledge that I introduce in Chapter 4. If I use that nugget over and over again in Chapters 5, 7, 8, and 9, I don't remind you about it in Chapter 12. But for other nuggets — ones that you don't read about repeatedly in this book — I provide cross references.

So in general, my advice is

- Read what interests you; skip what doesn't interest you.
- If you already know something, don't bother reading about it.
- If you're curious, don't be afraid to skip ahead. You can always sneak a peek at an earlier chapter if you really need to do so.

Conventions Used in This Book

Almost every technical book starts with a little typeface legend, and *Ruby on Rails For Dummies* is no exception. What follows is a brief explanation of the typefaces used in this book:

- New terms are set in *italics*.
- If you need to type something that's mixed in with the regular text, the characters you type appear in bold. For example: "Type **MyNewProject** in the text field."
- You also see this `computerese` font. I use computerese for Ruby code, filenames, Web page addresses (URLs), on-screen messages, and other such things. Also, if something you need to type is really long, it appears in computerese font on its own line (or lines).
- You need to change certain things when you type them. Words that you need to replace with your own words are set in *`italicized computerese`*. For instance, I might ask you to type

  ```
  class Anyname
  ```

  which means that you type **class** and then some name that you make up on your own.

What You Don't Have to Read

Pick the first chapter or section that has material you don't already know and start reading there. Of course, you might hate making decisions as much as I do. If so, here are some guidelines that you can follow:

- If you already know what kind of an animal Ruby on Rails is and you know that you want to use Ruby on Rails, skip Chapter 1 and go straight to Chapter 2. Believe me, I won't mind.
- If you already have Ruby on Rails, a database, and a Ruby program editor installed on your computer, skip Chapter 2 and go to Chapter 3.
- If you've seen one of the many Ruby on Rails demos or worked through a Ruby on Rails tutorial, move quickly through Chapter 3.

However, don't completely ignore Chapter 3. Some of the wording I use in Chapter 3 might be helpful, even if you've already been through a Rails demo or two.

- If you're a computer programmer, you might have already used Eclipse (for Java or for some other programming language). In that case, plan a quick excursion through Chapter 4. This book's examples use the RadRails integrated development environment, and RadRails is based on Eclipse.
- If you've never written programs in Ruby, Perl, or Smalltalk, set aside some time to read Chapters 5 and 6.

  These chapters cover some Ruby concepts, but the chapters don't describe the entire Ruby language. In these chapters, I highlight Ruby concepts that appear frequently in Rails code. I also emphasize some unusual features of Ruby — features that you don't find in other language families (in Java and C++, for example).

If you want to skip the sidebars and the Technical Stuff icons, please do. But try not to skip too many of my jokes. (I tell my kids that I write jokes for a living. They don't believe me. But even so, I'd appreciate your help in perpetuating this myth.)

Foolish Assumptions

In this book, I make a few assumptions about you, the reader. If one of these assumptions is incorrect, you're probably okay. If all these assumptions are incorrect . . . well, buy the book anyway.

- **I assume that you have access to a computer.** Here's the good news: You can run the code in this book on almost any computer. The only computers that you can't use to run this code are ancient things that are more than six years old (give or take a few years).
- **I assume that you can navigate through your computer's common menus and dialog boxes.** You don't have to be a Windows, Linux, or Macintosh power user, but you should be able to start a program, find a file, put a file into a certain directory . . . that sort of thing.

  On those rare occasions when you need to drag and drop, cut and paste, or plug and play, I guide you carefully through the steps. But your computer might be configured in any of several billion ways, and my instructions might not quite fit your special situation. So, when you reach one of these platform-specific tasks, try following the steps in this book. If the steps don't quite fit, consult a book with instructions tailored to your system or visit one of this book's Web sites for helpful hints. The URLs are `www.burdbrain.com/RubyOnRails` and `www.dummies.com/go/RonR1e`.

- **I assume that you've written some computer programs.** I've tried to make the book interesting for experienced programmers, yet accessible to people with only a modest amount of programming experience. I don't assume that you've written programs in any particular language or that you've hacked from midnight until dawn on the latest UNIX system. I assume only that you can compose loops, `if` statements, and other such things. (Of course, if you have no computer programming experience, you can start with my *Beginning Programming with Java For Dummies* book. Remember, the more of my books that you buy, the less debt I'll have when my kids finish college.)

  If you've written lots of programs in Visual Basic, Java, or C++, you'll discover some interesting plot twists in Ruby. The developer of Ruby took the best ideas in other programming languages, streamlined them, combined them, and reorganized them into a flexible, powerful new programming language. Ruby has many new, thought-provoking features. As you find out about these features, many of them will seem very natural to you. One way or another, you'll feel good about using Ruby.

How This Book Is Organized

This book is divided into subsections, which are grouped into sections, which come together to make chapters, which are lumped finally into four parts. (When you write a book, you get to know your book's structure pretty well. After months of writing, you find yourself dreaming in sections and chapters when you go to bed at night.) The parts of the book are listed here.

Part I: Nuts and Bolts

This part is your executive briefing. It includes a chapter that answers the question "What is Ruby on Rails?" and a chapter with a complete set of instructions on installing and running the software. It also has a jump-start chapter and a chapter with details about the RadRails integrated development environment.

Part II: Creating Code

Chapters 5 through 7 cover Ruby and HTML. Some of the material in Part II might be familiar to you. If so, you can skip some sections or read this stuff quickly. But don't read too quickly. Ruby is a little different from some other programming languages, and you might stumble upon some exciting new ideas.

Part III: Real Rails

This third part cuts to the chase. Rails has three components — Action Controller, Action View, and Active Record. The controller controls things (of course), the view displays things, and Active Record maintains all the data. Chapters 8 through 13 cover these three components and describe some interesting applications along the way.

Part IV: The Part of Tens

The Part of Tens is a little Ruby on Rails candy store. In the Part of Tens, you can find lists — online resources, hints about Ruby, and other interesting goodies.

Icons Used in This Book

If you could watch me write this book, you'd see me sitting at my computer, talking to myself. I say each sentence in my head. Most of the sentences I mutter several times. When I have an extra thought, a side comment, or something that doesn't belong in the regular stream, I twist my head a little bit. That way, whoever's listening to me (usually nobody) knows that I'm off on a momentary tangent.

Of course, in print, you can't see me twisting my head. I need some other way of setting a side thought in a corner by itself. I do it with icons. When you see a Tip icon or a Remember icon, you know that I'm taking a quick detour.

Here's a list of icons that I use in this book.

A tip is an extra piece of information — something helpful that the other books may forget to tell you.

Everyone makes mistakes. Heaven knows that I've made a few in my time. Anyway, when I think people are especially prone to make a mistake, I mark it with a Warning icon.

Question: What's stronger than a Tip icon, but not as strong as a Warning?

Answer: A Remember icon.

Occasionally I run across a technical tidbit. The tidbit might help you understand what the people behind the scenes (the people who developed Ruby on Rails) were thinking. You don't have to read it, but you might find it useful. You might also find the tidbit helpful if you plan to read other (more geeky) books about Ruby on Rails.

This icon calls attention to useful material that you can find online.

Where to Go from Here

If you've gotten this far, you're ready to start reading about Ruby on Rails. Think of me (the author) as your guide, your host, your personal assistant. I do everything I can to keep things interesting and, most importantly, help you understand.

If you like what you read, send me a note. My e-mail address, which I created just for comments and questions about this book, is `RubyOnRails@BurdBrain.com`. And don't forget — for the latest updates, visit one of this book's support Web sites. The support sites' addresses are `www.burdbrain.com/RubyOnRails` and `www.dummies.com/go/RonR1e`.

Part I
Nuts and Bolts

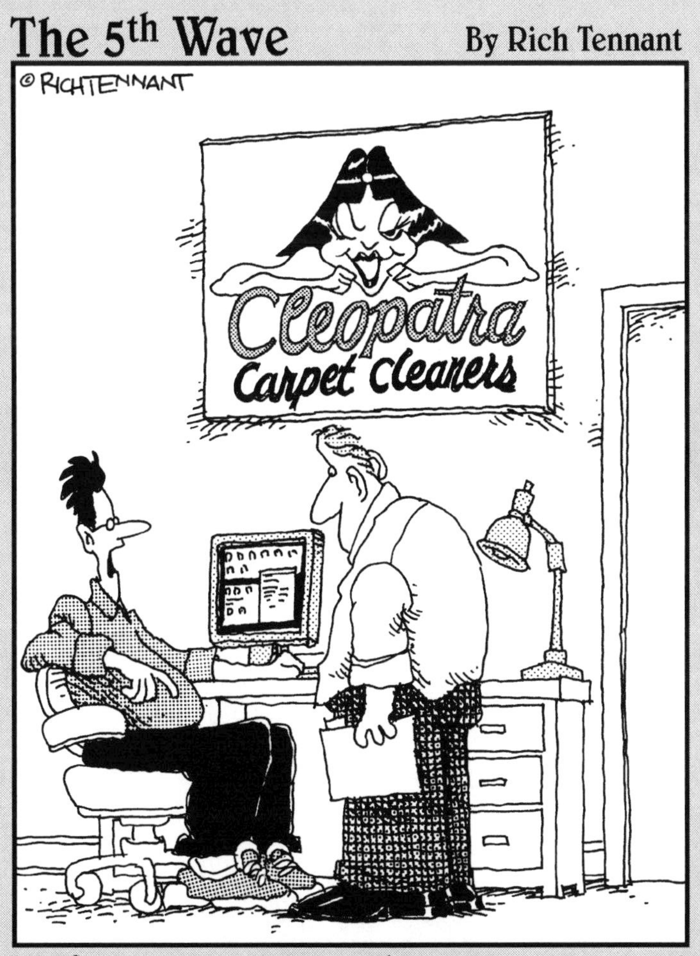

"So far our Web presence has been pretty good. We've gotten some orders, a few inquiries, and nine guys who want to date our logo."

In this part . . .

What's Ruby on Rails all about? And how do you install Ruby on Rails? And after installing it, how do you get started doing something with it? And what's really going on at Area 51 in Roswell, New Mexico?

This first part of the book answers the basic questions about Ruby on Rails. But "basic" doesn't mean "lame." For example, in Chapter 3, you create a complete Web application from scratch. You create the application in minutes, not hours. Then in Chapter 4, you find out what's at Area 51.

Chapter 1

Welcome to the World of Ruby on Rails

In This Chapter

- Understanding the need for agile software development
- Discovering Ruby's role in agile development
- Finding out how Rails fits in

Once upon a time, there were three little programmers. The programmers wrote code for the World Wide Web — code to give users access to a company's database.

The first programmer was in a hurry to write her code. She wrote simple code as quickly as she could. The second programmer wasn't quite in such a hurry. She used the traditional Waterfall methodology — a multistep process involving analysis, design, coding, testing, and deployment. The third programmer was careful and industrious. She used a heavyweight persistence framework such as Enterprise JavaBeans. She built her software to cover every possible contingency and to accommodate any future need.

As you might expect, this story has a big bad wolf. The wolf might have been a manager, a client paying for the software's creation, or a customer attempting to access the company's Web site. The wolf went in reverse order, visiting the careful and industrious programmer's Web site first.

Unfortunately, the wolf couldn't log onto the industrious programmer's site. Instead, he got the message: "This site is under construction." The careful, industrious programmer had completed only half of her work. The heavyweight persistence framework was difficult to learn and burdensome to use. Needless, to say, the wolf huffed and he puffed, and he blew the Web site down.

So the wolf visited the second programmer's Web site. The site was up and running, but certain aspects of the site didn't meet the wolf's needs. In following the Waterfall methodology, the second programmer had carefully planned every aspect of the project before beginning to write the code. But by the time the code was ready for testing, the project's requirements had shifted.

The second programmer was aware of her Web site's deficiencies. Through extended testing and use, she had learned that the original requirements were obsolete. But with all the code in place, the second programmer couldn't easily make major changes. All she could do was fix bugs and make the code run a bit faster. She promised that she'd update the requirements for version 2.0 of the system. But the wolf was impatient. He huffed and he puffed, and he blew the Web site down.

In desperation, the wolf visited the first programmer's Web site. She had built the site quickly and easily, using Ruby on Rails. In fact, her first prototype had been up and running in two days. Her co-workers had tested the prototype, critiqued the prototype's features, and told her what they expected in the next prototype.

The next prototype was ready sooner than anyone expected. Once again, co-workers tested the prototype, suggested improvements, and helped the programmer to refine her evolving requirements.

After several brief rounds of coding and testing, the Web site was ready for public use. The wolf enjoyed visiting the site because the site's look and feel reflected the way it had been designed. The site was nimble, intelligent, and easy to use. The site did the kinds of things the wolf wanted it to do because the programmer had gotten feedback on each prototype. Everyone was happy . . . for a while anyway.

To repay the Ruby on Rails programmer, the wolf offered to repair her house's leaking roof. Unfortunately, the wolf had a nasty accident. While he was working on the roof, he fell into the chimney and landed directly into a pot of boiling water. Goodbye, wolf!

But the Ruby on Rails programmer was happy. She had created a great Web site. And with all the time she'd saved using Ruby on Rails, she was able to climb up to the roof and repair the leak herself.

The end.

The Software Development Process

The world changes quickly. Ten years ago, when I taught programming to computer professionals, I wore a suit and a tie. Last month I taught the same course wearing a polo shirt and khakis.

This tendency for things to change goes way back. In the 1960s, programmers and managers noticed that commercial software tended to be very buggy. They analyzed large projects created by big businesses. They saw software development efforts going past deadline and over budget. They saw finished products that were terribly unreliable. Most computer code was difficult to test and impossible to maintain.

So they panicked.

They wrote books, magazine articles, and scholarly papers. They theorized. They devised principles, and they arrived at various conclusions.

After years of theorizing, they founded the discipline known as *software engineering*. The goal of software engineering is to discover practices that help people write good code. As disciplines go, software engineering is pretty good stuff. Software engineering encourages people to think about the way they create software. And when people think about the way they work, they tend to work better.

But in the 1970s, software engineering focused on methodologies. A *methodology* is a prescribed set of practices. Do this, then do that, and finally, do the other thing. When you're finished, you have a big software system. But do you have a useful software system?

In 1979, I worked briefly for a company in Milwaukee. On the day I arrived, the team manager pointed to the team's methodology books. The books consisted of two monstrous volumes. Together the volumes consumed about six inches of bookshelf. I remember the team manager's words as he pointed a second time to the books. "That's what we use around here. Those are the practices that we follow."

I spent several months working for that company. In all those months, no one ever mentioned the methodology books again. I would have cracked the books open out of curiosity. But unfortunately, excessive dust makes me sneeze. Had I found anyone on the team who knew the methodology, I probably would have learned how ponderous the methodology can be. No one wanted to wade through hundreds of pages of principles, rules, and flow diagrams. And if anyone did, they'd read about rigid systems — systems that encourage programmers to follow fixed procedures — systems that don't encourage programmers to listen, to adjust, or to change.

Agility

In 2001, a group of practitioners created the *Manifesto for Agile Software Development* (`www.agilemanifesto.org`). The Manifesto's signatories turned their backs on the methodologies of the past. Instead, they favored a nimble approach. Their principles put "individuals and interactions over processes and tools," and put "responding to change over following a plan." Best of all, they declared that "Simplicity — the art of maximizing the amount of work not done — is essential." According to these practitioners, the proof of the pudding is in the result. A process that doesn't end in a worthwhile result is a bad process, even if it's an orderly, well-established process.

The Agile Manifesto's signatories aren't opposed to the discipline of software engineering. On the contrary, they believe firmly in the science of software development. But they don't believe in unnecessary paperwork, required checklists, and mandatory diagrams. In other words, they don't like horse puckey.

Databases and the World Wide Web

By 2001, many businesses faced an enormous problem. Computers were no longer islands unto themselves. Customers visited Web sites, ordered goods, read headlines, updated records, posted comments, and downloaded songs. At one end was a Web browser; at the other end was a database. In between was lots of network plumbing. The problem was to move data from the browser to the database, and from the database to the browser. The movement must be efficient, reliable, and secure.

Imagine millions of people working on the same problem — moving data between a Web browser and a database. If everyone works independently, then millions of people duplicate each others' efforts. Instead of working independently, why not have people build on other people's work? Create a software framework for connecting Web browsers to databases. Provide hooks into the software so that people can customize the framework's behavior. An online order system uses the framework one way, and a social networking site uses the framework in its own, completely different way.

Throwing frameworks at the problem

By 2004, there wasn't just one framework for solving the Web/database problem. There were dozens of frameworks. New frameworks, with names such as Enterprise JavaBeans, Spring, Hibernate, and .NET, tackled pieces of the problem.

But most of the aforementioned frameworks had a serious deficiency. They didn't lend themselves to agile software development. Software created with one of these frameworks was fairly rigid. Planning was essential. Changes were costly.

What the world needed was a different framework — a framework for agile developers. The world needed a language that didn't put programmers in a box. The world needed software that could shift with a user's shifting needs. Let the major corporations use the older, heavyweight frameworks. An entrepreneurial company thrives with a more versatile framework. A small-to-medium-size company needs Ruby on Rails.

Along Comes Ruby on Rails

Think about your native language — the language you speak at home. Divide the language into two styles. You use one style when you speak to a close friend. ("Hi, buddy.") You use another, more formal style when you write to a potential employer ("Dear Sir or Madam . . .").

Talking to a close friend is an agile activity. You listen intently, but occasionally you interrupt. If your friend says something intriguing, you take time out to ask for more details. You don't try to impress your friend. You tune carefully to your friend's mood, and the friend tunes to your mood.

In contrast, writing a business cover letter is not an agile activity. You don't get feedback as you write the letter. You try to guess what the potential employer wants you to say, but you can never be sure. You use a formal writing style in case the employer is a stodgy old coot.

Now imagine using a formal style to speak to your friend. "If you have any questions about our next meeting at Kelly's Tavern, please don't hesitate to call me at the phone number on this napkin. I look forward to hearing from you soon. Yours truly, *et cetera, et cetera.*" Using formal language with your friend would slow the conversation to a crawl. You wouldn't pop your eyes open when you heard some juicy gossip. Instead, you'd plan each sentence carefully. You'd think about subject/verb agreement, hoping you didn't offend your friend with an awkward phrase or with some inappropriate slang.

Language isn't a neutral medium of expression. Language influences the nature of the message. A free-flowing style encourages free-flowing thought. In the same way, a flexible programming language complements an agile software development process.

Why Ruby?

Ruby is a computer programming language. You might be familiar with Basic, Java, C++, or some other programming language. In certain ways, all these languages are the same. They all provide ways for you to give instructions to a computer. "Move this value from that memory location to that other location on your hard drive." A computer language is a way of expressing instructions in a precise, unambiguous manner.

What makes Ruby different from so many other computer programming languages? In what way does Ruby support agile development?

Here's the answer: Ruby is a dynamically typed, interpreted, reflective, object-oriented language. That's a great answer, but what does it mean?

Ruby is dynamically typed

In many languages, you have to declare each variable's type. You write

```
int date;
date = 25092006;
```

The first line tells the computer that the `date` must store an integer — a whole number — a number without a decimal point — a number like `25092006`. Later in the same program, you might write

```
date = "September 25, 2006";
```

But the computer refuses to accept this new line of code. The computer flags this line with an error message. The value `"September 25, 2006"` isn't an integer. (In fact, "September 25, 2006" isn't a number.) And because of the `int date;` line, the non-Ruby program expects `date` to store an integer.

The word `int` stands for a type of value. In a *statically* typed language, a variable's type doesn't change.

In contrast, Ruby is *dynamically* typed. The following lines form a complete, valid Ruby program:

```
date = 25092006
date = "September 25, 2006"
```

(Yes, this program doesn't do anything useful, but it's a program nevertheless.)

Ruby's variables can change from being integers to being decimal values, and then to being strings or arrays. They change easily, without any complicated programming techniques. This flexibility makes Ruby a good language for agile software development.

Ruby is interpreted

Many commonly used programming languages are *compiled*. When the computer compiles a program, the computer translates the program into a very detailed set of instructions (a set more detailed than the set that the programmer originally writes).

So picture yourself developing code in a compiled language. First you write the code. Then you compile the code. Then you run the code. The code doesn't run exactly the way you want it to run, so you modify the code. Then you compile again. And then you run the code again. This cycle takes place hundreds of times a day. "Modify, compile, run." You get tired of saying it inside your head.

In contrast to the compiled languages, Ruby is *interpreted*. An interpreted language bypasses the compilation step. You write the code, and then you run the code. Of course you don't like the results. (That's a given.) So you modify and rerun the code. The whole cycle is much shorter. A piece of software (the Ruby *interpreter*) examines your code and executes that code without delay.

Which is better — compiled code or interpreted code? Believe it or not, the answer depends on your point of view. A computer executes compiled code faster than interpreted code. But as computer processing power becomes cheaper, the speed of execution is no longer such an important issue.

So step back from the processing speed issue and think about the speed of software development. With a compiled language, each modify-compile-run cycle is three steps long, compared with the two-step modify-run cycle in an interpreted language such as Ruby. But what's the big deal? How long can an extra compilation step possibly take?

The answer is that compilation can slow you down. Compilation can be time consuming, especially on a very large, complex project. Even a two-second compilation can be annoying if you perform the cycle several hundred times a day.

But aside from the time factor, the compilation step distances the programmer from the run of a program. Imagine writing a program in a compiled language, say in C++. The computer compiles your program to get a more detailed set of instructions. This detailed set of instructions isn't the same as your original program. It's a translation of your instructions. Instead of executing your program, the computer executes a translation.

Little to nothing gets lost in translation. But the fact that the computer doesn't run your original code makes a difference in the way you think about the development cycle. The immediate, hands-on feeling of an interpreted language gives an extra lift to the agile development mindset.

Ruby is reflective

A Ruby program can reflect upon its own code, like a philosopher reflecting on his or her own life. More specifically, a Ruby program can turn a string of characters into executable code and can do this somersault during the run of a program. Listing 1-1 contains an example:

Listing 1-1: Defining a Database Table

```
print "Enter some text: "
STDOUT.flush
text_input = gets
puts

print "You entered: "
print text_input
puts

print "Maybe you entered some Ruby code!\n"
print "I'll try to execute the text that you entered.\n"
print "The result of executing your text is "
eval text_input
```

Figures 1-1 and 1-2 show two different runs of the code in Listing 1-1. In each run the code prompts you to type some text. Ruby does two things with whatever text you type:

- Ruby echoes the text (displays the text a second time on the screen).
- Ruby interprets your text as Ruby code and executes the code if possible.

The second step (reinterpreting text as code) is difficult to do in other programming languages. Ruby makes it easy to reinterpret text as code, and this ease makes life better for computer programmers.

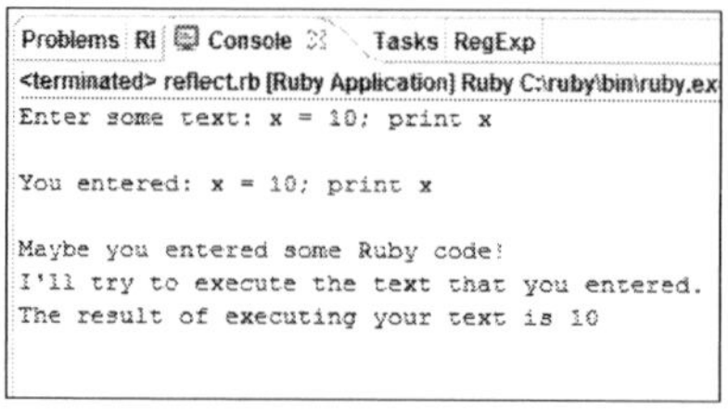

```
Problems  RI  Console  Tasks  RegExp
<terminated> reflect.rb [Ruby Application] Ruby C:\ruby\bin\ruby.ex
Enter some text: x = 10; print x

You entered: x = 10; print x

Maybe you entered some Ruby code!
I'll try to execute the text that you entered.
The result of executing your text is 10
```

Figure 1-1: A run of the code in Listing 1-1.

```
Problems  Ri  Console  Tasks  RegExp
<terminated> reflect.rb [Ruby Application] Ruby C:\ruby\bin\ruby.exe : reflect.rb
Enter some text: prod = 1; 5.times { |x| print prod *= x + 1, ' ' }

You entered: prod = 1; 5.times { |x| print prod *= x + 1, ' ' }

Maybe you entered some Ruby code!
I'll try to execute the text that you entered.
The result of executing your text is 1 2 6 24 120
```

Figure 1-2: Running the code with more complicated input.

Ruby is object-oriented

I describe object-oriented programming (OOP) in Chapter 6. So I don't want to spoil the fun in this chapter. But to give you a preview, object-oriented programming centers around nouns, not verbs. With object-oriented programming, you begin by defining nouns. Each *account* has a name and a balance. Each *customer* has a *name,* an *address,* and one or more *accounts.*

After describing the nouns, you start applying verbs. *Create* a new account for a particular customer. *Display* the account's balance. And so on.

Since the late 1980s, most commonly used programming languages have been object oriented. So I can't claim that Ruby is special this way. But Ruby's object-oriented style is more free-form than its equivalent in other languages. Again, for more details on object-oriented programming in Ruby, see Chapter 6.

Why Rails?

Rails is an add-on to the Ruby programming language. This add-on contains a library full of Ruby code, scripts for generating parts of applications, and a lot more.

The name *Ruby on Rails* is an inside joke. Since the year 2000, teams of Java programmers have been using a framework named *Struts.* The Struts framework addresses many of the problems described in this chapter — Web development, databases, and other such things. But the word *strut* means something in the construction industry. (A *strut* is a horizontal brace, and a sturdy one at that.) Well, a *rail* is also a kind of horizontal brace. And like *Ruby,* the word *Rail* begins with the letter *R.* Thus the name *Ruby on Rails.*

In spite of the name *Ruby on Rails,* you don't add Ruby on top of Rails. Rather, the Rails framework is an add-on to the Ruby programming language.

The following fact might not surprise you at all. What separates Rails from Struts and other frameworks is agility. Other frameworks used to solve the Web/database problem are heavy and rigid. Development in these other frameworks is slow and formal. In comparison, Rails is lightweight and nimble.

Author and practitioner Curt Hibbs claims that you can write a Rails application in one-tenth the time it takes to write the same application using a heavyweight framework. Many people challenge this claim, but the fact that Hibbs is willing to make the claim says something important about Rails.

Rails is built on two solid principles: convention over configuration, and Don't Repeat Yourself (DRY).

Convention over configuration

A Web application consists of many parts, and you can go crazy connecting all the parts. Take one small example. You have a variable named `picture` in a computer program, and you have a column named `image` in a database table. The computer program fetches data from the `image` table column and stores this data in the `picture` variable. Then the program performs some acrobatics with the `picture` variable's data. (For example, the program displays the picture's bits on a Web page.)

One way to deal with an application's parts is to pretend that names like `picture` and `image` bear little relation to one another. A programmer stitches together the application's parts using a *configuration file*. The configuration file encodes facts such as "variable `picture` reads data from column `image`," "variable `quotation` reads data from column `stock_value`," and "variable `comment_by_expert` reads data from column `quotation`." How confusing!

With dozens of names to encode at many levels of an application, programmers spend hours writing configuration files and specifying complex chains of names. In the end, errors creep into the system, and programmers spend more hours chasing bugs.

Rails shuns configuration in favor of naming conventions. In Rails, a variable named `image` matches automatically with a column of the same name in the database table. A variable named `Photo` matches automatically with a table named `photos`. And a variable named `Person` matches automatically with a table named `people`. (Yes, Rails understands plurals!)

In Rails, most configuration files are completely unnecessary. You can create configuration information if you want to break Ruby's naming conventions. But if you're lucky, you seldom find it necessary to break Ruby's naming conventions.

Don't Repeat Yourself (DRY)

Another important Rails principle is to avoid duplicating information. A traditional program contains code describing database tables. The code tells the rest of the program about the structure of the tables. Only after this descriptive code is in place can the rest of the program read data from the database.

But in some sense, the description of a database is redundant. A program can examine a database and automatically deduce the structure of the database's tables. Any descriptive code simply repeats the obvious. "Hey, everyone. There's a gorilla in the room. And there's an `image` column in the `photos` database table." So what else is new?

In computer programming, repetition is bad. For one thing, repetition of information can lead to errors. If the description of a database is inaccurate, the program containing the description doesn't work. (My HMO asks for my address on every claim form. But my address hasn't changed in the past ten years. Occasionally, the folks who process the claim forms copy my address incorrectly. They mail a reimbursement check to the wrong house. Then I make ten phone calls to straighten things out. That's a danger of having more than one copy of a certain piece of information.)

Aside from the risk of error, the duplication of information means more work for everyone. With traditional database programming, you must track every decision carefully. If you add a column to a database table, you must update the description of the database in the code. The updating can be time-consuming, and it discourages agility. Also, if each change to a database table requires you to dive into your code, you're less likely to make changes. If you avoid changes, you might not be responding to your customer's ever-changing needs.

Let's Get Going

You can read this chapter's lofty paragraphs until you develop a throbbing headache. But the meaning behind these paragraphs might be somewhat elusive. Do you feel different when you switch from C++ or Java to programming in Ruby? Does Rails really speed up the development cycle? Can you create an application in the time it takes to find a Starbucks in Manhattan? If you find these questions intriguing, please read on.

Chapter 2
Installing the Software

In This Chapter

- Installing the required software
- Testing that the software is installed properly
- Adding shortcuts to run the software quickly and easily

There was a young fellow named Nash
Whose software installing was rash.
He followed directions,
But skipped half the sections,
And caused his computer to crash.

Your system won't crash if you install Ruby on Rails incorrectly. The worst that can happen is that your Ruby program doesn't run. Well, worse than that, your Ruby program doesn't run, and you forget to send me an e-mail message asking me how to fix it. Remember, this author reads his e-mail!

Anyway, you don't have to read all the sections in this chapter. (In the limerick, I encourage you to read all the sections, but I do that only because "sections" rhymes with "directions." It makes a better limerick.) Instead, read enough directions to make sure you don't leave out any crucial steps. That means skimming for what you need to know, skipping descriptions of things you already know how to do, and backtracking occasionally when you stumble onto some unusual computer behavior.

Six Pieces of Software

I recommend that you install six different programs when you begin working with Ruby on Rails. You can get away with fewer programs or different programs, but the list of programs in this chapter includes the easiest, most convenient tools, which are

- The Ruby interpreter
- The Rails framework
- The Java runtime environment
- The RadRails integrated development environment
- The MySQL database system
- The MySQL Administrator program

All of these tools are free. (Yippee!)

Installing the Ruby Interpreter

To install Ruby on your computer, follow these steps:

1. **Visit `http://rubyforge.org/projects/rubyinstaller`.**

   The software that you download from `http://rubyforge.org/projects/rubyinstaller` runs only on Windows. If you're running Linux, try `http://rubyforge.org/projects/ruby` instead. If you're a Macintosh user, visit `http://hivelogic.com/articles/2005/12/01/ruby_rails_lighttpd_mysql_tiger`.

2. **Click the Download link.**

   Figure 2-1 shows the Download link as it appears in the summer of 2006. The name of the software is One-Click Installer. By the time you read this book, the Ruby people might have changed the Web page, and the link might look different. (For that matter, the steps for finding the Download link might be different.)

   If in doubt, do the things that you'd usually do to find a download link at a Web site. If all else fails and you can't find the link, check this book's Web page for up-to-date information.

   The Download link should lead you to a list of Ruby interpreters with version numbers like 1.8.4 and 1.8.5.

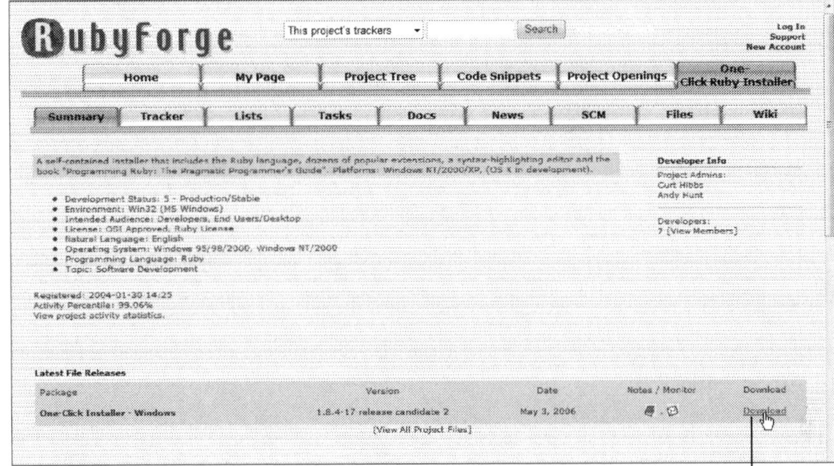

Figure 2-1: The link for downloading the Ruby interpreter.

3. **Find the highest-numbered version with the word *stable* in its description. Click this version's link to begin the download.**

   Your Web browser might ask whether you want to save or run the file.

4. **Click Run to run the installation file.**

   Alternatively, you can click Save to save the installation file on your hard drive. Then you can find the installation file's icon and double-click the icon to start running this file.

5. **Respond to any prompts during the installation.**

   You might see a dialog box asking whether you really want to install this potentially dangerous program. If you're downloading the program from `http://rubyforge.org`, the chance that the program contains a virus (or any other malicious code) is very, very small.

   At some point in the installation, you might also be given a list of components to install, including Ruby itself, something named SciTE, and other things. (See Figure 2-2.) The installation program permanently selects the Ruby check box. (That's good, because to work with Ruby on Rails, you need this Ruby software.) But make sure that you also select the RubyGems check box. Later in this chapter, you use the RubyGems component to help you install Rails.

6. **When the installation is complete, click Finish.**

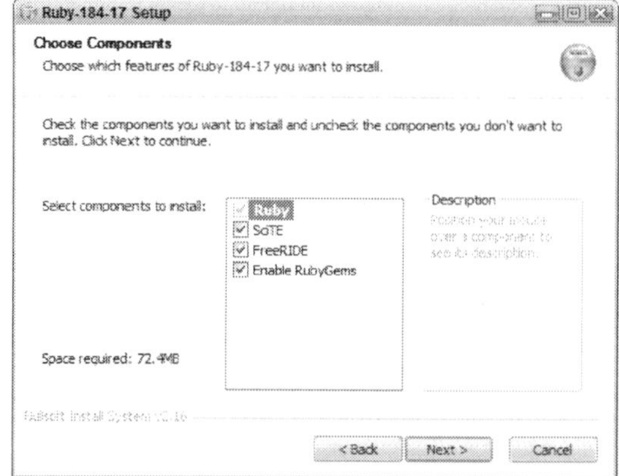

Figure 2-2: The installer offers you a choice of components.

Testing the Ruby installation

After installing the Ruby interpreter, you should test your new interpreter to make sure that it's installed properly. This section shows you how to perform a test.

Steps 1 and 2 apply only to computers running Microsoft Windows. If you use Linux or Mac OS X, visit this book's Web site for more specific instructions.

1. **If you run Windows XP, choose Start⇨Run. If you run Windows Vista, simply choose Start.**

   A small Run dialog appears.

2. **If you run Windows XP, type** cmd **in the Run dialog's text field. If you run Windows Vista, type** cmd **in the Start Search field. Then, in both cases, press Enter.**

   A white-on-black window appears. This is your computer's *command window.* The text `C:\WINDOWS\system32\cmd.exe` appears in the command window's title bar.

   A blinking cursor appears inside the command window.

3. **In the command window, type** irb **and then press Enter.**

   The letters *irb* stand for *interactive Ruby.* This `irb` command fires up a very easy-to-use interface to the Ruby programming system. (See Figure 2-3.)

   For now, you can ignore the cryptic prompt `irb(main):001:0>`.

Figure 2-3: The interactive Ruby interpreter (irb).

```
C:\Windows\system32\cmd.exe - irb
Microsoft Windows [Version 6.0.5384]
(C) Copyright 1985-2005 Microsoft Corp.

C:\Users\bburd>irb
irb(main):001:0> _
```

4. **Type** puts "Hello" **and then press Enter.**

   You've just told Ruby to display the word `Hello`. Ruby displays `Hello`, followed by some other junk. (See Figure 2-4.)

Figure 2-4: Ruby responds by displaying the word *Hello.*

```
C:\Windows\system32\cmd.exe - irb
Microsoft Windows [Version 6.0.5384]
(C) Copyright 1985-2005 Microsoft Corp.

C:\Users\bburd>irb
irb(main):001:0> puts "Hello"
Hello
=> nil
irb(main):002:0>
```

5. **Type** quit.

   Typing **quit** ends the execution of the irb interface.

Troubleshooting the Ruby installation

The instructions in this troubleshooting section are primarily for Windows users. If you're a Mac or Linux user, visit this book's Web site.

When you type `irb`, you might get a message saying that `'irb' is not recognized as an internal or external command`. If so, try the following:

- **Open a new command window (as in Steps 1 and 2). Then try typing** irb **again.**

  If this works, it's because the Ruby installation didn't reconfigure any command windows that you already had open. From this time onward, any command window that you open anew will properly interpret your `irb` request.

- **Type** dir c:\ruby\bin\irb* **in a command window.**

  In the computer's response, you should see `irb` and `irb.bat`. If you don't see these, you probably didn't install Ruby properly. Try installing Ruby again. (I know. It's a pain in the neck to install software twice. But what else can you do?)

  If the computer's response includes `irb` and `irb.bat`, the most likely cause of the `'irb' not recognized` error is that the Ruby installation failed to change your system's path. (See the next bullet for details about the system's path.)

- **Type** set path **in a newly opened command window.**

  Somewhere in the computer's wordy response, you should see something about `ruby\bin`. If you don't, type the following:

  ```
  c:\ruby\bin\irb
  ```

  Typing `c:\ruby\bin\irb` should start the Ruby interpreter. (You should see the kind of text shown earlier in Figure 2-3.) If typing `c:\ruby\bin\irb` works for you, you have three choices:

  - Get into the habit of typing `c:\ruby\bin\irb` (instead of plain old `irb`) whenever you want to run irb from a command window.
  - Find out how to permanently add `c:\ruby\bin` to your system's path.
  - Ignore the problem, because when you run the examples in this book, you don't use the command window very often.

Installing Rails

After installing Ruby, the installation of Rails goes fairly quickly.

1. **Make sure you have a working connection to the Internet.**

   Visit `www.burdbrain.com`, just to make sure!

2. **If you run Windows XP, choose Start⇨Run. If you run Windows Vista, simply choose Start.**

   A small Run dialog appears.

3. **If you run Windows XP, type** cmd **in the Run dialog's text field. If you run Windows Vista, type** cmd **in the Start Search field. Then, in both cases, press Enter.**

   The (by now familiar) white-on-black command window appears.

4. **In the command window, type the following line, and press Enter:**

   ```
   gem install rails -r -y
   ```

   With this command, you tell your computer to use *gem* — an installation-managing program for Ruby add-ons. In particular, you tell gem to install Rails (though the command is `rails`, lowercase). The `-r` part of the command tells gem to get the Rails program remotely (from the Internet, that is). The `-y` part of the command tells gem to install other programs — programs that your computer needs in order for Rails to work properly.

A typical gem session is shown in Figure 2-5.

Figure 2-5: Installing Rails.

The gem installer has all kinds of nice features. To find out about these features, open a command window and type **gem help**, **gem help commands**, or **gem help examples**.

Installing Java

Hey, wait a minute! Ruby is a computer programming language, and Java is a different computer programming language. What does Java have to do with Ruby?

Here's the story. When you create Ruby on Rails programs, it helps to work inside an *integrated development environment* (IDE). An IDE is like a text editor, but smarter. An IDE organizes your code into projects, runs your code with a few mouse clicks, and displays the code's output in a nice panel. In general, an IDE removes the programming grunt work and makes you more productive.

The best IDE for writing Ruby on Rails code is a program named RadRails, and RadRails is written partially in Java. So before you can use RadRails, you have to install Java. Fortunately, the people at Sun Microsystems have simplified the installation of Java.

1. **Visit `www.java.com`.**
2. **Find and click the Java download link.**

   I don't bother putting a screenshot of the link in this book. The Web page layout changes quite often. Sun Microsystems wants you to download Java, so they feature the download link very prominently near the top of the Web page.

   After you click the link, Java downloads and installs itself. You don't even leave your Web browser's window.
3. **As the installation proceeds, select all the defaults, including the ones that warn you about potentially malicious software.**

   When the dust settles, Java is installed on your computer.

Installing RadRails

RadRails is a cool program developed by Kyle Shank, Marc Baumbach, and Matt Kent. RadRails is built on top of Eclipse, another cool program (a program that most of the world uses as a Java IDE).

In my unending quest to make things easy for you, I've created my own editions of RadRails (for Windows, Linux, and Macintosh computers). The customized editions come with all the code from this book. The customized Windows edition also has a neat plug-in named Wicked Shell (created by Stefan Reichert). With Wicked Shell, you can jump seamlessly from Ruby development to the command window (introduced earlier in this chapter in the "Testing the Ruby installation" section).

To install my custom version of RadRails, do the following:

1. **Visit this book's Web site.**
2. **Look for the link to my version of RadRails (whichever link is appropriate for your computer's operating system).**
3. **Click the Download link.**

   In response, your computer probably asks you whether you want to save the file.

4. **Say "yes" to saving the file.**

   RadRails slithers down onto your computer's hard drive as one big Zip file. You have to extract the contents of this file to some handy place on your hard drive. Here's one way to do it:

5. **Double-click the downloaded Zip file.**

   When you double-click, you get to see what's inside the Zip file. This Zip file contains lots of stuff, but all that stuff is inside one folder — a folder named radrails.

   To find the radrails folder, you might have to double-click twice — once on a `radrails-0.6-win32.zip` icon and then a second time on a `radrails-0.6-win32` icon (without the `zip`). One way or another, you should work your way down to a folder whose name is plain old radrails.

6. **Right-click the radrails folder and then click Copy.**
7. **Open My Computer.**
8. **Right-click the C: drive and then click Paste.**

Steps 5 through 8 work with plain old Windows XP and Windows Vista systems. If your computer has a third-party Zip-file-handling program (WinZip, or some other such thing), the way you deal with the Zip file might differ from the steps described in this section.

Those pesky filename extensions

The filenames displayed in the Browse for Files or Folders dialog box can be misleading. You might browse your hard drive in Steps 3 and 4 and see the name `radrails`. Instead of just `radrails`, the file's full name is `radrails.exe`. You might even notice two `radrails` branches. What you don't see is that one branch's real name is `radrails`, and the other's real name is `radrails.exe`.

The ugly truth is that Windows and its dialog boxes can hide parts of filenames. This awful feature tends to confuse people. So, if you don't want to be confused, modify the Windows Hide Extensions feature. To do this, you have to open the Folder Options dialog box. Here's how:

- **In Windows XP with the control panel's default (category) view:** Choose Start⇨Control Panel⇨Appearance and Themes⇨Folder Options.
- **In Windows Vista with the control panel's default (category) view:** Choose Start⇨Control Panel⇨Appearance and Personalization⇨Folder Options.
- **In Windows XP or Windows Vista with the control panel's classic view:** Choose Start⇨Control Panel⇨Folder Options.

In the Folder Options dialog box, click the View tab. Then look for the Hide File Extensions for Known File Types option. Make sure that this check box is *not* selected.

After following this section's steps, you have a folder named radrails on your computer's hard drive. That's all you do to install RadRails on your computer. There's no setup program to run, no dreaded DLLs to install, no Windows registry settings to change — nothing like that.

Creating a RadRails shortcut on your desktop

This section applies only to computers running Microsoft Windows. If you use Linux or Mac OS X, visit this book's Web site for more specific instructions.

Having a RadRails shortcut on your desktop might be helpful. Here's how you can create one:

1. **Right-click any uninhabited space on your system's desktop.**

   A contextual menu appears.

2. **Choose New⇨Shortcut.**

   A Create Shortcut wizard appears. The wizard has a Browse button.

3. **Click the Browse button.**

   This step opens the familiar Browse for Files or Folders dialog box.

   In Windows Vista, the dialog box's title bar reads Browse for Files or Folders. But in Windows XP, the dialog box's title bar reads Browse For Folder. The Vista title is more accurate because, in this section's steps, you browse for a file, not for a folder. Despite the confusing title bar, this section's steps work in both Windows XP and Windows Vista.

4. **Browse to the inside of the directory in which you installed RadRails.**

   If you followed the previous section's steps to the letter, you can reach this directory by expanding My Computer, then expanding the C: drive branch within My Computer, and then expanding the subbranch of C: named `radrails`.

5. **Inside the `radrails` directory, select the branch named `radrails` (or `radrails.exe`).**

   If you find something named `radrails.exe`, you're in very good shape. If you don't see `radrails.exe`, the thing you want is simply labeled `radrails`. It's inside a folder of the same name (radrails). It's a leaf on the tree. It has a pretty icon — an icon that doesn't look like a folder. (The icon is either blue or red.) See Figure 2-6.

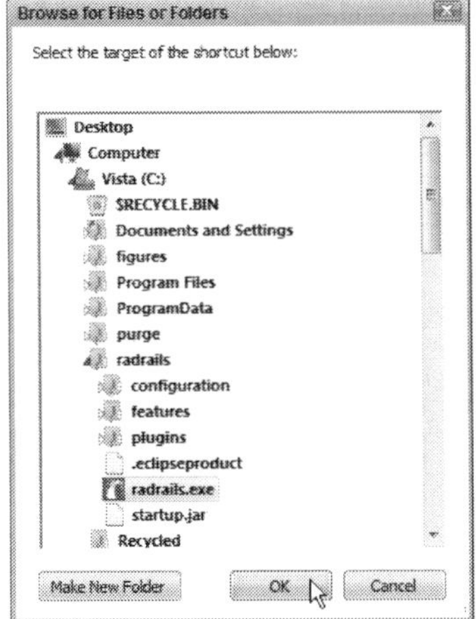

Figure 2-6: Finding the RadRails program.

After finding the correct `radrails` branch, you're almost finished creating a desktop shortcut.

6. **In the Browse For Files or Folders dialog box, click OK.**

   This step brings you back to the Create Shortcut Wizard.

7. **Click Next.**

   In response, the second page of the wizard appears. The second page asks if you want to change the name of the shortcut. You can accept the default name, change the name to kaploozamamma, or do whatever you want with the name.

8. **When you finish naming your newborn baby shortcut, click Finish.**

   The shortcut appears on your desktop. Now it's time to run RadRails.

Testing RadRails

It's time to take RadRails for a test drive. Here's how you do it:

1. **Double-click the desktop shortcut that you created in the preceding section.**

   RadRails starts running. The RadRails splash screen appears for an uncomfortably long time. (All Eclipse-based programs take longer than average to start running. Relax! It's worth the wait.)

Finally, a Workspace Launcher dialog box appears. (See Figure 2-7.)

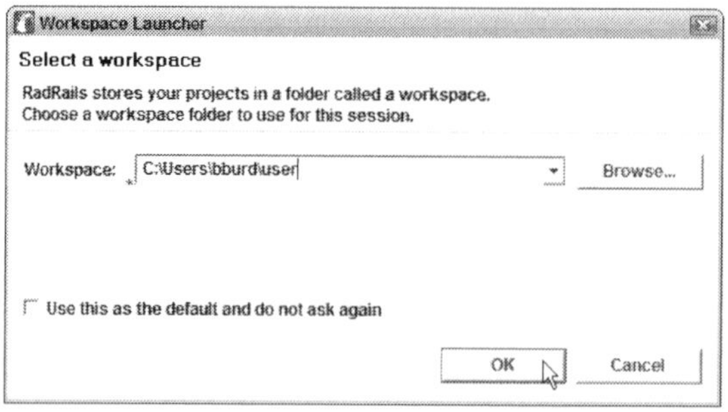

Workspace Launcher
Select a workspace
RadRails stores your projects in a folder called a workspace.
Choose a workspace folder to use for this session.
Workspace: C:\Users\bburd\user Browse...
Use this as the default and do not ask again
OK Cancel

Figure 2-7: The RadRails workspace launcher.

2. **Click OK to accept the default workspace folder.**

   . . . or don't click OK. Change the workspace folder and see if I care! The point is that the default workspace folder is fine, and any other place you choose on your hard drive is fine, too.

   After clicking OK, the RadRails workbench (shown in Figure 2-8) opens in full glory. When you see the workbench, you know that you've successfully installed RadRails.

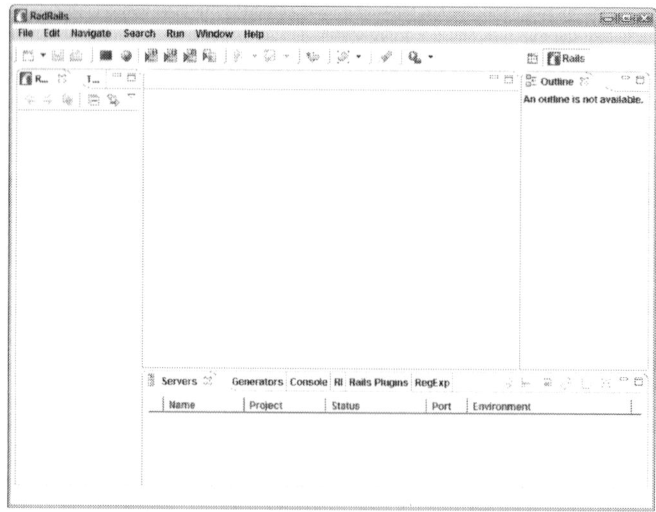

Figure 2-8: The RadRails workbench.

Troubleshooting the RadRails installation

If you follow the steps to install and test RadRails and you don't see the workbench in Figure 2-8, something's wrong. But don't panic! Most RadRails installation problems have one of four causes:

- **You might have downloaded and installed the wrong version of RadRails.**

  RadRails comes in three flavors — Windows, Macintosh, and Linux. If you run Windows, double-check your RadRails download to make sure that the filename contains the letters `win`. For a Macintosh installation, look for `mac` in the filename. And for Linux, check for `linux`.

- **You might not have installed Java properly.**

  If you see a message containing words like `No Java Virtual machine was found`, you might have skipped something in this chapter's "Installing Java" section. I recommend repeating the steps in that section, looking carefully at the instructions on the `www.java.com` Web site.

- **You might not have unzipped the RadRails download correctly.**

  Check to make sure that you have a folder named radrails. Then check within that folder for a file named `radrails` (or `radrails.exe`). Also within the radrails folder, check for subfolders named configuration, features, and plug-in. If you can't find these things, revisit Steps 5 to 8 at the start of this chapter's "Installing RadRails" section.

- **The file that you're trying to run might not be `radrails.exe`.**

  In the section entitled "Creating a RadRails shortcut on your desktop," Step 5 instructs you to look for something named `radrails` or `radrails.exe`. Between `radrails` and `radrails.exe`, you might have become confused. (The confusion isn't your fault. It's the Windows operating system's fault.) If you see `radrails` but not `radrails.exe`, follow the instructions in the sidebar entitled "Those pesky filename extensions." The steps in that sidebar should help clear up the problem.

Configuring RadRails

A section near the start of this chapter presents steps for installing a Ruby interpreter. And in this section, you install RadRails. The RadRails integrated development environment uses your installed Ruby interpreter. So before

RadRails can do its thing, you have to point RadRails to the Ruby interpreter. Here's what you do:

1. **Launch RadRails.**

   For details, see the section entitled "Testing RadRails."

2. **Choose Window⇨Preferences.**

   The Preferences dialog box appears.

3. **In the Preferences dialog box's navigation tree, expand the Ruby branch. Then, in the Ruby branch, select Installed Interpreters.**

   In response, RadRails displays a big Installed Interpreters panel. (See Figure 2-9.)

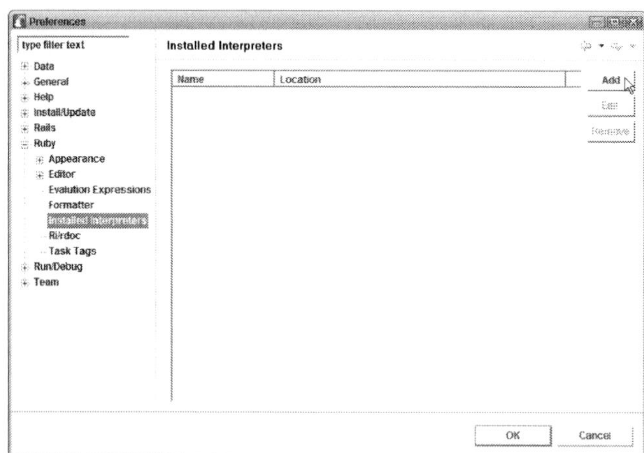

Figure 2-9: The Installed Interpreters panel.

4. **Click Add.**

   The Add Interpreter dialog box appears. (See Figure 2-10.)

Figure 2-10: The Add Interpreter dialog box.

5. **Make up any name and type it into the Interpreter Name field. Then click the Browse button to start filling in the Location field.**

   If you run Windows and you didn't change any defaults when you installed Ruby, you can browse to the `C:\ruby\bin` directory and select `ruby` (or `ruby.exe`). When you finish browsing, the Add Interpreter dialog box should look like the one in Figure 2-10.

6. **Click OK to close the Add Interpreter dialog box.**

   In response, the Preferences dialog box's Installed Interpreters panel comes to the fore. The panel displays your `C:\ruby\bin\ruby.exe` location. (See Figure 2-11.)

Figure 2-11: The Installed Interpreters panel has an interpreter in its list.

7. **Make sure that the new check box (the check box for the location `C:\ruby\bin\ruby.exe`) is selected.**

   Again, see Figure 2-11.

8. **In the Preferences dialog box's navigation tree, expand the Rails branch. Then, in the Rails branch, select Configuration.**

   In response, RadRails displays a Configuration panel. (See Figure 2-12.)

9. **Click the topmost Browse button to fill in the Rails Path field.**

   If you run Windows and you didn't change any defaults when you installed Ruby, you can browse to the `C:\ruby\bin` directory and select `rails`.

10. **Click the next Browse button to fill in the Rake Path field.**

    If you're lucky, you might find a `rake` entry in the `C:\ruby\bin` directory. If you're not lucky, you might have to browse for a `rake` entry in a directory named `C:\ruby\lib\ruby\gems\1.8\gems\rake-0.7.1\bin` (or something like that). In Figure 2-12, I'm not lucky.

11. **Click OK to close the Preferences dialog box.**

Figure 2-12: The Rails Configuration panel.

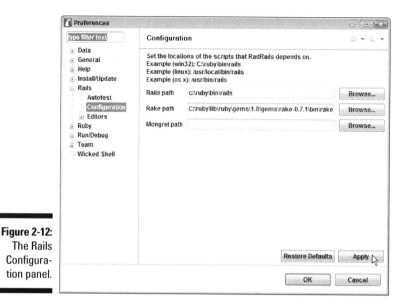

Congratulations! By following this section's instructions, you've effectively molded RadRails to suit your needs. RadRails is ready to work for you.

Installing MySQL

Rails is a framework for making Web pages communicate with databases. So to work with Rails, you need database software. If you already have database software, you can probably use that software with Rails. Rails talks to all kinds of databases, including Oracle, MySQL, DB2, Postgres, Firebird, SQLServer, and SQLite databases. In this book, I emphasize MySQL because Ruby on Rails and RadRails have built-in MySQL support. Besides, MySQL is free.

I haven't found any software to make Rails talk to a Microsoft Access database. But there are plenty of ways to convert an Access database to some other kind of database. My favorite trick is to launch Microsoft Access, open the database in question, and then choose File⇨Export. In the Save As Type drop-down list, I select Text Files and save the database with the `.csv` (comma separated value) extension. Almost every other kind of database, including MySQL, has facilities for importing files of type `.csv`. (There are usually several `.csv` options to choose from, so sometimes you have to experiment a bit before you import the data correctly. Be patient, and you'll figure it out.)

To install MySQL on your computer, follow these steps:

1. **Visit `http://dev.mysql.com/downloads/mysql`.**

2. **Find the link for downloading the Windows Essentials version of MySQL.**

   As the name suggests, Windows Essentials is all you need for running MySQL on Windows. This Windows Essentials bundle has none of the extra (possibly confusing) features that you get when you download the full Windows MySQL program.

   Once again, if you run Linux, a Mac OS, or some other non-Windows operating system, you need to follow a slightly different set of instructions. The `http://dev.mysql.com/downloads/mysql` page has downloads for many different operating environments, so scroll down the page to find the download that's right for your system. You might not see a download dubbed "Essentials," but you can certainly find a download for your computer's operating system.

3. **Click the Download link.**

   Proceed with the download as you would with most other programs. When the download is complete, you double-click the downloaded file to begin execution of the installation program.

   When the installation finishes, the program asks whether you want to begin configuring MySQL.

4. **Make sure that the Configure MySQL check box is selected. Then click Finish.**

   The MySQL Server Instance Configuration Wizard appears.

5. **Click Next over and over again to accept *most* of the defaults.**

   Notice the word *most* in this step. Strictly speaking, you can't just keep clicking Next and do nothing else. At one point in the configuring of MySQL, you're presented with the Modify Security Settings check box. (See Figure 2-13.) If you leave this check box selected (which is the default), you have to make up a username and password. You can't click Next until after you've typed these two things into their respective text fields.

Figure 2-13: The Security Settings page of the MySQL Server Instance Configuration Wizard.

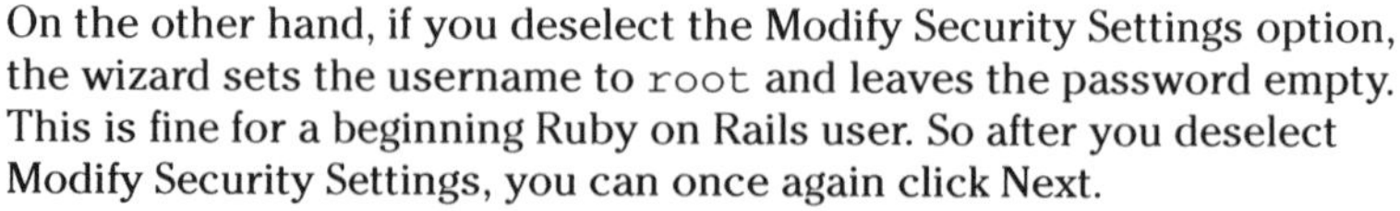

On the other hand, if you deselect the Modify Security Settings option, the wizard sets the username to `root` and leaves the password empty. This is fine for a beginning Ruby on Rails user. So after you deselect Modify Security Settings, you can once again click Next.

For a real-life application, your password should never be empty.

When you deselect the Modify Security Settings option, the wizard grays out the username and password fields, making it look as if there's no username and no password. Yes, there's no password, but the username is `root`.

At one point, the MySQL Server Instance Configuration Wizard offers you the option to Enable TCP/IP Networking. You should accept the default (enabling TCP/IP networking with port number 3306). On another of the wizard's pages, you should accept the Install As Windows Service default, with the Launch the MySQL Server Automatically check box selected. (A Windows service is like any other Windows program except that a Windows service runs constantly in the background, without muss or fuss.) Change these settings only if you have experience installing a database and you know how to deal with non-standard settings.

6. **On the last page of the configuration wizard, click Execute.**

   In response, MySQL configures your new database.

7. **Click Finish to execute the configuration wizard.**

Database terminology

People toss around the word *database* as if it's a Frisbee or one my out-of-print books. But at this early stage, when you're first installing MySQL, it helps to distinguish between terms like *database* and *database server.* Here are the terms you need to know, from the bottom upward:

A *table* is a collection of rows. For example, a table named `employees` may have 50 rows — a row for each employee in the company. A table also has several columns (also called *fields*). The `employees` table may have fields called `firstname`, `lastname`, `jobtitle`, `salary`, and so on.

A *database* is a collection of tables. For example, the `xyzcompany` database may have tables named `employees`, `customers`, `suppliers`, and so on.

With only a database and nothing else on your system, the database is useless. To read data from the database and write data to it, you need a special program called a *database server.* These servers typically come from big companies, such as Microsoft, Oracle, and IBM. Of course, some servers come from smaller, open source organizations such as MySQL.

The kind of server you have determines the kind of database that you use. That's because each server encodes and decodes data in its own way. The ones and zeros in an Oracle database are different from the ones and zeros in a Microsoft database, even if the information stored in the two databases (the employees' names, job titles, and salaries) is exactly the same. When Microsoft SQL Server stores part of an employee's name, it may store 01101010. But when IBM DB2 stores the same name, it may store 10010001. That's why, when you refer to a database, you usually specify the database's type — Microsoft SQL Server, DB2, or in most of this book's examples, MySQL.

So far you have a database — a bunch of information sitting passively on your computer — and a database server, which reads from and writes to the database. What else? Well, a company's accounting application needs to get salaries from the database, reduce each salary (except the CEO's) by 10 percent, and put the new updated information back into the database. This accounting application is called a *database client.* To interact with the database, this client software sends requests to the server software. In turn, the server fulfills the request (reads from the database or writes to the database) and sends results back to the client.

The whole business can take place on several different computers (with the client on one computer, the server on another, and the database itself on a third). Or, the way you're setting up the software in this chapter, the whole affair can take place on only one computer. Your computer houses the database and runs both the client and the server. Even so, the client must send explicit requests to the server. Same machine or not, the client and server are separate programs, each with its own specific role. (See the following figure.)

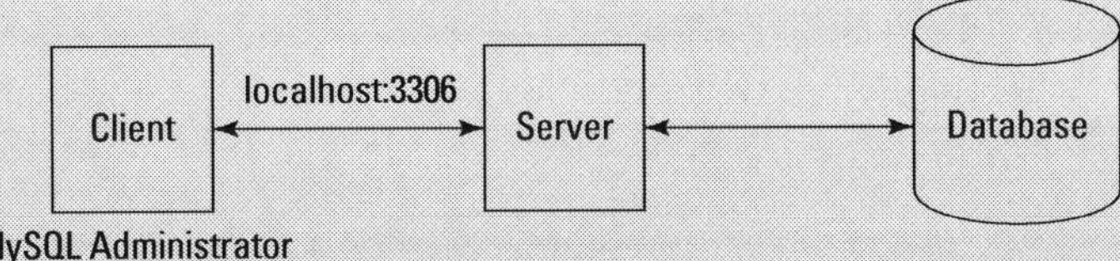

There's a tried and true way of sending requests and other messages from one program to another. It's called *TCP/IP* (Transmission Control Protocol/Internet Protocol). Besides connecting your computer to the Internet, TCP/IP can also connect your database client to your database server. When you communicate by using TCP/IP, you specify a bunch of things, including a *host name* and a *port number.* For instance, when you visit Google, your browser specifies the host `www.google.com` with port number 80. It's like tuning to channel 80 on your `www.google.com` TV.

When you run both the MySQL server and a client program on the same computer, the client sends requests to host name `localhost` and port number 3306. The word `localhost` means "the same computer as the client," but the port number 3306 is somewhat arbitrary. You can change this default number as long as you change the setting in both the server and the client's dialog boxes. (Of course, you should never reuse a number that's already in use by another program, like that magic number 80. If you're not sure about port numbers, you're best off sticking with the 3306 default.)

Finally, the term *database administrator* usually refers to a person — a highly paid techie at a large firm — who makes important decisions, attends lots of meetings, and is surrounded by swarms of underlings. But in this book, the term *MySQL Administrator* refers to a program — a special piece of client software. This MySQL Administrator program provides a user-friendly interface to the database server. You tell MySQL Administrator to perform setup tasks and maintenance tasks. In turn, MySQL Administrator sends requests to the database on your behalf.

Installing MySQL Administrator

Working within the Rails framework, you can do almost anything with a database. You can add tables, drop tables, add rows, modify values, and do all sorts of nice things. There's just one thing you can't do — create a database. To create a new database, you need MySQL's own administrative tools.

The easiest tool to use is named MySQL Administrator. Here's how you get it:

1. **Visit `http://dev.mysql.com/downloads/administrator`.**

   This is the main download page for the MySQL Administrator tool.
2. **Click the download link for your particular operating system.**

   Windows users: Click the link labeled Windows. No surprise there.
3. **Choose to save the download on your computer's hard drive.**
4. **When the download is complete, run the downloaded file in order to begin the installation.**
5. **Accept the license agreement, the defaults, and all that other stuff.**

   In response, the software installs MySQL Administrator on your computer.

Testing your MySQL installation

If you've followed the steps in the preceding two sections, you're ready to test MySQL. Here's what you do:

1. **Choose Start➪All Programs➪MySQL➪MySQL Administrator.**

   A preliminary dialog box opens. In the text fields, you tell the Administrator program how to connect to your MySQL database. (See Figure 2-14.)

Figure 2-14: The MySQL Administrator preliminary dialog box.

Once again, if you don't do Windows, you have to modify Step 1. See this book's Web site for hints.

2. **If you followed the steps in this chapter's "Installing MySQL" section, you can accept all the dialog box's defaults. Simply click OK. (Again, see Figure 2-14.)**

   The main MySQL Administrator window opens. (See Figure 2-15.) If you get this far, your MySQL installation is a success.

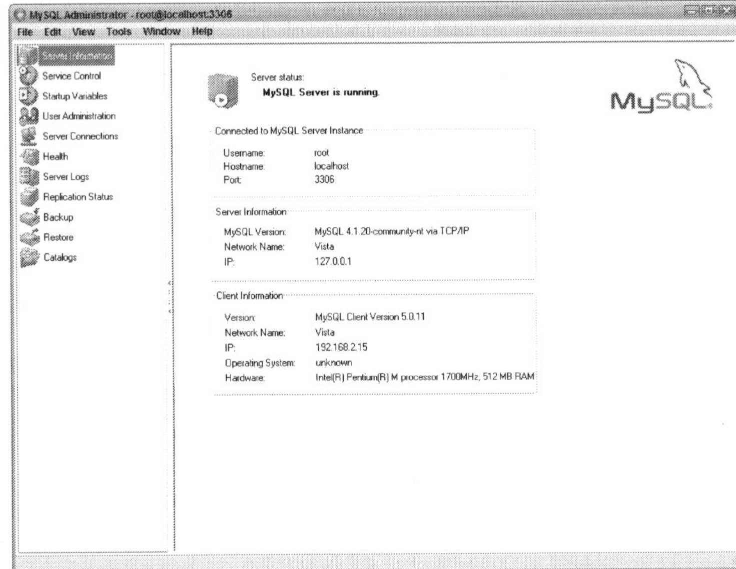

Figure 2-15: The main MySQL Administrator window.

If you don't see the window in Figure 2-15 (if you get a message saying `Could not connect to the specified instance` or some other frightening thing), you have to troubleshoot your database connection. Fortunately, troubleshooting the connection is the topic of the next section.

Troubleshooting your database connection

What do you do if you can't connect to your database? (That is, what do you do besides scream?) A number of things can keep you from connecting. This section has some troubleshooting tips.

This section's steps emphasize Microsoft Windows. If you're a Linux or Macintosh user, visit this book's Web site.

Advice for travelers

Several years ago, I was asked to give a talk on database connectivity in Dublin, Ireland. Normally, I'd get some funding from my employer and travel on a very low budget. But this time, I decided to bring along my family and some of my in-laws. My family members booked hotel rooms in several cities and planned for us to caravan from city to city for a week before my presentation.

Wouldn't you know it? When I arrived in Ireland, I turned on my notebook computer and found that I couldn't connect to my database. While my family members toured the city, I sat in the hotel room trying to get the database software working.

The next day, we drove from Waterford to Galway. I spent the day with my fist clenched nervously on the car's shift lever (which was on my left, not my right). When we arrived in Galway, I unpacked my computer and began working with the database. Much later that night, my family members (happy travelers that they were) returned to the hotel room. "Any luck?" they asked. "Not yet," I said. "But I think I'm getting closer."

On we marched, from day to day, from city to city. Each day I got what I called "closer." But each day I failed to connect to the database. The database was installed. The software for getting data from the database was installed. But the software couldn't communicate with the database. "Database connection failed," it said.

The morning of the conference, I got out of bed, thinking about nothing in particular. My mind wandered, and I asked myself, "Are blank spaces allowed in the database names?" I turned on my computer to check it out. Sure enough, when I removed the blank space, my database software connected instantly. When I gave the talk at the conference, everything went well.

You might think that the point of this story is "Don't try to connect to a database. It'll just make you miserable. Besides, you'll spend a lot of money on a vacation, and you'll miss seeing any of Ireland." Well, that's not the point of the story. The point is "Don't travel with your family and your in-laws."

Or maybe the point of the story is "Don't be discouraged. Connecting to a database can be tricky. Even more-experienced people run into some stumbling blocks." If you have trouble connecting, don't despair. Double-check the instructions, ask a friend, check the online discussion groups, try a different computer, or send me an e-mail. One way or another, you'll get things running.

Is the database server running?

To find out whether the database server is running, do the following:

1. **Choose Start➪All Programs➪MySQL➪MySQL Administrator.**

   The preliminary dialog box opens.

2. **While holding down Ctrl, click Skip.**

Holding down Ctrl turns the Cancel button into a Skip button! (Never in a million years would you discover this fact on your own. You have to read about it somewhere.)

When you press Skip, MySQL Administrator opens in *configure-service mode.* In configure-service mode, the Administrator program doesn't ask for settings (as it does in Step 1 of the "Testing your MySQL installation" section). Instead, the Administrator program searches your computer for any run of the MySQL server.

3. **In the upper-left panel of MySQL Administrator, select Service Control.**

   After selecting Service Control, you should see a `MySQL Service is running` message (like the message in Figure 2-16). Alternatively, you might see the `MySQL Service is stopped` message (which is easily fixed) or the `No Service selected` message (which isn't great, but also isn't the worst thing in the world).

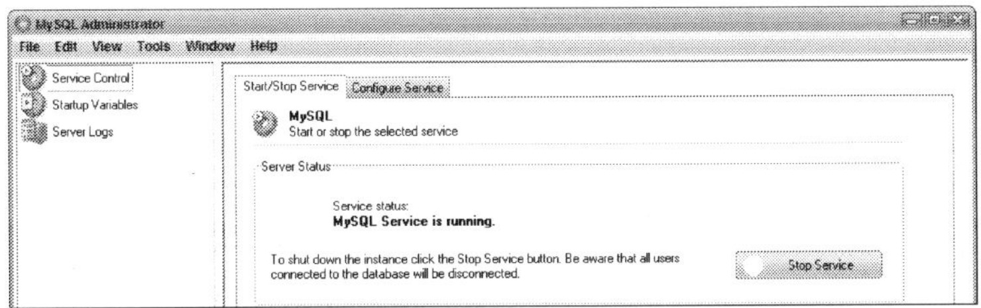

Figure 2-16: MySQL Administrator confirms that the server is running.

   - If you see `MySQL Service is stopped`, you should also see a Start Service button. Click the Start Service button, and then things should be okay. Repeat the steps in the "Testing your MySQL installation" section.
   - If you see `No Service selected`, you didn't successfully install MySQL as a Windows service.

     To fix the problem, choose Start➪All Programs➪MySQL➪MySQL Server➪MySQL Server Instance Config Wizard. In response, MySQL restarts the dialog box from Step 4 of the "Installing MySQL" section, earlier in this chapter. Repeat the steps in that section (from Step 5 onward) and then repeat the steps in the "Testing your MySQL installation" section.

Are the server and the administrator programs using the same settings?

Look again at Figure 2-14. The dialog box in Figure 2-14 tells the MySQL Administrator client how to talk to the MySQL server. In that dialog box, the item in each text field must match whatever value the server expects. (The client can't see the server if the client watches CNN while the server sings on MTV.)

In Figure 2-14, the MySQL Administrator client is being told to use port 3306 on the localhost computer (on the same computer that's running the MySQL Administrator client program). To log onto the database, MySQL Administrator tries username `root` with no password.

So to check for matching settings, you look at two things — the client settings and the server settings. First, check the client settings:

1. **Restart MySQL Administrator as you do in Step 1 of the "Testing your MySQL installation" section.**

   There are at least two ways to launch MySQL Administrator. The way you launch in this step isn't the same way you launch in the next set of steps!

2. **In the preliminary dialog box, verify that the values are the same as the values you see in Figure 2-14.**

   The values in Figure 2-14 are `localhost`, `3306`, `root`, and no password.

3. **If you see anything different, change it to `localhost`, `3306`, `root`, and no password. Then, click OK and see what happens.**

If that doesn't fix the problem, check the server settings:

1. **Restart MySQL Administrator in configure-service mode, as you do in Steps 1 and 2 of the section entitled "Is the database server running?"**

   The MySQL Administrator program starts immediately (without showing you a preliminary settings screen).

2. **In the left panel of MySQL Administrator, select Startup Variables.**

   After selecting Startup Variables, a bunch of tabs appear in the main body of the MySQL Administrator window.

3. **Select the General Parameters tab.**

4. **Make sure that Disable Networking is not selected and that the TCP Port is 3306. (See Figure 2-17.) If either of these items is incorrect, fix it.**

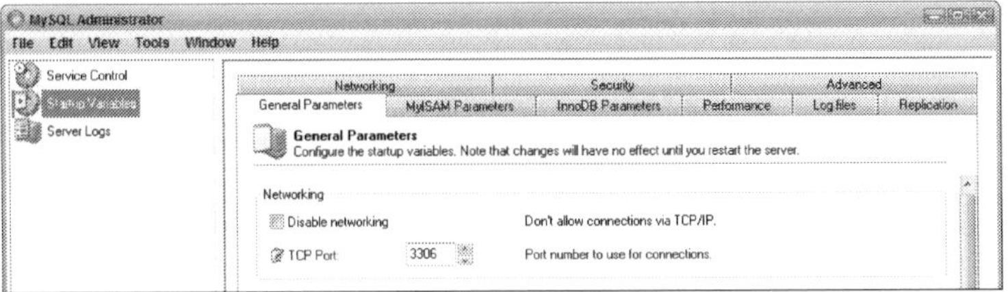

Figure 2-17: Checking the MySQL server settings.

You don't have to check the host name (`localhost`) or the username (`root`). So the only remaining item to check is the password. To be precise, you don't actually check the password. Instead, you set the password to its original default (to no password, that is).

To set the server's password, rerun the MySQL configuration wizard. Here's how:

5. **Choose Start⇨All Programs⇨MySQL⇨MySQL Server⇨MySQL Server Instance Config Wizard.**

   In response, MySQL restarts the dialog box from Step 4 of the "Installing MySQL" section.

6. **Repeat the steps in the "Installing MySQL" section (from Step 5, onward) making sure to deselect Modify Security Settings when that check box appears.**

That should fix the problem. Repeat the steps in the "Testing your MySQL installation" section. I think you'll be pleasantly surprised.

If all else fails, I suggest uninstalling MySQL, deleting the directory that once contained MySQL, and then reinstalling MySQL. Remember, installing software is fun. (Okay, it's not always fun. But sometimes, it's necessary.)

Chapter 3

Details on Rails

In This Chapter

- Creating a new database
- Creating a Web interface to a database
- Using the Web interface to create, list, and modify database entries

June 21, 2006, 12:06 p.m. EST* — Ruby on Rails For Dummies — *Author's note to self: *Every technical book begins with a quick-start chapter — a chapter that quickly guides the reader through a simple but powerful example. The chapter's purpose is to show the reader how, with little effort, a person can easily create an interesting, useful application. Why not do something different in* Ruby on Rails For Dummies*? Consider not including a quick-start chapter. Instead, dive right into the detailed material in Chapter 3.*

June 21, 2006, 12:33 p.m. EST* — Ruby on Rails For Dummies — *Author's note to self: *Made a brief effort to avoid having a quick-start chapter and to dive right into the details. It was painful to write and would have been impossible to comprehend. I'm returning to Plan A. Chapter 3 will be a quick-start chapter. Chapter 3 will show the reader how, with little effort, a person can easily create an interesting, useful Ruby on Rails application.*

To be perfectly frank, I feel guilty writing this chapter. It's not that I don't like quick-start chapters. I love quick-start chapters. For many books, the quick start is the only part that I read. (This applies mostly to technical books, but in some cases it applies to general non-fiction, fiction, books about politics for which I already have an opinion, owner's manuals, mortgage contracts, students' term papers, and on occasion, a single sentence that someone says to me.)

The problem with this quick-start chapter is that Ruby on Rails makes a quick start too easy. There's no sport in writing a quick-start example. With a little practice, you can put up a Web interface to a database in just a few minutes. What could be quicker than that?

Creating a Database

In this section, you create an employee database using MySQL Administrator. (For info about installing MySQL Administrator, see Chapter 2.)

1. **Choose Start➪All Programs➪MySQL➪MySQL Administrator.**

   The MySQL Administrator program displays its preliminary dialog box. (See Figure 3-1.)

Figure 3-1: The preliminary MySQL Administrator dialog box.

2. **In the preliminary dialog box, click OK to accept the defaults.**

   As in Figure 3-1, the defaults are `localhost` for the server host, `3306` for the port, and `root` as the username. The Password field is empty.

   After you click OK, the main MySQL Administrator window opens. The window is divided into two panes — a narrow pane on the left and a wider pane to the right. The pane on the left contains a list. The wider pane contains information about the MySQL server.

3. **In the list pane (on the left) click Catalogs.**

   A list of catalogs appears. At first, this list includes only two catalogs — `mysql` and `test`. (See Figure 3-2.)

MySQL Administrator displays the words *database, catalog,* and *schema.* What's the difference? At this point in the process, there's no difference at all. A schema is the structure underlying a particular database. But who cares? When you click Catalogs, you see a list of databases. And the title of the list of databases is "Schemata." No, the word *schemata* isn't the name of some strange curse from a cheap horror movie. *Schemata* is the plural of *schema.* So if you want to sound cool, you say *schemata,* not *schemas.* I don't want to sound cool, so I say *database.*

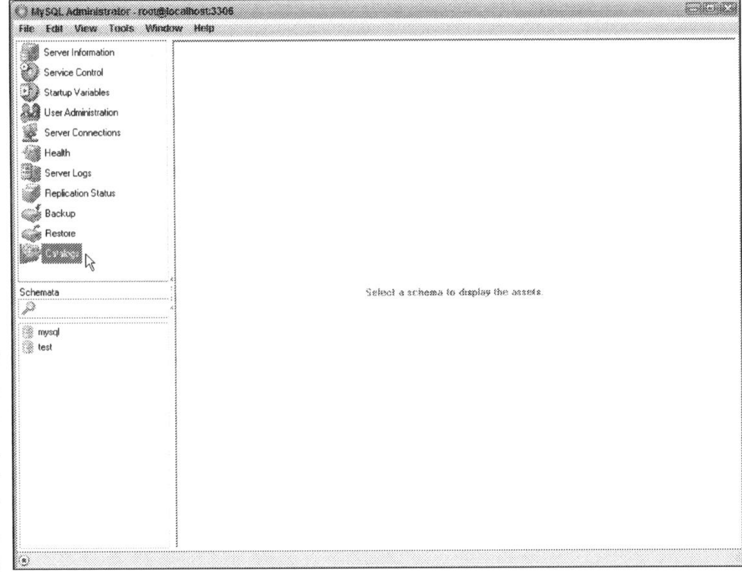

Figure 3-2: The main MySQL Administrator window.

4. **Right-click anywhere inside the list of catalogs (databases). Then, in the resulting contextual menu, select Create New Schema.**

   In response to your selection, the Create New Schema dialog box appears. (See Figure 3-3.)

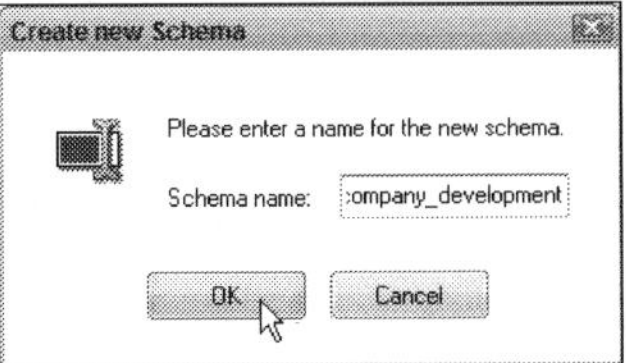

Figure 3-3: The Create New Schema dialog box.

5. **In the Schema Name field, type** company_development. **Then click OK.**

   In the list of catalogs, a brand-new `company_development` entry appears. (See Figure 3-4.)

   This step creates a database named `company_development`. The `company` part describes the information that you intend to store in the database. The `development` part indicates that this is a sample database to use while you develop a new application.

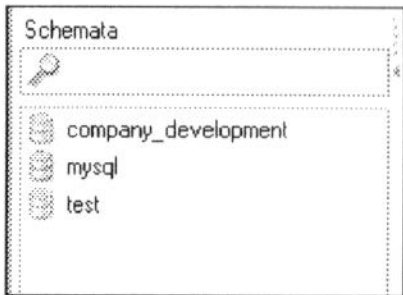

Figure 3-4: Look! A company_ development database!

The alternatives to `development` are `test` and `production`. You use a `company_test` database to test the code after you've developed it. Eventually, you use the `company_production` database to process the company's real-life data.

Put an underscore (_) between the words `company` and `development`.

6. **Close MySQL Administrator. (Choose File➪Close.)**

   You can leave MySQL Administrator open if you want, but you won't use it for the remainder of this chapter.

Creating a New Ruby on Rails Project

RadRails is an integrated development environment for Ruby on Rails. (See Chapter 2.) Like most other integrated development environments, RadRails separates your code into *projects*. A typical project contains all the code related to one application. (That explains the word *project* clearly. Now what does *one application* mean?)

In this chapter, you create a project named `company` — a project whose code processes information about a particular company. In another project, you might house a much simpler application. For example, you might store the code and images required to run a simple computer game. One way or another, each project tends to be a complete, self-contained entity. (Of course, in this complex computing world, nothing is ever really self-contained. So please take my description of the word *project* with a grain of salt.)

1. **Double-click the RadRails shortcut icon on your desktop to launch RadRails.**

   The RadRails workbench appears on-screen.

   If you haven't yet created a desktop shortcut for RadRails or (Heaven forbid) you haven't yet installed the RadRails software, flip back to Chapter 2.

The RadRails workbench is divided into four parts. The leftmost part displays the Rails Navigator view. You recognize the Rails Navigator view by the label on the tab near the top of Figure 3-5.

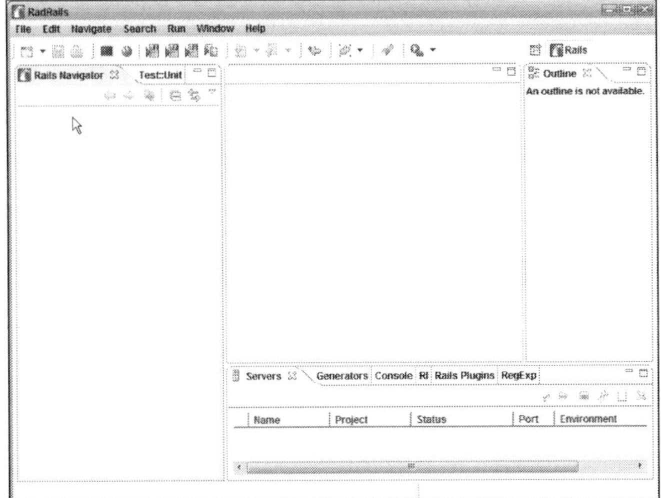

Figure 3-5: The RadRails workbench.

2. **Right-click inside the Rails Navigator view. In the resulting contextual menu, choose New➪Project.**

   The New Project dialog box appears. (See Figure 3-6.)

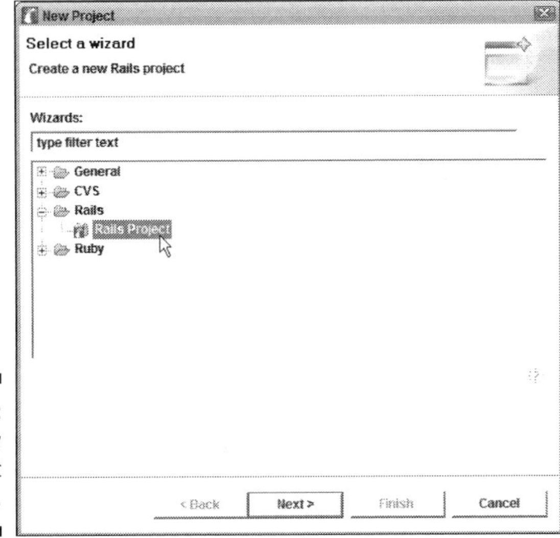

Figure 3-6: The New Project dialog box.

3. **In the New Project dialog box, select Rails Project from the navigation tree and then click Next.**

   In response, the New Rails Project dialog box appears. (See Figure 3-7.)

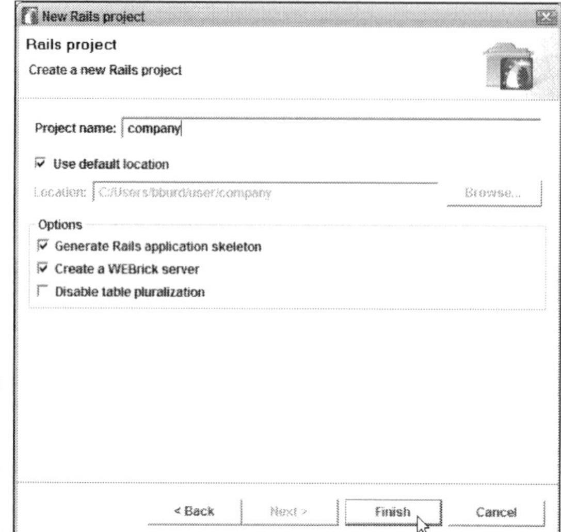

Figure 3-7: The New Rails Project dialog box.

Under certain circumstances, you can compress Steps 2 and 3 into one step. The contextual menu in Step 2 might have a New⇨Rails Project option. If so, you can select the Rails Project option and then skip Step 3.

4. **In the Project Name field of the New Rails Project dialog box, type** company.

   The name of the project matches part of the database name. In a project named `company`, Rails automatically creates references to three database names: `company_development` (which you create in the previous section), `company_test`, and `company_production`.

5. **Still in the New Rails Project dialog box, make sure that the Use Default Location, Generate Rails Application Skeleton, and Create a WEBrick Server check boxes are all selected. Also, make sure that the Disable Table Pluralization check box is deselected.**

   You can do some fancy things with all these check boxes. But in this book, I avoid fancy things. I try to keep it simple.

6. **Click Finish.**

The New Rails Project dialog box disappears. A new branch, labeled `company`, appears in the Rails Navigator view. And a new item (labeled `companyServer`) appears in the Servers view. (See Figure 3-8.)

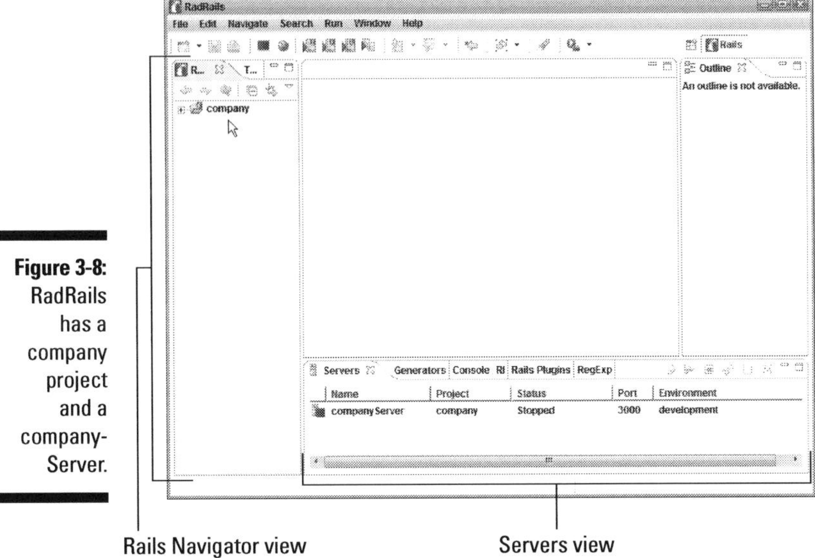

Figure 3-8: RadRails has a company project and a company-Server.

At this point, servers abound. You have the database server described in Chapter 2. In addition, you have a Web server (named `companySer`that shows up in Figure 3-8. For more information about these servers, see Chapter 11.

Running Your New Rails Project (Already!)

In the preceding section, you create a bare-bones Rails project. Bare as its bones may be, the project has enough equipment for you to start testing your work.

In a few steps, you check to make sure that the new `companyServer` runs properly.

1. **Select the `companyServer` row in the RadRails Servers view.**

   For help finding the Servers view, refer to Figure 3-8.

2. **Click the Launch Browser icon in the Servers view's toolbar.**

   The Launch Browser icon looks like a tiny globe. (See Figure 3-9.)

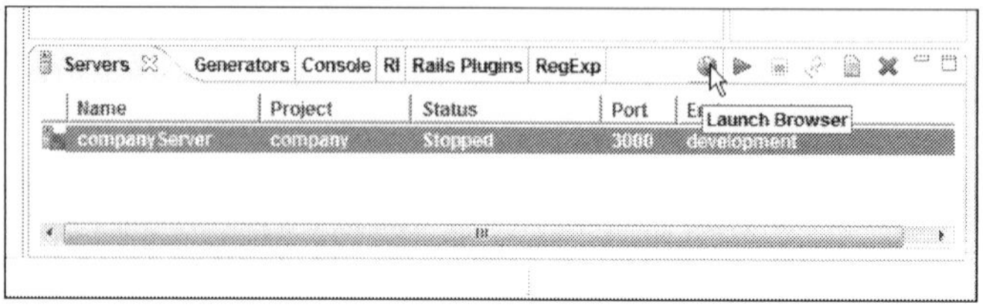

Figure 3-9: Launching a Web browser.

   In response to your click, RadRails displays a message: `. . . your server is currently stopped. Do you want to start the server?`

3. **Click Yes.**

   A this point, you might see a standard Windows Security Alert asking whether you really, really, reeeeeeally want to let the Ruby interpreter have access to your innocent little Web server.

4. **In the Windows Security Alert dialog box, click Unblock.**

   The server starts, and RadRails displays a small Web browser. The page in the Web browser starts with `Welcome aboard . . . You're riding the Rails!` (See Figure 3-10.)

   Working busily behind this Welcome page lies more code than you might think. Your computer is running a Web server (the `companyServer`), and the server is feeding the new Welcome page to the Web browser. Using Rails, you make all this stuff happen by clicking your mouse and typing a few words. Not bad!

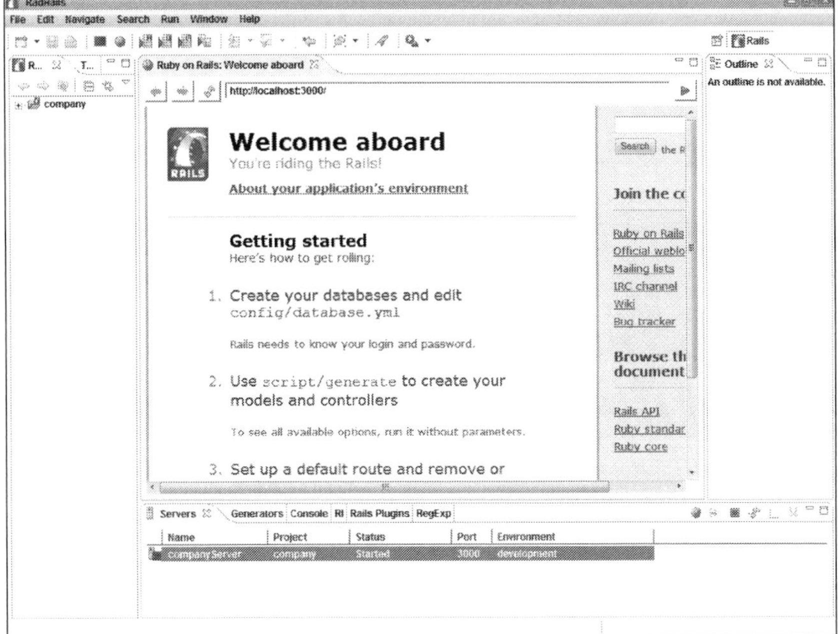

Figure 3-10: Your new application's Welcome page.

Creating a Model

To deal with your `company_development` database, Rails uses a *model.* Think of a model as a piece of code — a Ruby program whose structure mirrors the structure of a database table.

Rails is based on the celebrated Model/View/Controller (MVC) framework. For details about MVC, see Chapter 8.

You might think that creating a model means writing a bunch of Ruby code. But you don't have to write any code. Rails makes the creation of model code a cinch. Here's how:

1. **In the Rails Navigator view, select the `company` project branch.**

   See Figure 3-11.

Figure 3-11: Selecting a project in the Rails Navigator view.

2. **Near the bottom of the RadRails workbench, select the Generators tab. (You find the Generators tab in the same part of the RadRails workbench as the Servers tab.)**

   Your selection brings the Generators view to the foreground. (See Figure 3-12.) With this view, you tell Rails to generate things (models, for example).

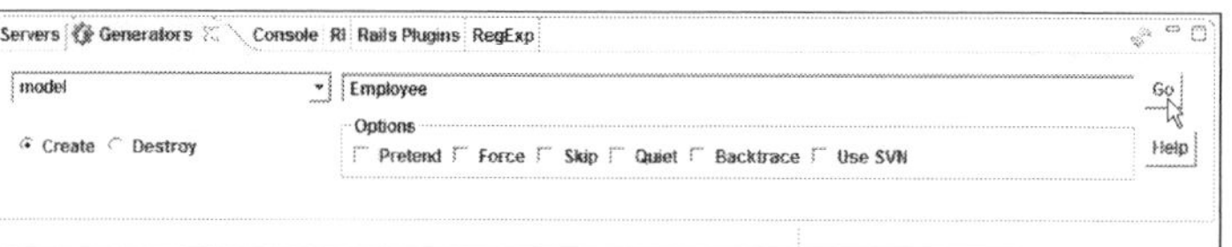

Figure 3-12: The Generators view.

3. **In the Generators view's drop-down list, select Model.**
4. **In the radio button group, select Create.**
5. **In the text field, type** Employee.

   With Steps 3–5, you prepare to create a model for a table named `employees`. Sure, you haven't even created an `employees` table yet. But the lack of a database table doesn't bother Rails.

   The Generators view has some other options (labeled Pretend, Force, Skip, and so on). You can leave these things deselected.

   Before proceeding to Step 6, look at the Rails Navigator view. Make sure that you haven't accidentally changed the selection you made in Step 1 (selecting the `company` project branch). I admit, if you have only one project, you're not likely to be selecting the wrong branch. But when you become proficient and have several projects, it's easy to select the wrong branch. (I ought to know. I selected the wrong project when I first prepared these instructions!) So don't wait until you have 20 or 30 projects. Start developing the habit of double-checking your Rails Navigator selection.

6. **In the Generators view, click Go.**

   After you click Go, the Generators view gets covered up by another view — the Console view. Within this Console view, you see Rails doing its thing. As shown in Figure 3-13, Rails creates an `employee.rb` file, an `employee_test.rb` file, and so on. These are Ruby program files.

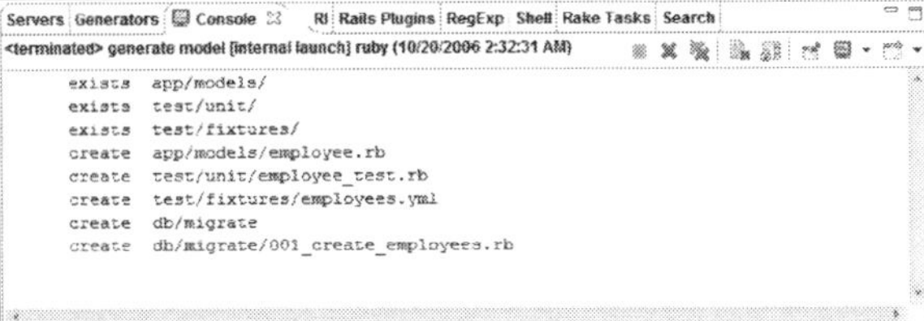

Figure 3-13: The Console view shows the progress as Rails generates a model.

   In fact, if you poke around inside the Rails Navigator tree, you find new branches for the newly created files.

7. **Expand the `company` branch. Within the `company` branch, expand the `app` branch. Finally, within the `app` branch, expand the `models` branch.**

   Inside the `models` branch, you see an `employee.rb` branch. This branch represents the newly created `employee.rb` Ruby code file.

8. **Double-click the `employee.rb` branch.**

   An editor appears. (See Figure 3-14.) The editor displays the Ruby code in the `employee.rb` file.

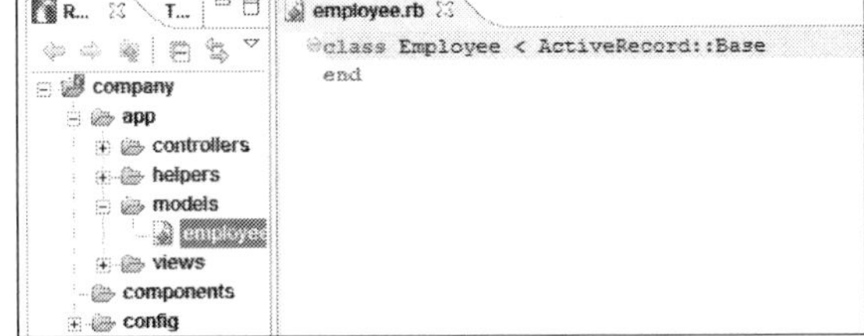

Figure 3-14: The employee.rb model file.

The code in Figure 3-14 is very brief. The code has only two lines with nothing very specific to companies or employees. What an anticlimactic end to the creation of this important thing called a model! But don't be fooled. This simple code contains a lot of good stuff, by virtue of its relationship to `ActiveRecord::Base`. But that story must wait until Chapter 9.

Creating a Database Table

In the preceding section, you create an `Employee` model — a Ruby program whose structure mirrors the structure of a database table. But remember — at this point in your work, your database has no table! You've created a database, but you haven't yet created a database table. There's no structure for the model to mirror.

You must add a table to your database. When you do, the table's columns (employee name, employee salary, and so on) are the table's structure.

To create a table, Rails provides a migration mechanism. A *migration* is a Ruby program that creates tables, adds columns to tables, and does other nice things to databases. Here's how it works:

1. **In the Rails Navigator view, expand the `company` branch. Within the `company` branch, expand the `db` branch. Finally, within the `db` branch, expand the `migrate` branch.**

   Inside the `migrate` branch, you see a `001_create_employees.rb` branch. This branch represents the new `001_create_employees.rb` Ruby code file.

2. **Double-click the `001_create_employees.rb` branch.**

   An editor appears. (See Figure 3-15.) The editor displays the Ruby code in the `001_create_employees.rb` file.

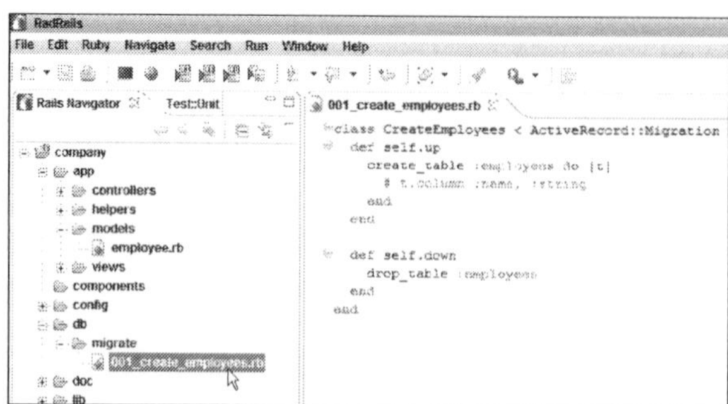

Figure 3-15: The migration file.

3. **Add lines to the `001_create_employees.rb` file.**

   Add the `t.column` lines as follows.

```
class CreateEmployees < ActiveRecord::Migration
  def self.up
    create_table :employees do |t|
      # t.column :name, :string
      t.column :name, :string
      t.column :hiredate, :date
      t.column :salary, :float
      t.column :fulltime, :boolean
      t.column :vacationdays, :integer
      t.column :comments, :text
    end
  end

  def self.down
    drop_table :employees
  end
end
```

   If you don't enjoy typing, you can omit some of the new `t.column` lines. After all, if your practice database doesn't have a `vacationdays` column, no one cares.

   Check the lines that you type before proceeding to the next step. Check spelling, capitalization, and punctuation. Look for `:string` instead of `:String`. Look for `t.column :name, :string` instead of `t.column, :name :string`.

4. **When you're done checking your typing, choose File⇨Save.**

   Your changes to the migration file are now safe and sound.

5. **In the lower-right pane of the RadRails workbench, select the Rake Tasks tab.**

   The Rake Tasks view appears. (See Figure 3-16.)

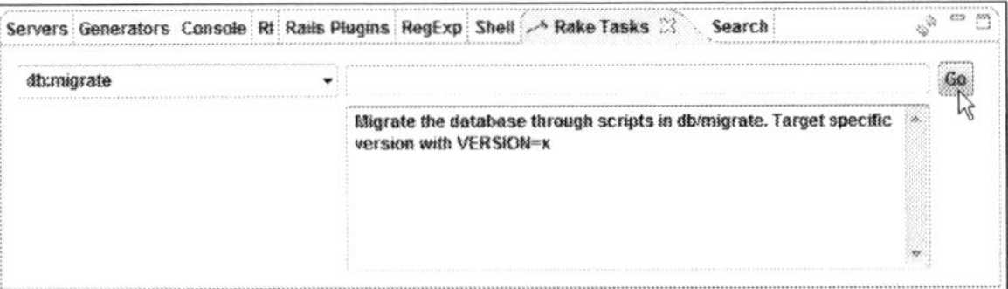

Figure 3-16: The Rake Tasks view.

6. **In the Rake Tasks view's drop-down list, select db:migrate. (See Figure 3-16.)**

What kinds of columns are you creating?

The migration code in Step 3 tells Rails to create a database table. The table contains six columns. Each column has a *name* and a *type*. The name identifies the column, and the type describes the kind of value that may be stored in that column's entries.

In the code of Step 3, the column names are `name`, `hiredate`, `salary`, `fulltime`, `vacationdays`, and `comments`. Never mind that the first column's name is `name`. If I had planned ahead, I would have called this column `familyname`, or something like that. But unfortunately, I didn't plan ahead.

In the code of Step 3, the types of values stored in the columns' entries are `string`, `date`, `float`, `boolean`, `integer`, and `text`. The word `string` stands for a short string of characters. The word `date` stands for a calendar date. The word `float` stands for a number with some digits to the right of the decimal point (a number like 23999.95). The word `boolean` stands for either true or false. (True, this employee is full time; or false, this employee isn't full time.) The word `integer` stands for a number with no digits to the right of the decimal point (a number like 60). Finally, the word `text` stands for a potentially long string of characters.

If you think about it, the choices for column types make sense. An employee's name isn't likely to be more than 30 characters long. A salary might have cents (digits to the right of the decimal point). Even a salary like 25000.00 has digits to the right of the decimal point, although both of the digits are zeros. A number of vacation days is normally a whole number. (An employee with 15.27 vacation days is rare, just as an employee with 2.5 children tends not to want anyone to know about it.) And a comment might be a large number of characters, especially for some employees that I've met.

If you're a fan of databases, you know that each kind of database supports certain types of values. In MySQL, a Rails `string` is of type `VARCHAR(255)`. A Rails `boolean` is of type `TINYINT(1)`. The other Rails types in the code of Step 3 have the same names as their corresponding MySQL types.

In the Rake Task view, make sure that the text field to the right of the drop-down list is empty. Don't worry about any text (or the lack of text) in the big text area below the text field.

7. **In the Rake Tasks view, click Go.**

   In response, Ruby on Rails creates an `employees` table. Rails guesses the table name `employees` from your model name `Employee`. (Rails is good at guessing names. From a model named `Person`, Rails would create a table named `people`!)

   To confirm the table's creation, the RadRails Console view displays some `migrating` and `migrated` messages. (See Figure 3-17.) If you want more confirmation, you can launch MySQL Administrator and examine the newly created table.

```
Servers Generators Console RI Rails Plugins RegExp
rake migrate
(in C:/Users/bburd/user/company)
== CreateEmployees: migrating ==================================================
-- create_table(:employees)
   -> 0.3520s
== CreateEmployees: migrated (0.3520s) =========================================
```

Figure 3-17: Confirmation that RadRails performed a migration.

In Step 7, you run the migration code, but you don't run the code directly. Instead, you invoke something called Rake, which calls the migration code on your behalf. To discover more about Rake, visit `http://rubyforge.org/projects/rake`.

Creating a Scaffold

In common English, the word *scaffold* has two meanings. A scaffold can be a temporary structure for supporting builders while they work. A scaffold can also be a platform with a noose — a place for hanging criminals.

In Rails, the word `scaffold` stands for a temporary Web page. The page provides simple connectivity to the database, helping you to develop your application. (With a Rails scaffold, you may execute some commands, but you don't execute any criminals.) Think of the scaffold as a quick prototype — a proof-of-concept for your Web interface. Or, if you're like many developers, you can use the scaffold as a basis for your application. You start with the scaffold, add more functionality, customize the menus, pretty it up a bit, and Presto! You have a complete Web application.

In this section, you create a scaffold for the `company` project. You repeat the steps from this chapter's "Creating a Model" section. But this time, you build a scaffold instead of a model:

1. **In the Rails Navigator view, select the `company` project branch.**
2. **Near the bottom of the RadRails workbench, select the Generators tab.**

   Your selection brings the Generators view to the foreground. In the next few steps, you set up the parameters in the Generators view. You can follow along in Figure 3-18.

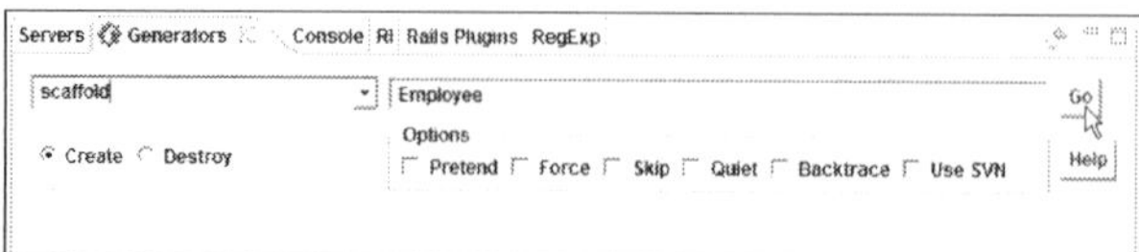

Figure 3-18: Creating a scaffold.

3. **In the Generators view's drop-down list, select Scaffold.**
4. **In the radio button group, select Create.**
5. **In the text field, type** Employee.

   The Generators view has some other options (labeled Pretend, Force, Skip, and so on). You can leave these things deselected.

   With Steps 3–5, you're preparing to create a scaffold for your `Employee` model.

   Before proceeding to Step 6, look back at the Rails Navigator view. Make sure that you haven't accidentally changed the selection you made in Step 1 (selecting the `company` project branch).

6. **In the Generators view, click Go.**

   In the Console view, RadRails shows the progress of the scaffold creation. (See Figure 3-19.) When the creation is complete, you can view the scaffold's code.

```
Terminal
company> ruby script/generate scaffold Employee
   exists  app/controllers/
   exists  app/helpers/
   create  app/views/employees
   exists  test/functional/
dependency  model
   exists   app/models/
   exists   test/unit/
   exists   test/fixtures/
identical   app/models/employee.rb
identical   test/unit/employee_test.rb
identical   test/fixtures/employees.yml
   create  app/views/employees/_form.rhtml
   create  app/views/employees/list.rhtml
   create  app/views/employees/show.rhtml
   create  app/views/employees/new.rhtml
   create  app/views/employees/edit.rhtml
   create  app/controllers/employees_controller.rb
   create  test/functional/employees_controller_test.rb
   create  app/helpers/employees_helper.rb
   create  app/views/layouts/employees.rhtml
   create  public/stylesheets/scaffold.css
```

Figure 3-19: The terminal shows the progress as Rails generates a scaffold.

In this chapter's "Creating a Model" section, I mention that Rails uses a Model/View/Controller framework. When Rails creates a scaffold, much of the scaffold's code is inside the Controller part of the framework. So to see some of the scaffold's code, you can look at a controller file. Here's how:

1. **Expand the `company` branch in the Rails Navigator view. Within the `company` branch, expand the `app` branch. Finally, within the `app` branch, expand the `controllers` branch.**

   Inside the `controllers` branch, you see an `employees_controller.rb` branch. This branch represents the newly created `employees_controller.rb` Ruby code file.

2. **Double-click the `employees_controller.rb` branch.**

   The code defines what it means to list employees, to show one employee, to add a new employee, and so on. (See Figure 3-20.) This `employees_controller.rb` file works in conjunction with other files (also created as part of the scaffold) to present a Web interface to the database.

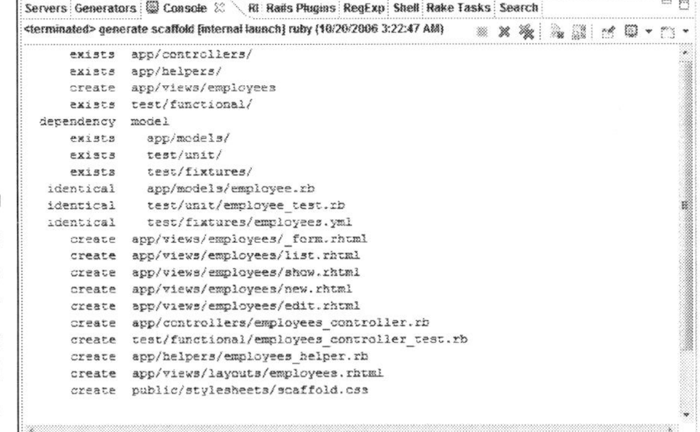

Figure 3-20: The controller file contains scaffold code.

Using the New Web Interface

Every story has a climax; every joke has a punch line. This section is the climax to the story you've been developing throughout this chapter. With some pointing, clicking, and a minimal amount of typing, you've built a modest (but complete) application. The application includes a database and a Web interface to the database. Here's how to test your application:

1. **Repeat the steps in the section entitled "Running Your New Rails Project (Already!)."**

   RadRails displays a small Web browser. The page in the Web browser starts with `Welcome aboard . . . You're riding the Rails!` (Refer to Figure 3-10.) In the browser's address field, you see `http://localhost:3000/` (or something similar).

2. **To the text in the browser's address field, add** employees/new **and then press Enter.**

   The text in the address field should be `http://localhost:3000/employees/new`.

   In the browser window, you see a shiny, new, custom Web page for adding an employee to the database. (See Figure 3-21.) Rails creates this page according to your specifications.

   The RadRails Web browser is a component borrowed from Microsoft Internet Explorer. And Internet Explorer doesn't allow you to abbreviate `http://localhost:3000` by writing `localhost:3000`. You get an error page if you omit the `http://` prefix.

3. **Fill in the fields on the New Employee page. (Again, refer to Figure 3-21.)**

Figure 3-21: The New Employee page.

4. **Click Create at the bottom of the New Employee page.**

   In the browser window, a Listing Employees page appears. (See Figure 3-22.) The Listing Employees page has only one employee (the employee that you create in Step 3). But you can add more employees.

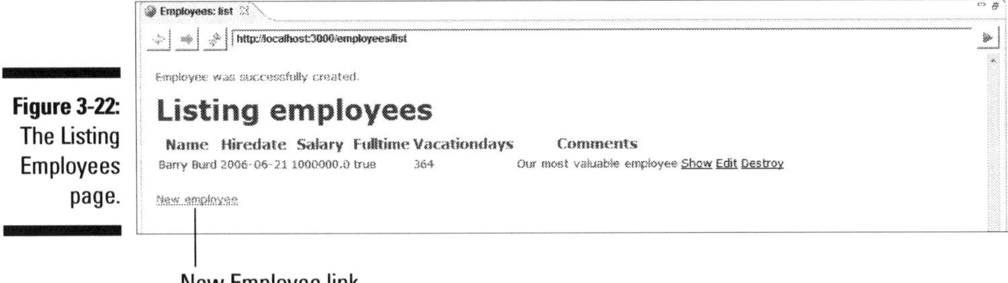

Figure 3-22: The Listing Employees page.

5. **Click the Web page's New Employee link.**

   In response, the browser redisplays the New Employee page.

6. **Fill in the fields on the New Employee page (this time, for a different employee).**

7. **Click Create at the bottom of the New Employee page.**

   The Listing Employees page reappears. This time, the page lists two employees. (See Figure 3-23.)

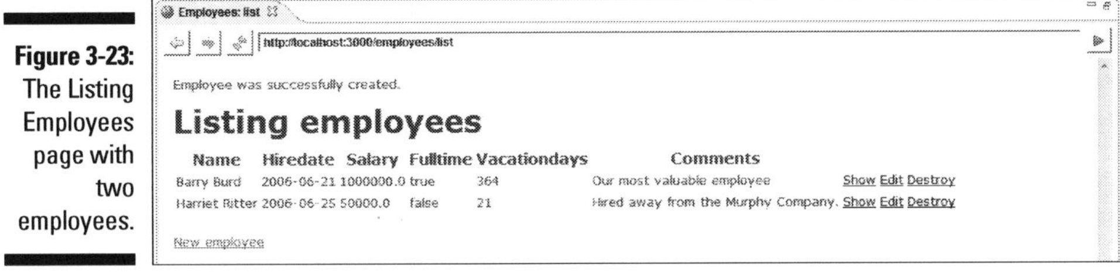

Figure 3-23: The Listing Employees page with two employees.

   Notice the Show, Edit, and Destroy links to the right of each employee's information.

8. **Click the Show link for one of the employees.**

   After clicking Show, you see a page like the one in Figure 3-24. The body of the page has information about the company's favorite employee, and the bottom of the page has links for editing and for returning to the list of all employees.

Figure 3-24: The Show page for one employee.

9. **Experiment further with the Show, Edit, and Destroy links.**

   Using these links, you can perform the four basic database operations — Create, Read, Update, and Destroy. So common are these operations that they have their own acronym. They're called the CRUD operations. (I suppose that calling them CRUD operations is better than calling them the SCUM operations. Would that be Search, Create, Update, and Modify? Or how about calling them the DIRT operations? That's Delete, Interrogate, Read, and Tally. Anyway, if you talk about databases, you're stuck with the term CRUD.)

The goal of this chapter was to create and test a scaffold — a simple prototype for what may become a complex Web interface.

But maybe this chapter's prototype isn't so simple. The prototype solves all kinds of problems that you face when you create Web pages, and the scaffold pages do some very useful tasks. The scaffold pages list items, create items, edit items, and so on. That's what online shopping carts do. It's also what online guest books and discussion forums do. It's what millions of Web sites do every day.

Chapter 4

Using RadRails

In This Chapter

- Navigating the RadRails workbench
- Performing common tasks
- Heading off trouble (if trouble occurs)

RadRails is an integrated development environment (IDE) for Ruby on Rails. In the name RadRails, the *Rad* stands for "Rapid application development" (and, of course, *Rails* stands for "Rails"). RadRails is based on the Eclipse platform — an open source effort that forms the basis for many IDEs.

Words, Words, Words

In many of this book's examples, I ask you to do this-or-that by using RadRails. So to make things easy for you (well, for me, actually), I start by establishing some RadRails terminology. Some of this terminology is familiar stuff for you. Some other terminology might be new.

- **Workbench:** The RadRails desktop. (See Figure 4-1.) The workbench is the environment in which you develop code.
- **Area:** A section of the workbench. The workbench in Figure 4-1 has four areas. (See Figure 4-2.)
- **View:** A part of the workbench that displays information for you to browse and modify. A view can fill up an area in the workbench. For instance, in Figure 4-1, the Outline view fills up the rightmost area. Also in Figure 4-1, the six different views share the bottommost area. (The Servers, Generators, Console, RI, Rails Plugins, and RegExp views share the bottommost area.)

Many views display information as lists or trees. For example, in Figure 4-1, the Rails Navigator and Outline views contain trees, whereas the Servers view contains a list.

You can use a view to make changes to things. For instance, to delete a file named `useless_code.rb`, find the `useless_code.rb` file in the Rails Navigator view. (The Rails Navigator view lives along the left side of the RadRails workbench. See Figure 4-1.) Right-click the `useless_code.rb` branch. Then, in the resulting contextual menu, choose Delete.

- **Editor:** Another part of the workbench (besides a view) that displays information for you to modify. The workbench in Figure 4-1 has two editors. The editors' names are `employees_controller.rb` and `application.rb`. All editors share the same area — called the *editor area,* of course — but reside on distinct tabs that you then bring to the fore with a single mouse click.

  A typical editor displays the lines of text in a file (the way a word processor displays the lines of text in a document). But some editors surprise you and display information in a more elaborate format.

Like other authors, I occasionally become lazy and use the word *view* when I really mean *view or editor.* When you catch me doing this, just shake your head and move onward. When I'm being very careful, I use the official terminology. I refer to views and editors as *parts* of the workbench. Unfortunately, this *parts* terminology doesn't stick in people's minds very well.

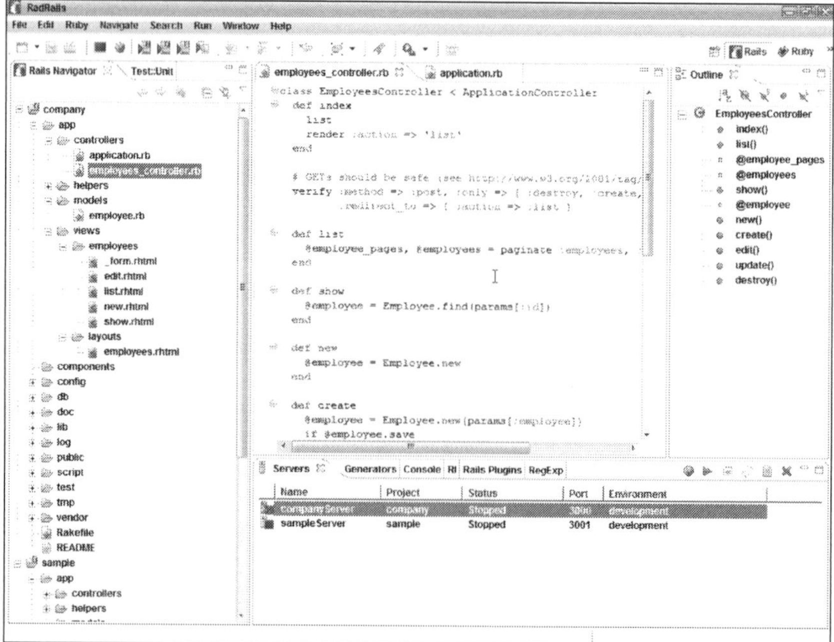

Figure 4-1: The RadRails workbench often looks like this (but not always).

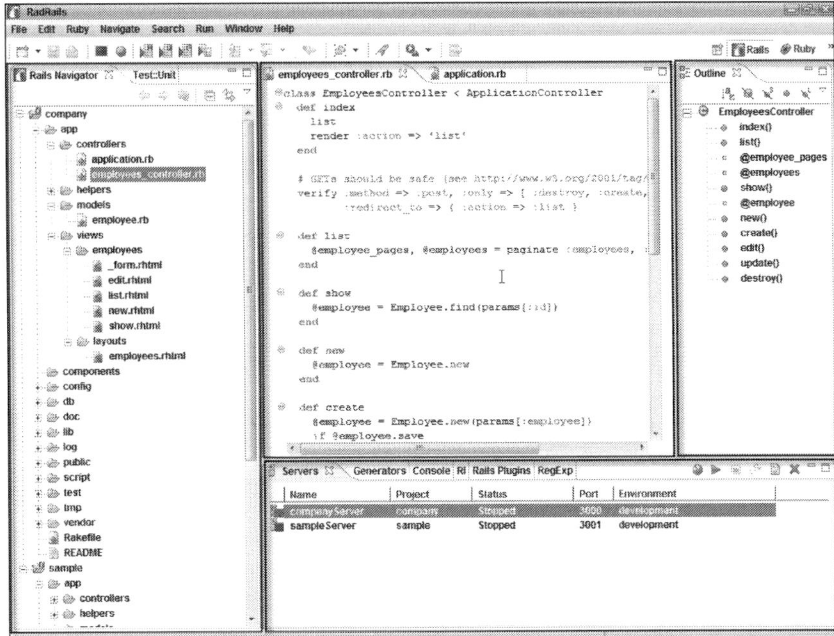

Figure 4-2: The workbench is divided into areas.

What's inside a view or an editor?

The next several terms deal with individual views, editors, and areas.

- **Toolbar:** The bar of buttons (and other little things) at the top of a view. See Figure 4-3.
- **Menu button:** A downward-pointing triangle in the toolbar. When you click the menu button, a drop-down list of actions appears. (See Figure 4-4.) The list of actions varies from one view to another.
- **Close button:** A button that gets rid of a particular view or editor. See the big, hollow X icons to the right of the words `Rails Navigator` and `employees_controller.rb` in Figure 4-4.

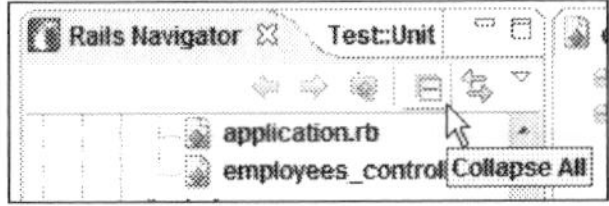

Figure 4-3: The Collapse All button in the Rails Navigator view's toolbar.

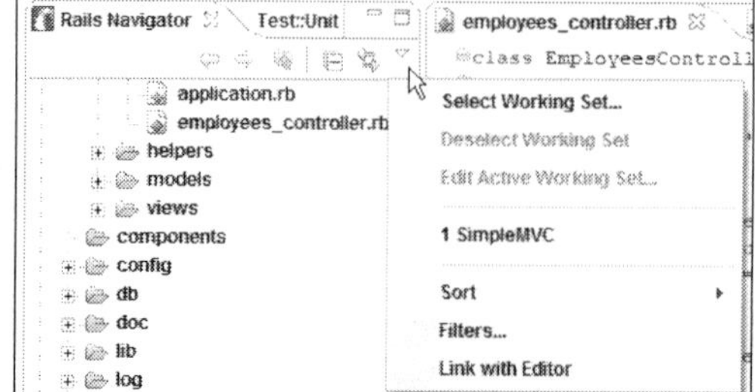

Figure 4-4: Clicking a view's menu button.

- **Chevron:** A double arrow indicating that other tabs should appear in a particular area (but that the area isn't wide enough). The chevron in Figure 4-5 has a little number 3 beside it. The 3 tells you that, in addition to the two visible tabs, three other tabs are invisible. Clicking the chevron brings up a menu containing the labels of all five tabs.
- **Marker:** Tiny icons along the left edge of the editor area.

  In Figure 4-6, a marker to the left of `puts "Hello` looks like a circle with an X inside it. The marker indicates that the line `puts "Hello` contains a Ruby *syntax error.* That is, the line `puts "Hello` isn't a grammatically correct Ruby statement.

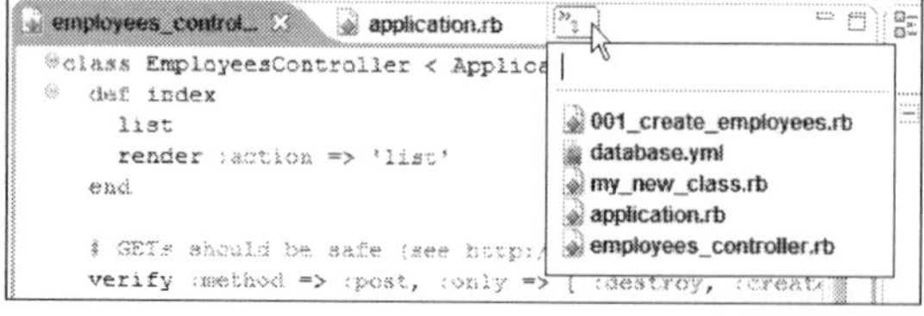

Figure 4-5: Clicking the chevron reveals the labels of all the editors' tabs.

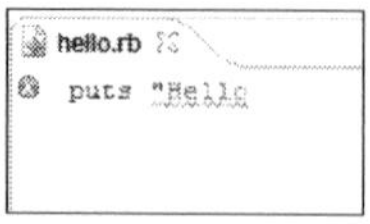

Figure 4-6: A marker accompanies unmatched quotation marks.

Understanding the big picture

The next two terms deal with the overall look and feel of RadRails:

- **Layout:** An arrangement of certain views (along with the editor area) on the workbench. The layout back in Figure 4-1 has nine views — two in the left area, one in the right area, and six in the bottom area. But additional views are available. (See the section entitled "Showing a view.")
- **Perspective:** A handy way of referring to a very useful layout. If a particular layout is really useful, someone gives that layout a name. And if a layout has a name, you can use the layout whenever you want.

  For instance, the workbench of Figure 4-1 displays the Rails perspective. The Rails perspective is useful for creating and editing Rails projects. By default, the Rails perspective contains nine views, with the arrangement shown in Figure 4-1.

  Along with all these views, the Rails perspective contains an editor area. (Sure, the editor area has several tabs, but the number of tabs has nothing to do with the Rails perspective.)

  To find out about another perspective — the Ruby perspective — see this chapter's "Changing the perspective" section.

To all this user interface vocabulary, add two more terms:

- **Workspace:** A directory in which RadRails stores your work. You can choose one directory or another each time you launch RadRails. (For details, see Chapter 2.)
- **Project:** One application comprising a collection of files and folders. The Rails Navigator view back in Figure 4-1 lists two projects: `company` and `sample`. As the view shows, each project contains several folders and files.

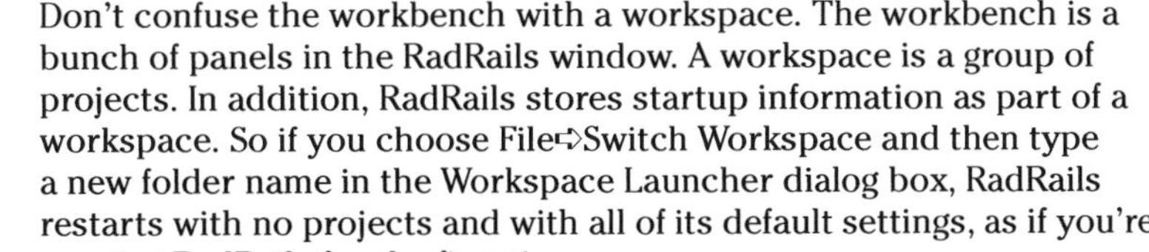

Don't confuse the workbench with a workspace. The workbench is a bunch of panels in the RadRails window. A workspace is a group of projects. In addition, RadRails stores startup information as part of a workspace. So if you choose File➪Switch Workspace and then type a new folder name in the Workspace Launcher dialog box, RadRails restarts with no projects and with all of its default settings, as if you're running RadRails for the first time.

Some Common RadRails Tasks

The preceding sections tell you the names of all the doohickeys and thingamabobs on the RadRails workbench. The rest of this chapter tells you what you can do with all those doohickeys and thingamabobs.

Changing the perspective

Figure 4-7 shows the upper-left corner of the RadRails workbench. The Rails icon is part of the *perspective bar.* The Rails icon's inlaid look indicates that the workbench is currently in the Rails perspective. To change to another perspective, do the following:

Figure 4-7: Clicking the Open Perspective button.

1. **Click the Open Perspective button, as shown in Figure 4-7.**
2. **In the resulting pop-up menu, look for the name of the perspective that you want to activate.**

   In Figure 4-7, the only easily accessible alternative to the Rails perspective is the Data perspective. But what if the perspective you want to activate is the Ruby perspective?
3. **If you don't find the perspective you want, click Other.**

   The Select Perspective dialog box appears. (See Figure 4-8.)
4. **Select Ruby. Then click OK.**

   The Ruby perspective (shown in Figure 4-9) opens before your eyes. The Ruby perspective is useful for developing and testing plain old Ruby programs (code that's not necessarily associated with Rails). By default, the Ruby perspective has the eight views shown in Figure 4-9, along with an editor area for Ruby code.

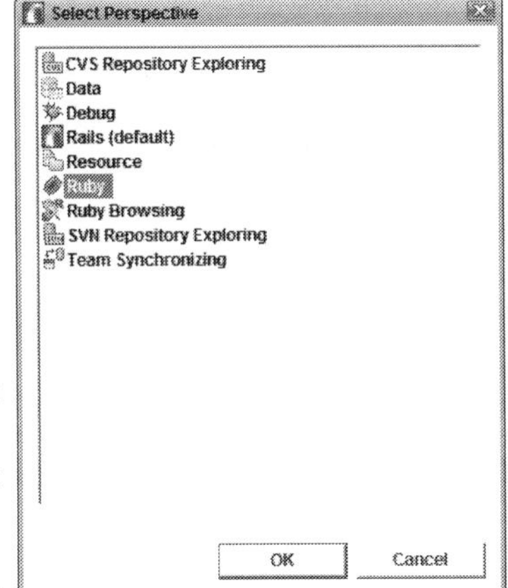

Figure 4-8: The Select Perspective dialog box.

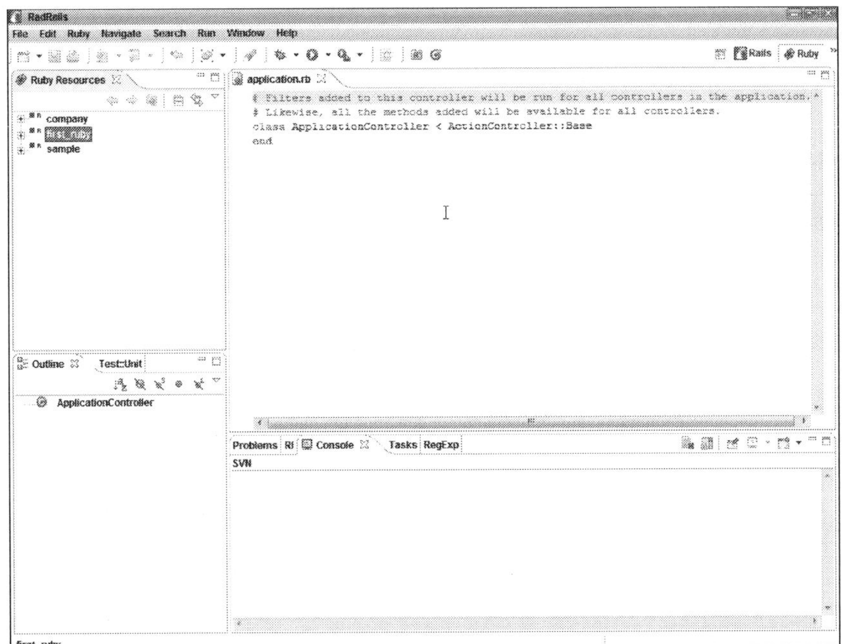

Figure 4-9: The Ruby perspective.

Showing a view

Each view has its own Close button, and occasionally you might press the Close button by accident. You can follow these steps to reopen a view or to open a previously unopened view:

1. **Choose Window➪Show View, as shown in Figure 4-10.**

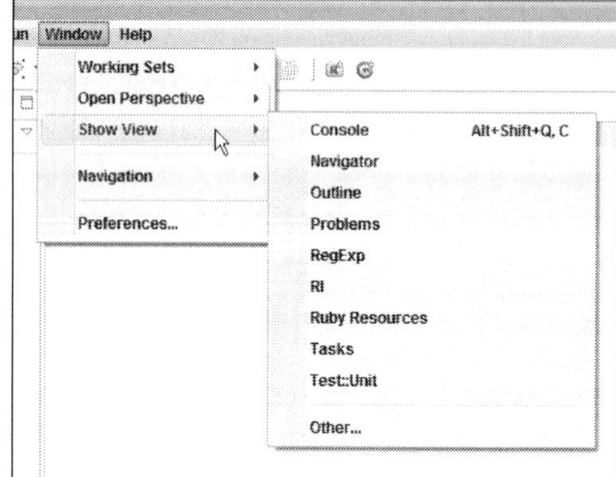

Figure 4-10: A choice of views.

2. **In the resulting submenu, look for the name of the view that you want to open.**

   In Figure 4-10, the views named in the submenu include the Console, the Rails Navigator, and so on. You can show a view by choosing one of these alternatives. But what if you want to show a view that isn't listed in the submenu?

3. **If you don't find the view you want to open, click Other.**

   The Show View dialog box appears. (See Figure 4-11.)

4. **In the Show View dialog box, navigate to the view that you want to open.**

   To find the view that you want to open, you might have to expand a branch in the Show View dialog box's tree. In Figure 4-11, I went for the Shell view (one of two views in the Wicked Shell category).

   Wicked Shell isn't available in the standard version of RadRails (the version that you download from `www.radrails.org`). You can try adding the Wicked Shell plug-in to a standard download of RadRails. But over time, Eclipse becomes available in different releases (releases 3.1.2, 3.2, and so on). Changes between releases can make the installing of Wicked Shell a bit tricky. So, for a surefire way of getting RadRails with Wicked Shell, download the customized version of RadRails from this book's Web site.

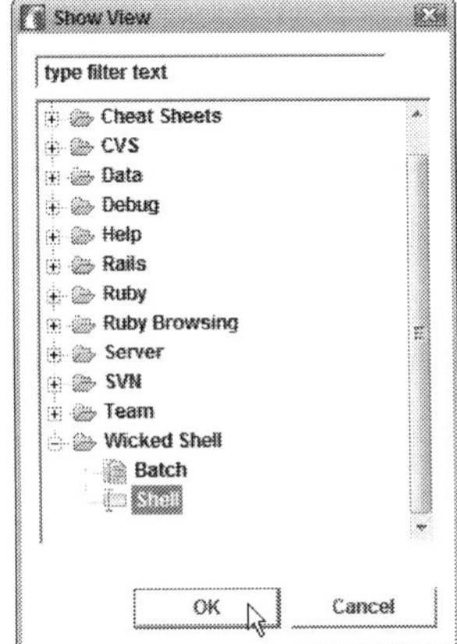

Figure 4-11: The Show View dialog box.

Only the Windows version of my customized RadRails download has the Wicked Shell plug-in. The Linux and Macintosh versions don't include Wicked Shell. Even so, a Linux or Macintosh user can follow this section's steps to open any available RadRails view.

5. **Click OK.**

   The selected view appears in the RadRails workbench. Figure 4-12 shows the Shell view.

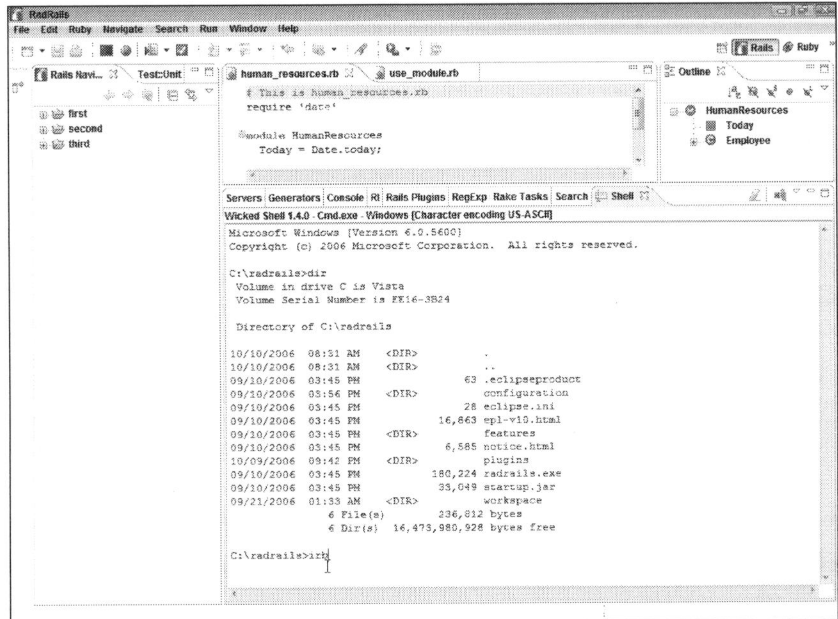

Figure 4-12: The Shell view.

Using a wizard to create something

Chapter 3 describes a quick way to create a certain kind of project (a Rails project). This section describes a more general way to create things.

1. **Select a project in the Rails Navigator or Ruby Resources view.**

   Whatever you create will be inside this project. (Of course, if the thing you want to create is a brand-new project of some kind, skip this step!)

2. **In the RadRails main menu, choose File⇨New.**

   A Select a Wizard dialog box appears. (See Figure 4-13.) The dialog box offers several choices (several kinds of things that you can create).

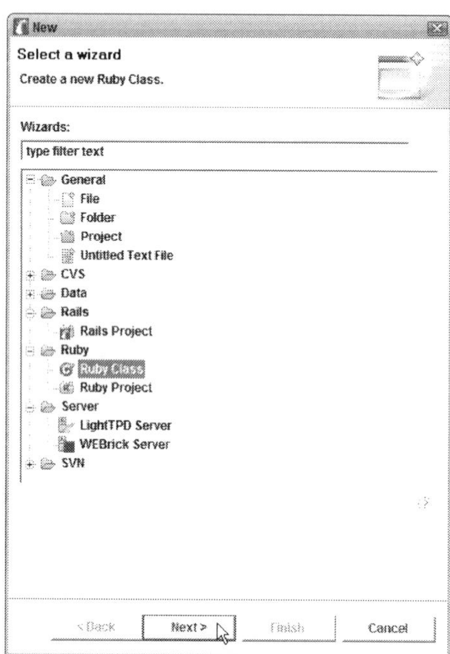

Figure 4-13: Pick your poison.

3. **Select one of the items in the dialog box and then click Next or Finish.**

   In Chapter 3, I choose Rails Project. But in Step 2, I choose Ruby Class. The Finish button in Figure 4-13 is grayed out, so I can't click Finish. Instead, I click Next. In response, RadRails displays a New Ruby Class dialog box. (See Figure 4-14.)

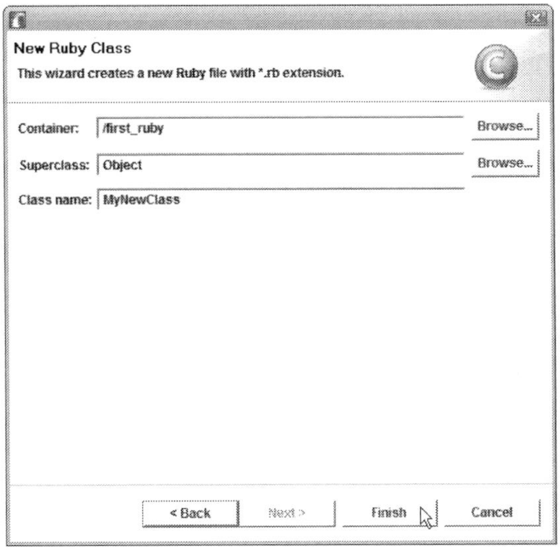

Figure 4-14: The New Ruby Class dialog box.

4. **Fill in any required fields (and select any other required items) in the dialog box.**

   In Figure 4-14, I accept the defaults. In particular, I leave `MyNewClass` in the Class name field.

   I also leave `/first_ruby` in the Container field. (In this case, the word *Container* is a fancy name for *directory* or *folder.* When it's created, my new Ruby class will live in a folder named `first_ruby`, and will be part of a project named `first_ruby`.)

5. **Click Next to move to the next wizard page. Alternatively, click Finish.**

   In Figure 4-14, the Next button is grayed out. So instead of clicking Next, I click Finish. When I click Finish, the wizard disappears. In the Ruby Resources view, I see the new Ruby file's name (`my_new_class.rb`). And in the editor area, I see some skeletal Ruby code. (See Figure 4-15.)

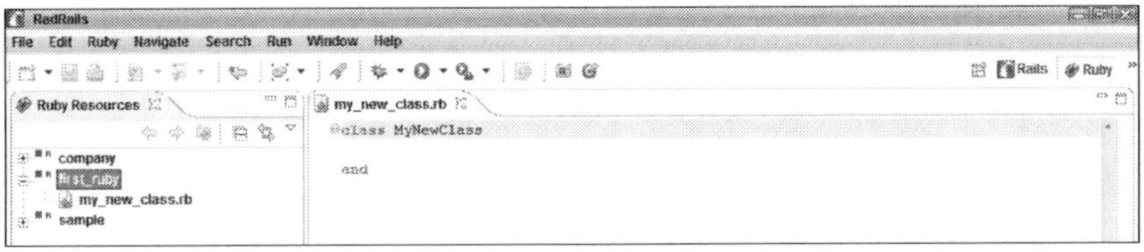

Figure 4-15: RadRails creates a Ruby file.

Using the Shell view

Eclipse is a very versatile platform with many avenues for customization and enhancement. And because RadRails is an offshoot of Eclipse, a developer can add new views, new features, and make all kinds of useful contributions.

Stefan Reichert created the Wicked Shell plug-in for Eclipse. He also helped me install Wicked Shell on RadRails. This plug-in gives you easy access to the computer's command window. Using Wicked Shell, you can quickly perform some system tasks without leaving the RadRails environment. (Refer to Figure 4-12.) Wicked Shell also gives you alternative ways of performing some Rails-related tasks. For example, in Chapter 3, you create a database by using MySQL Administrator and create a table by using Rails migration. If you prefer the good old command line over these fancy tools, you can accomplish the same tasks in Wicked Shell, as I show in the figure below.

Using Wicked Shell (or your system's command window) means remembering instructions to type. But for tasks that you perform frequently, remembering and typing instructions can be easier than opening windows and clicking buttons. And if you already know the SQL query language, the shell can save you from some laborious pointing and clicking. You can use the GUI tools or the shell. It's your choice.

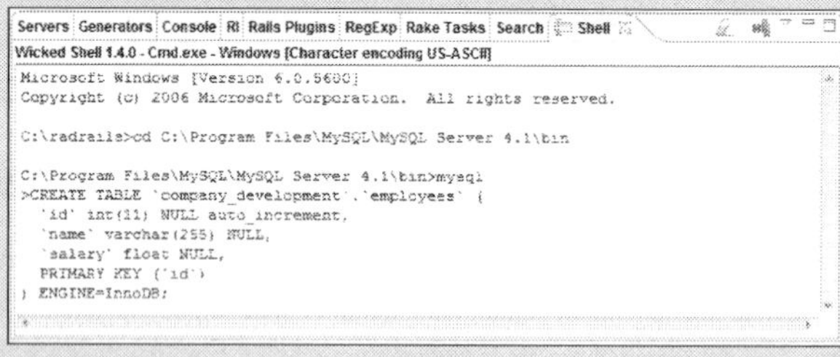

Using the Generators view to create something

In Chapter 3, you use the New Rails project wizard to create a project. But in the same chapter, you use the Generators view to create a model. One task uses a wizard, and the other task uses a view. There are reasons why you create one thing with a wizard and another thing with a view, but in the end, the reasons aren't air-tight. That's just the way RadRails works.

The preceding section describes the way you use a wizard to make something new (a new project or a new file, for example). This section describes the way you use the Generators view to make something new:

1. **Open the Rails perspective.**

   For details, see this chapter's "Changing the perspective" section.

2. **In the Rails Navigator view, select a project branch.**

   In Figure 4-16, I select the branch for a project named `sample`.

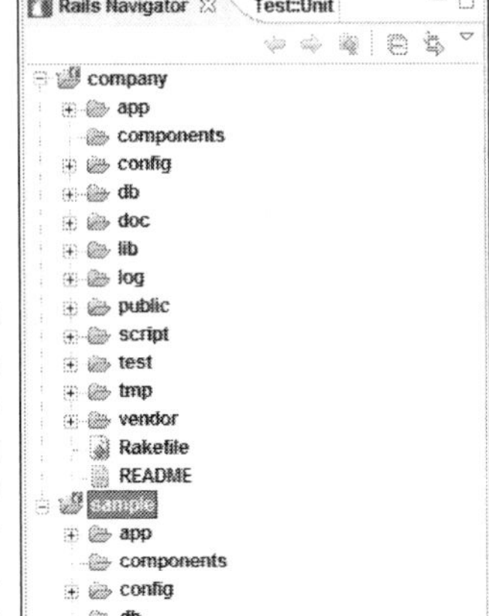

Figure 4-16: Selecting a project in the Rails Navigator view.

3. **Near the bottom of the RadRails workbench, select the Generators tab.**
4. **Make the appropriate choices in the Generators view.**

   In Figure 4-17, I make choices as follows:

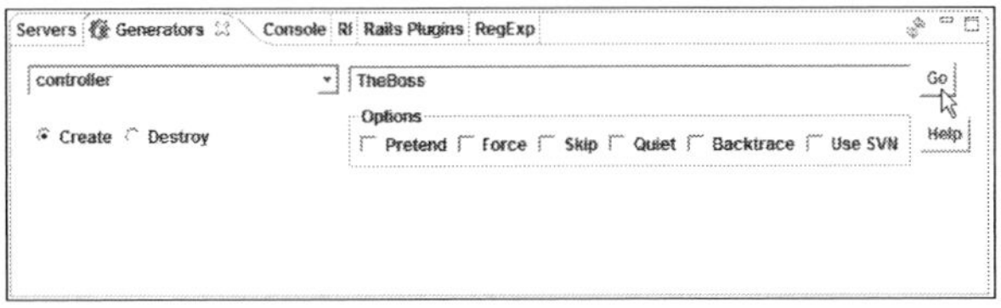

Figure 4-17: Generating a controller.

   - In the drop-down list, I select the Controller option.
   - Among the radio buttons, I select the Create option.
   - In the text field, I type **TheBoss** (the name of this particular controller).
   - I leave the check boxes deselected.

5. **In the Generators view, click Go.**

   RadRails generates the new model, the new scaffold, the new controller, or whatever else you asked RadRails to generate.

Editing an existing file

When you work with Ruby (or with any programming language, for that matter), you have to write and edit instructions in files. This section tells you how to do that.

1. **Navigate to a file's branch in one of the workbench's views.**

   In this chapter's "Using a wizard to create something" section, you create a file named `my_new_class.rb` in a Ruby project named `first_ruby`. (Refer to Figure 4-15.)

   So in Figure 4-18, with RadRails in the Ruby perspective, I navigate to the `first_ruby\my_new_class.rb` file's branch in the Ruby Resources view.

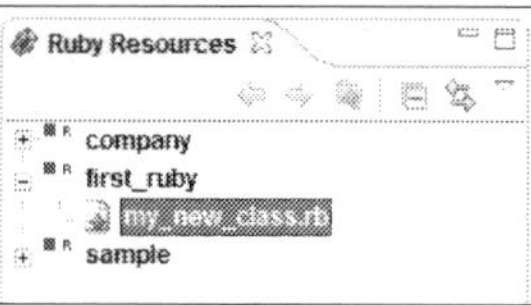

Figure 4-18: A branch in the Ruby Resources view.

   Notice how I can use a backslash to refer to a branch in a view's tree. I can extend this notation to several levels. For example, to refer to the `employee.rb` file in Figure 4-19, I write `company\app\models\employee.rb`.

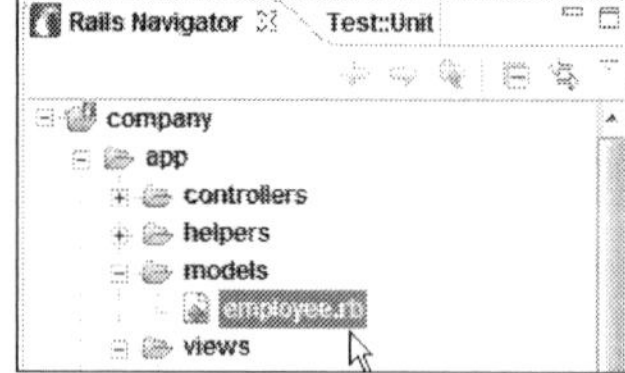

Figure 4-19: A branch in the Rails Navigator view.

2. **Double-click the branch.**

   The file's content appears in the editor window.

3. **Type any changes that you want to make to the file's content.**

   In Figure 4-20, I type `puts "Hello"` after the word `end`.

4. **Save the changes by choosing File➪Save.**

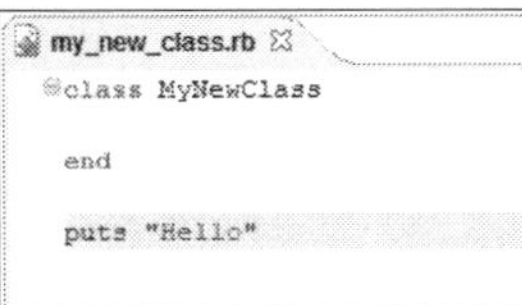

Figure 4-20: Adding a line to the code in Figure 4-15.

Instead of double-clicking, as in Step 2, you can right-click a filename in the Rails Navigator or Ruby Resources view. In the resulting contextual menu, choose Open With. In response, RadRails displays a submenu containing a list of editors. You can open the file with any of these alternative editors.

Running a Ruby program

In Chapter 3, you run some Rails code by visiting a Web page in a browser. In the next few steps, you do something similar, but you don't use Rails or a Web browser. Instead, you run some Rails-less Ruby code.

1. **Open the Ruby perspective.**

   For details, see this chapter's "Changing the perspective" section.

2. **Create a new Ruby Class file.**

   For details, see this chapter's "Using a wizard to create something" section. In that section, you create a file named `my_new_class.rb`.

3. **Edit the Ruby Class file.**

   For details, see this chapter's "Editing an existing file" section. In that section, you edit `my_new_class.rb`.

4. **Select the Ruby Class file in the Ruby Resources view.**

   Back in Figure 4-18, I select the `first_ruby\my_new_class.rb` branch in the Ruby Resources view.

5. **Choose Run⇨Run As⇨Ruby Application. (See Figure 4-21.)**

   In response, RadRails runs your `my_new_class.rb` program. A Console view appears in the bottommost area of the RadRails workbench. Inside that Console view, your program displays its output. (See Figure 4-22.)

   If you follow this section's steps but you don't see `Hello` in the Console view, try some of the steps in this chapter's "Troubleshooting the Run of a Ruby Program" section.

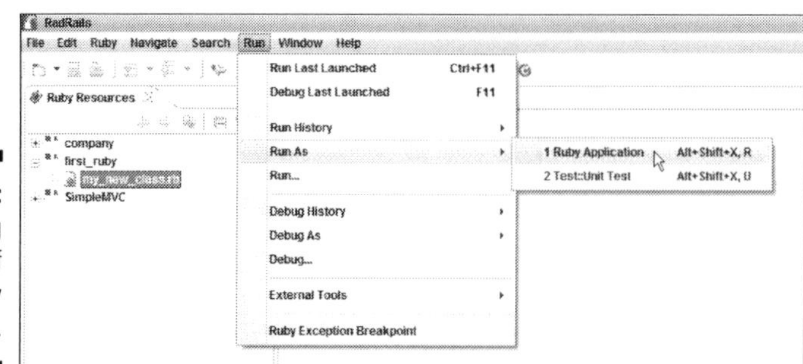

Figure 4-21: Launching the run of a Ruby program.

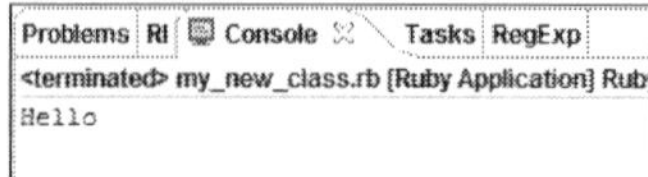

Figure 4-22: A Ruby program's output.

When you choose Run As, RadRails analyzes the file you want to run, and offers you a list of possibilities based on that analysis. As you saw in Figure 4-21, RadRails offers two choices — Ruby Application and Test::Unit Test. Occasionally, RadRails doesn't offer the choice that you want. You might want Ruby Application, but the only choice that you see is Test::Unit Test. In that case, check to make sure that you selected the file you want to run in Step 4. As an alternative, you can right-click the *editor* containing the file that you want to run. Then, in the resulting contextual menu, choose Run As➪Ruby Application.

Visiting a URL

Rails is all about creating Web sites, so RadRails comes with its own built-in Web browser. This section describes the use of the RadRails browser.

1. **Open the Rails perspective.**

   For details on opening a perspective, see this chapter's "Changing the perspective" section.

2. **Select one of the servers in the Servers view.**

   Refer to Figure 4-1.

3. **Click the Launch Browser icon in the Servers view's toolbar.**

   The Launch Browser icon looks like tiny globe.

4. **Click Yes in response to any "Do you want to start the server?" message.**

A Web browser appears in the editor area. The URL in the browser's address field is something like `http://localhost:3000/`. (For the Web server in your first Rails project, the URL is `http://localhost:3000/`. For the Web server in your second Rails project, the URL is `http://localhost:3001/`. RadRails adds 1 to the port number for every newly created Web server.)

5. **Change the URL in the browser's address window.**

   For example, to see a list of employees in the Rails project of Chapter 3, change `http://localhost:3000/` to `http://localhost:3000/`*`employees/list`*. To see a Webcam in Barry Burd's office or pictures of soft, furry bunnies hidden at Area 51, replace `http://localhost:3000/` with *`www.burdbrain.com`*.

The RadRails Web browser is a component borrowed from Microsoft Internet Explorer. And Internet Explorer doesn't allow you to abbreviate `http://localhost:3000` by writing `localhost:3000`. You get an error page if you omit the `http://` prefix.

Customizing RadRails

You can change the way RadRails behaves. Here's how:

1. **Choose Window⇨Preferences.**

   A Preferences dialog box appears. (See Figure 4-23.)

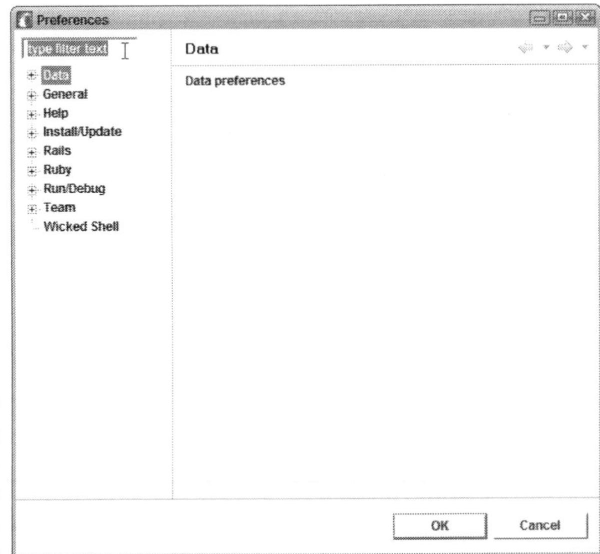

Figure 4-23: The Preferences dialog box.

2. **In the upper-left corner of the dialog box, look for a field containing the words "type filter text."**

   Again, see Figure 4-23.

3. **Replace the words "type filter text" with a word that describes the feature that you want to customize.**

   For example, to change the way editors work, type **editor**. In the panel on the left side of the Preferences dialog box, RadRails displays items having to do with editors. (See Figure 4-24.)

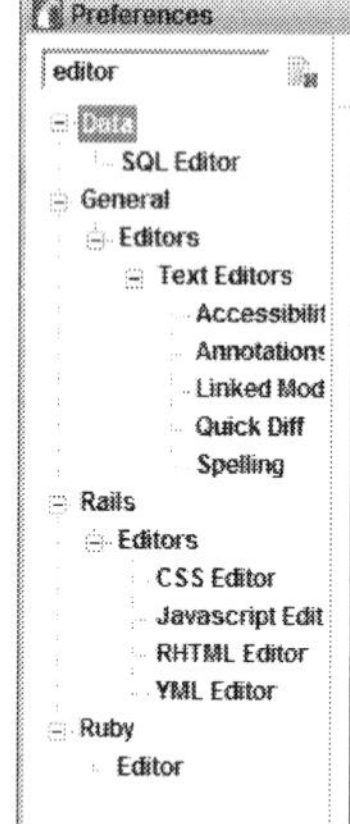

Figure 4-24: Editor preferences.

4. **Select an item in the panel on the left side of the dialog box.**

   When you select an item, RadRails shows you a list of choices relating to that item. For example, if you select the Editors item in the Rails branch, RadRails offers to stop its automatic closing of braces, parentheses, and quotation marks.

For another example of RadRails customization, read about the Installed Interpreters preference in Chapter 2.

Troubleshooting the Run of a Ruby Program

If, after all your efforts, you don't get the result shown in Figure 4-22, you don't have to suffer endlessly. The following sections have a few things you can check.

Does your Ruby code have a syntax error?

In Figure 4-6, I type `puts "Hello` with an opening quotation mark but no closing quotation mark. With unmatched quotation marks, the `puts "Hello` statement makes no sense to the Ruby interpreter. RadRails marks the error with a marker and puts a jagged red underline beneath the suspicious part of the code. (Again, refer to Figure 4-6.)

This statement `puts "Hello` has a *syntax error,* very much like a grammatical error in an English language sentence. If you make a grammatical error in English, people can probably figure out what you're trying to say. But like the headmaster in a 1940s school for wayward boys, the Ruby interpreter accepts only syntactically correct statements — nothing else.

Does your Ruby code have a semantic error?

Linguist Noam Chomsky once said that "Colorless green ideas sleep furiously." No, he wasn't crazy. He was giving an example of a grammatically correct sentence that makes absolutely no sense. It's called a *semantic error;* the word *semantic* refers to meaning.

Consider the following one-line Ruby program:

```
puts "Hello"
```

This program has no errors. With properly matched quotation marks, Ruby displays the word `Hello`.

Now consider the following two-line Ruby program:

```
Hello = 10
puts Hello
```

This program has no errors. Without any quotation marks, Ruby displays the value represented by the name `Hello`. The output is `10`.

But try to run the following one-line Ruby program.

```
puts Hello
```

If you try to run this one-line program, you get the message shown in Figure 4-25. Without any quotation marks around `Hello`, Ruby thinks you're trying to display whatever value is contained in a placeholder named `Hello`. And because there's no statement saying `Hello = 10` (or saying that `Hello` equals anything at all), the placeholder `Hello` has no value. This one-line program makes no sense.

The nasty thing is that the RadRails editor doesn't put a marker beside this line. This single line of code is grammatically correct because, when it's preceded by `Hello = 10`, this line makes sense. This one-line program has a semantic error, not a syntax error.

Figure 4-25: Sorry, pal! You have a semantic error.

Did you tell RadRails where to find a Ruby interpreter?

In Chapter 2, I ask you to fuss with the Installed Interpreters preference in RadRails. If you forget to do this, then when you try to run a Ruby program, you get a nasty error message.

The message might be "Before running a Ruby application, please specify an interpreter using the ruby interpreter preferences page." Alternatively, you might see "An error occurred while trying to launch a ruby application. There is currently no ruby interpreter defined. Use preferences to define and select the active interpreter." One way or another, I recommend that you check Chapter 2 for the section on configuring RadRails.

Did you point RadRails to the correct location of the Ruby interpreter?

What if you try to run a Ruby application and something very strange happens? Windows Notepad opens, or a lamp in your living room starts to flicker. One possible cause is that, when configuring the RadRails Installed Interpreters preference, you chose a program that's not a Ruby interpreter. To fix this, go back to the section in Chapter 2 on configuring RadRails. Make sure that the Ruby Interpreter's location ends in `ruby.exe`.

RadRails doesn't always respond quickly when you change an Installed Interpreters preference. Deselecting one check box and selecting another check box might have little or no effect. You might have to completely remove the unwanted interpreter from the list. In extreme cases, you might have to remove all interpreters from the list, and then rebuild the list from scratch. In any case, I recommend restarting RadRails before you try the new interpreter.

Part II
Creating Code

"What I'm looking for are dynamic Web applications and content, not Web innuendoes and intent."

In this part . . .

You can go a long way in Ruby on Rails with very little coding. For example you can create a complete Web application by typing less than 200 characters. (Yes, I've counted the characters.)

But to understand how an application works or to customize an application, you need to know some Ruby programming. You must also understand how to use HTML tags to compose Web pages. This part of the book describes all that stuff.

Chapter 5

Ruby One's Day

In This Chapter

- Exploring Ruby fundamentals
- Controlling flow in a Ruby program
- Using Ruby collections

I don't like to make fun of people (at least not in print). But several years ago I was conversing with someone I didn't like. We were talking about computer programming languages. He was finishing a course on C language fundamentals, and he wanted me to give him some advice. Which programming language should he learn next?

I thought for a moment. Then I asked him which languages he eventually wanted to learn. "All of them," he replied.

Sorry, no one can learn all computer programming languages. The world has thousands of computer languages. You can narrow down the list. Depending on how you count, at least 20 of these languages are "major" computer languages. But no one becomes expert in all 20 of them.

I would have advised this fellow to learn Ruby, but unfortunately, I couldn't. The year was 1982, and Ruby hadn't yet been invented. The Ruby programming language dates back to around 1993. The brainchild of Yukihiro "Matz" Matsumoto, this language crept onto the scene the way most one-person efforts do. Some people read about the language, and a few people became excited about it. By 2004, when Ruby on Rails came along, many computer professionals had heard the name *Ruby*, but most didn't know much about the language.

But as time goes on, Ruby is becoming more and more popular. Rails has pushed Ruby into the computer programming limelight. And with Ruby, people are discovering something that they seem to have forgotten — that computer programming can actually be fun.

Hello, Again

As they say, "You gotta start somewhere." In this section, you start with some small details — things to remember the next time you play a Ruby trivia game.

Listing 5-1 contains an introductory Ruby program. A run of the program is shown in Figure 5-1.

Listing 5-1: A Simple Ruby Program

```
# This file's name is intro.rb

puts "Hello, world!"
numOfCoins = (10 + 20) * 2 / 3
puts "You have #{numOfCoins} coins."
puts 'You have #{numOfCoins} coins.'
puts 'You have ' + numOfCoins.to_s + ' coins.'
```

Figure 5-1: I know! I have 20 coins. Enough, already!

```
Problems  RI  Console  Tasks  RegExp
<terminated> intro.rb [Ruby Application] Ruby C:\ruby\bin\ruby.exe : intro.rb
Hello, world!
You have 20 coins.
You have #{numOfCoins} coins.
You have 20 coins.
```

You can run the code in Listing 5-1. You can also experiment with what happens when you modify the code. For details, see the section about running a Ruby program in Chapter 4.

The Ruby interpreter ignores everything on a line that comes after a pound sign (unless the pound sign occurs inside a string of characters). So the first line in Listing 5-1 is a *comment*. The Ruby interpreter doesn't try to execute the words `This file's name is intro.rb`. (That's good, because those words mean nothing to the Ruby interpreter!)

A glimpse of a Ruby method

In Ruby, a *method* is a sequence of statements. Each method has a name. You can execute the method's statements by writing the method's name. You can define your own methods, execute methods written by other programmers, or execute methods defined in the standard Ruby library.

In Listing 5-1, the second nonblank line has a call to the standard Ruby `puts` method. Like other methods, a call to Ruby's `puts` method may have *parameters* (also known as *arguments*). If you call `puts "Hello, world!"`, the string `"Hello, world!"` is one of the `puts` method's parameters. When you call the `puts` method, Ruby displays each parameter's value in the RadRails Console view (or in some other place, depending on your Ruby environment).

The `puts` method takes as few or as many parameters as you want to give it. If you type `puts` on a line with no parameters, Ruby displays a blank line. If you type `puts "Hello", "There"`, Ruby displays two lines — one line with the word `Hello`, and another line with the word `There`. (On a call to the `puts` method, Ruby displays each parameter on a line of its own.)

For more on Ruby methods, see this chapter's "Using Methods" section.

Variables and values

In Listing 5-1, the word `numOfCoins` is called a *variable*. You can assign values to variables and perform arithmetic on numeric values.

When you do arithmetic, an asterisk (`*`) denotes multiplication. Listing 5-1 uses a few of Ruby's arithmetic operations. Other operations include more exotic things such as exponentiation (`**`), remainder upon division (`%`), bit inversion (~), shifting (>> and <<), and three-way comparison (<=>).

What I call "remainder upon division" is commonly called the *modulo* operator. And (get this!) the three-way comparison is often called the *spaceship* operator.

Any chunk of code that represents a value is called an *expression*. Sure, the chunk `(10 + 20) * 2 / 3` from Listing 5-1 is an expression. (The expression's value is 20.) But what about the entire statement `numOfCoins = (10 + 20) * 2 / 3`? Is that an expression too?

Yes. In Ruby, more things than you might guess are expressions. The line

```
puts (numOfCoins = (10 + 20) * 2 / 3)
```

in a Ruby program causes it to display the number `20`. The value of a Ruby assignment is the same as the value being assigned.

Ruby strings

The last three lines of Listing 5-1 illustrate some tricks you can perform using Ruby strings. In particular, the code `#{numOfCoins}` is called an *interpolated expression*. Ruby may evaluate the expression and then substitute the expression's value in the middle of the string. To be more precise,

- Ruby performs the substitution within a string that's enclosed in double-quotation marks.
- Ruby doesn't substitute within a string that's enclosed in single quotation marks.

So in Figure 5-1, the program's output has three `You have ... coins` lines.

- In the first of these lines, Ruby substitutes `20` for `#{numOfCoins}`.
- In the second line, the corresponding line of code contains a singly quoted string. So Ruby doesn't substitute.
- The third `You have ... coins` line comes from a more traditional technique (a technique shared by many other computer languages). In Listing 5-1, the last call to `puts` contains a three-part string. Plus signs (+) paste the three parts together. In the middle part, the variable `numOfCoins` isn't enclosed in quotation marks. So Ruby evaluates `numOfCoins` and obtains the value `20`.

The only problem is that this value `20` is a number, not a string. Ruby doesn't know how to add a string to a number. So if you type `'You have ' + numOfCoins + ' coins.'` in your code, then Ruby spits back an error message. In Listing 5-1, you fix this problem with a call to Ruby's `to_s` method.

Every number has a `to_s` method. You apply a number's `to_s` method by writing the number, followed by a dot, followed by `to_s`. In Listing 5-1, `numOfCoins` is a number, but `numOfCoins.to_s` is a string. Ruby knows what it means to apply a plus sign to strings, so the expression `'You have ' + numOfCoins.to_s + ' coins.'` is legal in Ruby.

In Ruby, a plus sign (+) is an *overloaded* operator. The plus sign has several different meanings — one meaning for numbers, another meaning for strings, a third meaning for arrays, and so on. For strings, the plus sign performs *concatenation*. If you write `"Barry " + "A. " + "Burd"`, the concatenated result is one string — `"Barry A. Burd"`.

Working with Values

Most programming languages have several ways to assign values to variables, and several ways to display values. In this regard, the Ruby language is no exception.

Listing 5-2: Counting Coins

```
numOfCoins = 6
NumOfCoins = 10
print "NumOfCoins: ", NumOfCoins, "\n"
print "numOfCoins: ", numOfCoins, "\n"

numOfCoins = numOfCoins + 1
numOfCoins += 1
print "After two increments, numOfCoins is ",
  numOfCoins, "\n"

NumOfCoins = 24
print "After reassignment, NumOfCoins is ",
  NumOfCoins, "\n"
```

Ruby is *case-sensitive*. So in a Ruby program, the names `numOfCoins` and `NumOfCoins` stand for two different (unrelated) things. The fourth line in Listing 5-2 displays the number `6` in spite of the earlier assignment of `10` to `NumOfCoins` (starting with an uppercase `N`). For evidence, see Figure 5-2.

```
Problems RI Console Tasks RegExp
<terminated> variable_constant.rb [Ruby Application] Ruby C:\ruby\bin\ruby.exe : variable_constant.rb
NumOfCoins: 10
numOfCoins: 6
After two increments, numOfCoins is 8
After reassignment, NumOfCoins is 24
C:/Users/bburd/user/first/variable_constant.rb:11: warning: already initialized constant NumOfCoins
```

Figure 5-2: Some success (followed by a bit of failure).

Ruby uses two separate queues for the output in Figure 5-2. One queue is for the ordinary (expected) output. The other queue is for error messages and warnings. Like the waiting lines in a store, the queues might be processed at slightly different rates. So the warning in Figure 5-2 might not always be the last line of output.

Displaying values

The code in Listing 5-2 calls Ruby's `print` method. Unlike the `puts` method, the `print` method doesn't automatically display its parameters on separate lines. For example, the fourth line in Listing 5-2 adds `"numOfCoins: ", numOfCoins` to the output shown in Figure 5-2. In this output, the characters `numOfCoins:` and the number `6` appear on the same line.

One way to force a line break in a `print` call is to add `"\n"` to the `print` call. Taken together, the symbols `\n` form an *escape sequence* — a group of symbols representing some useful, hard-to-represent character.

When you place the `\n` escape sequence between double-quotation marks, the escape sequence stands for a line break. So, each `print` call in Listing 5-2 ends with a line break (preparing for the next `print` call to begin on a brand-new line of output).

Ruby substitutes a line break for `\n` only when `\n` is between double-quotation marks (`"`). When `\n` is between single quotation marks (`'`), Ruby doesn't perform a substitution. In other words, the statement `print "One\ntwo\nthree\n"` displays three lines of output, but the statement `print 'One\ntwo\nthree\n'` displays only one line (the line containing `One\ntwo\nthree\n`).

Besides `\n`, Ruby has several other escape sequences: `\t` for tab, `\a` for beep, and so on. The business about single and double quotation marks applies to all Ruby's escape sequences.

The last `print` statement in Listing 5-2 continues from one line to the next. Normally, a Ruby statement ends when a line ends. But if the line isn't a complete statement or if the line ends with a backslash (\), the statement continues on the next line. The next-to-last line in Listing 5-2 ends with a comma, so Ruby decides that this line isn't a complete statement. Ruby looks on the last line (`NumOfCoins, "\n"`) for the rest of the statement.

Assigning values

Listing 5-2 contains two statements that have exactly the same effect. The statement `numOfCoins += 1` does the same thing that `numOfCoins = numOfCoins + 1` does (adds 1 to the value of `numOfCoins`). In fact, the second statement (with `+=`) is an abbreviation for the first statement (with `+ 1`). So anything you do to redefine the plus sign applies automatically to `+=` as well.

Unlike C++ and Java, Ruby has no post-increment or pre-increment operators. In Ruby, you can't write `numOfCoins++`. Sorry about that.

In Ruby, a name beginning with a lowercase letter is a *variable* and a name beginning with an uppercase letter is a *constant*. In Listing 5-2, `numOfCoins` is a variable and `NumOfCoins` is a constant. But notice, a Ruby constant's value can change! At the top of Listing 5-2, I assign `10` to `NumOfCoins`. Then, near the bottom of Listing 5-2, I assign a different value, `24`, to `NumOfCoins`. In response, Ruby changes the value of `NumOfCoins` (from `10` to `24`), but because `NumOfCoins` is a constant, Ruby issues a warning. In Figure 5-2, Ruby warns you "already initialized constant NumOfCoins."

Going with the Flow

Like so many other languages, Ruby has `if` statements and loops. Both `if` statements and loops control the flow of a program's execution. Listing 5-3 has both an `if` statement and a loop. Figure 5-3 shows a run of the code in Listing 5-3.

Listing 5-3: Repeating and Making Choices

```
3.times do
  print "Enter a value: "
  STDOUT.flush
  value = gets.to_i

  if value == 1
    puts "one"
  elsif value == 2
    puts "two"
  else
    puts "many"
  end

  puts
end
```

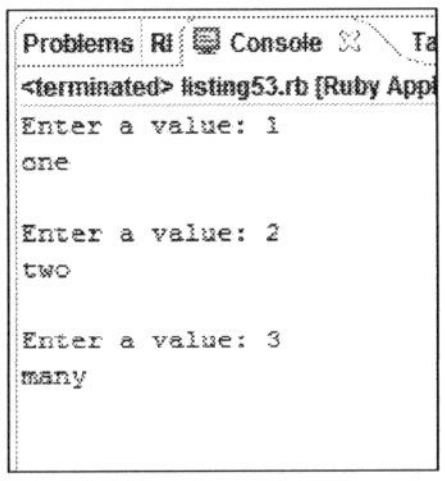

```
Problems  Ri  Console  Ta
<terminated> listing53.rb [Ruby Appl
Enter a value: 1
one

Enter a value: 2
two

Enter a value: 3
many
```

Figure 5-3: Turning numbers into words.

The `if` statement in Listing 5-3 starts by comparing `value` to `1`. If the comparison is favorable (that is, if `value` equals `1`), Ruby displays `one` and jumps down to the `puts` statement. When the comparison with `1` isn't favorable, the `if` statement marches on to compare `value` to `2`.

If the comparison with `2` is favorable (that is, if `value` equals `2`), Ruby displays `two` and jumps down to the `puts` statement. But when the comparison with `2` isn't favorable, Ruby executes whatever code is between `else` and `end`. If `value` is neither `1` nor `2`, this program displays the word `many`.

The whole process (the execution of the `if` statement with its comparisons and printing) takes place three times in Figure 5-3. The reason for this repetition is that the `if` statement is inside a loop. The loop starts with `3.times do`, and ends with the last line in Listing 5-3. (I have more to tell you about this `3.times` business. See Chapter 6.)

In Ruby, the assignment operator is a single equal sign (`=`), and comparison for equality is a double equal sign (`==`). Every programmer goofs once in a while and uses a single equal sign in an `if` statement's comparison clause. But the expression `value = 1` (with a single equal sign) doesn't do what you expect it to do. The expression `value = 1` assigns `1` to `value`. What's worse, the expression `value = 1` is always true because, in Ruby, all numbers are considered to be true. Even the number 0 is true. So whenever you mistakenly ask Ruby `if value = 1`, Ruby considers `value = 1` to be true. The moral of the story is, don't write `if value = 1`. Instead write `if value == 1`.

In Ruby, a double ampersand (`&&`) stands for *and,* an exclamation point (`!`) stands for *not,* and a double pipe (`||`) stands for *or.* So you can combine simple conditions to obtain complex conditions. For example, the expression

```
age >= 13 && !(time_of_day < 18 || reply == 'Yes')
```

is true as long as the first condition (`age` is greater than or equal to `13`) is true and both remaining conditions (`time_of_day` is less than `18` and the `reply` is `'Yes'`) are false. Here's another way to say the same thing: The whole expression is true as long as `age` is greater than or equal to `13`, and it is not true that either `time_of_day` is less than `18` or that `reply` is `'Yes'`. How about that?

Getting input from the keyboard

Listing 5-3 contains a call to Ruby's `gets` method. The `gets` method accepts input from the keyboard (in this program, a number such as `1`, `2`, or `3`). But `gets` interprets whatever you type as a string of characters. If you type `2`, then the value of plain old `gets` is the string `"2"`. Unfortunately, the string `"2"` isn't the same as the number `2`, so with plain old `gets`, a comparison such as `value == 2` always fails. (The comparison fails because Ruby compares the string `"2"` with the number `2`.)

To fix this problem, Listing 5-3 calls Ruby's `to_i` method. (The name `to_i` stands for "to integer.") Every string has a `to_i` method. In Listing 5-3, `gets` is a string (such as `"2"`). But `gets.to_i` is a number (such as `2`). Listing 5-3 assigns `gets.to_i` to the variable named `value`, so `value` is a number (such as `2`) and the comparison `value == 2` makes sense.

You can apply `to_i` to any string, not only to strings of digits. If you apply `to_i` to an alphabetic string, then `to_i` returns 0.

In Listing 5-3, the line `STDOUT.flush` ensures that the RadRails Console displays the program's output correctly. Without `STDOUT.flush`, RadRails does all its reading before it does any of its writing. The result is that lines of the program's output seem to appear out of sequence. This nasty effect happens only when the program contains a `gets` call. Furthermore, the effect happens only in RadRails. (You can run a Ruby program from your operating system's command line. If you do, the call to `STDOUT.flush` in Listing 5-3 is optional.)

Using keywords

A *keyword* is a word that has the same meaning in all Ruby programs. Listing 5-3 uses the keywords `do`, `if`, `elsif`, `else`, and `end`. Some other keywords that you encounter in this book's examples include the words `class`, `false`, `module`, `nil`, `self`, `super`, `true`, `unless`, `until`, `while`, and `yield`.

As a general rule (subject to exceptions), the names of things aren't Ruby keywords. For example, method names such as `puts` and `print` aren't keywords. Ruby defines these names in its standard library. But with a little code, you can change the meanings of these names.

When you make up names for things in a Ruby program, don't use any of Ruby's keywords. A statement such as `do = 20` isn't legal as far as Ruby is concerned.

In Ruby, the word `false` is a keyword. The comparison `if false` is never true. The word `nil` is also a keyword. The keyword `nil` stands for a *nothing object* — an object that happens not to be anything (whatever that means). In a Ruby comparison, `nil` is the same as `false`. So `if nil` is never true.

Flowing the other way

Ruby has many variations on the `if` statement and the loop. Like so many other languages, Ruby has a `while` loop. (See Listing 5-4 and also the output of Listing 5-4 in Figure 5-4.)

Listing 5-4: A while Loop

```
i = 10
while i >= 0
  print i, " bottles of beer on the wall.\n"
  i -= 1
end
```

```
Problems  RI  Console  Tasks  RegExp
<terminated> loops.rb [Ruby Application] Ruby C:\
10 bottles of beer on the wall.
9 bottles of beer on the wall.
8 bottles of beer on the wall.
7 bottles of beer on the wall.
6 bottles of beer on the wall.
5 bottles of beer on the wall.
4 bottles of beer on the wall.
3 bottles of beer on the wall.
2 bottles of beer on the wall.
1 bottles of beer on the wall.
0 bottles of beer on the wall.
```

Figure 5-4: A classy program runs its course.

Ruby's `until` loop does roughly the same things as Ruby's `while` loop. For example, the code in Listing 5-5 produces the same output as the code in Listing 5-4.

Listing 5-5: An until Loop

```
i = 10
until i < 0
  print i, " bottles of beer on the wall.\n"
  i -= 1
end
```

Going with the glow (or glowing with the flow)

In addition to `while` loops, `until` loops, and other loops, Ruby has *modifiers*. A modifier is like an `if` statement or a loop. But a modifier applies to only one statement. And you write the modifier after the statement that it modifies. The code in Listing 5-6 contains two modifiers.

Listing 5-6: An until Modifier

```
i = 1
i += 7 until i > 30
puts i if i % 2 == 0
```

The output of the code in Listing 5-6 is the number `36`. The program starts with `i` equal to `1`, then adds `7` to `i` (making `i` equal to 8), then adds `7` a few more times until `i` becomes 36. The looping stops because 36 is greater than 30.

On the last line of Listing 5-6, Ruby compares `36 % 2` with `0`. Remember that the percent sign (`%`) represents the remainder upon division. When you divide 36 by 2, you get the remainder 0. (In fact, when you divide any even number by 2, you get the remainder 0.) On the last line of Listing 5-6, the condition `i % 2 == 0` is true. So the program displays the value of `i`, which is 36.

An `if` statement, a `while` loop, or an `until` loop may contain one or more statements. But a modifier applies to only one statement.

Ruby has a `for` loop. For example, the output of code in Listing 5-7 is `1 5 9 4 fish`.

Listing 5-7: A for Loop

```
for value in [1, 5, 9, 4, "fish"] do
  print value, " "
end
```

Ruby also has a ternary conditional expression. The expression is called *ternary* because it takes three parameters. A ternary expression has the following form:

```
condition_to_test ? value_when_true : value_when_false
```

Listing 5-8 contains the ternary expression `i != 1 ? 's' : ''`. When `i != 1` is true, the ternary expression's value is `'s'`. But when `i != 1` is false, the ternary expression's value is `''` (two single quotes surrounding nothing — a string containing no characters). The output of Listing 5-8 is shown in Figure 5-5.

Listing 5-8: Making Decisions the Easy Way

```
i = 10
while i >= 0
  print i, " bottle#{i != 1 ? 's' : ''} of beer ",
    "on the wall.\n"
  i -= 1
end
```

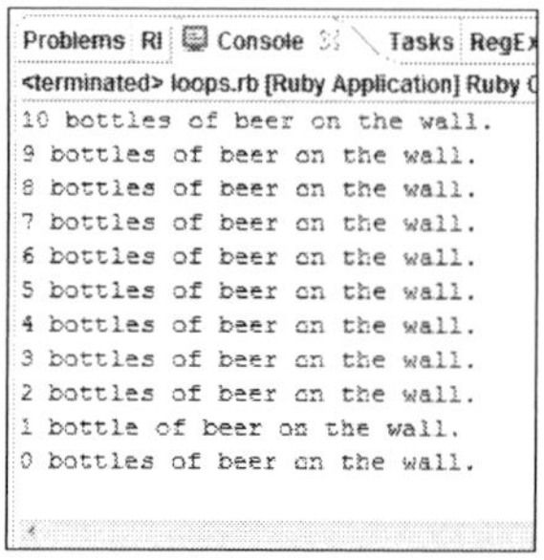

```
Problems RI Console Tasks RegEx
<terminated> loops.rb [Ruby Application] Ruby
10 bottles of beer on the wall.
9 bottles of beer on the wall.
8 bottles of beer on the wall.
7 bottles of beer on the wall.
6 bottles of beer on the wall.
5 bottles of beer on the wall.
4 bottles of beer on the wall.
3 bottles of beer on the wall.
2 bottles of beer on the wall.
1 bottle of beer on the wall.
0 bottles of beer on the wall.
```

Figure 5-5: The output for one bottle is grammatically correct.

Bunches of Things

Ruby has two structures that collect individual values into groups of values. One structure, familiar to people who program in other languages, is an *array*. The other (less familiar) structure is called a *hash*.

Arrays

An array is an indexed collection of things. Listing 5-9 gives you an example.

Listing 5-9: Keeping Track of a Hotel's Guests

```
how_many_in_room = [2, 3, "closed for repair", 0, 1]
how_many_in_room += [2]

puts "Displaying individual elements:"
puts how_many_in_room[0]
puts how_many_in_room[5]
puts

puts "Stepping through elements:"
for count in how_many_in_room
  puts count
end
puts

puts "Stepping through indices:"
for room_number in 0..10
  print room_number, " ",
    how_many_in_room[room_number], "\n"
end
```

Here are some observations about the code in Listing 5-9:

- **A Ruby array may contain values of any type.**

  The array in Listing 5-9 contains several integer values and one string value. In many other languages, you can't mix integers and strings in a single array.

- **An array has no fixed size.**

  The second line of Listing 5-9 enlarges the `how_many_in_room` array by adding a new element to the existing array. If you want, you can add 1,000 new elements. Ruby doesn't care.

- **An array's indices start with 0.**

  In Listing 5-9, the array's initial element, `how_many_in_room[0]`, stores the value 2. (See Figure 5-6.)

- **You can step through an array's elements using a loop.**

  Listing 5-9 steps through the `how_many_in_room` array with the `for count` loop.

- **You can step through an array's indices.**

  The last loop in Listing 5-9 has `room_number` going from 0 to 10, inclusive. This `0..10` expression is called a *range*. You can use ranges almost anywhere in your code, not only in `for` loops.

  Ruby has two notations for ranges — a notation that uses two dots, and a notation that uses three dots. These different notations have slightly different meanings. The range `0..5` (with two dots) stands for the numbers 0 to 5 *inclusive*. But the range `0...5` (with three dots) stands for the numbers 0 to 4 (excluding the 5).

```
Problems RI Console Tasks RegExp
<terminated> bunches.rb [Ruby Application] Ruby C:
Displaying individual elements:
2
2

Stepping through elements:
2
3
closed for repair
0
1
2

Stepping through indices:
0 2
1 3
2 closed for repair
3 0
4 1
5 2
6 nil
7 nil
8 nil
9 nil
10 nil
```

Figure 5-6: Listing the numbers of people in hotel rooms.

Ruby arrays are rich and varied creatures. You can do dozens of things with Ruby arrays that you can't do with other languages' arrays. For details, visit `http://www.ruby-doc.org/core/classes/Array.html`.

Hashes

A hash is like an array, except that a hash's indices aren't necessarily numbers. More precisely, a *hash* is a collection of key/value pairs. Each pair is called an *entry*. The hash

```
{'Book' => 20.00, 'Shirt' => 15.00, 'Cup' => 10.00}
```

contains three entries. In one entry, `'Book'` is the key and `20.00` is the value. In another entry, `'Shirt'` is the key and `15.00` is the value. Listing 5-10 illustrates some features of Ruby hashes.

Listing 5-10: Using a Hash

```
price_of =
  {'Book' => 20.00, 'Shirt' => 15.00, 'Cup' => 10.00}
price_of['Car'] = 15000.00

puts "Displaying a value:"
printf("$%5.2f", price_of['Book'])
puts; puts

puts "Displaying entries:"
for one_thing in price_of
  print one_thing, "\n"
end
puts

puts "Displaying keys and values:"
for first_thing, second_thing in price_of
  printf("%s\t$%5.2f\n", first_thing, second_thing)
end
```

Figure 5-7 shows a run of the code in Listing 5-10. In Listing 5-10, a hash named `price_of` begins its life with three entries. But the hash gains a fourth entry (for `'Car'`) on a subsequent line of code.

You use brackets to refer to a particular entry's value. So in Listing 5-10, the expression `price_of['Car']` stands for the a new `'Car'` entry's value, and the expression `price_of['Book']` stands for the `'Book'` entry's value.

Problems RI Console Tasks
<terminated> bunches_2.rb [Ruby Applicat
Displaying a value:
$20.00
Displaying entries:
Shirt15.0
Cup10.0
Car15000.0
Book20.0
Displaying keys and values:
Shirt $15.00
Cup $10.00
Car $15000.00
Book $20.00

Figure 5-7: Displaying hash keys and values.

Hashes and loops

The `for` loops in Listing 5-10 are interesting. Both loops cycle through the entries in the `price_of` hash. But in the first loop, the variable `one_thing` stands for an entire hash entry. And in the second loop, the variables `first_thing` and `second_thing` stand for the two parts of an entry (the key and the value).

The chosen variable names have nothing to do with this. (Replacing `one_thing` by `fred` everywhere in the first `for` loop doesn't change the way this code works.) The code works because, in the first line of each `for` loop, Ruby counts the variables and figures out what each variable signifies.

Writing the fine print

If you've written programs in C or C++, you feel at home with Ruby's `printf` method. The method's first parameter is a *format string*. The format string's cryptic codes tell Ruby how to display the remaining parameters. In particular, in the code `%5.2f`, the `5` tells Ruby to take at least five characters (including the decimal point) to display a number. Also, in `%5.2f`, the `2` tells Ruby to display two digits to the right of the decimal point. So in Figure 5-7, Ruby displays `$20.00`, not `$20.0` and not `$20.000`.

TECHNICAL STUFF

With the format code `%5.2f`, the number `5` is merely advisory. If the number being displayed requires only four characters, Ruby pads the number with a blank space. If the number being displayed requires ten characters, Ruby ignores the `5` and displays ten characters.

The `printf` call in the second `for` loop illustrates some facts about Ruby's format strings. A format string may contain more than one format code. The string `"%s\t$%5.2f\n"` contains two format codes — the code `%s` to display the value of `first_thing`, and the code `%5.2f` to display the value of `second_thing`. The code `%s` stands for any string, and indeed, the value of `first_thing` is a string.

The format string `"%s\t$%5.2f\n"` contains other characters — characters that aren't format codes. In this format string, `\t` stands for a tab, `$` stands for itself (a dollar sign to be displayed), and `\n` stands for a line break.

A typical Ruby statement is exactly one line of code. But a statement can straddle several lines. And you can separate two statements with a semicolon. If you do, you can squeeze two (or more) statements on a line. In Listing 5-10, the line `puts;  puts` contains two Ruby statements.

Using Methods

A Ruby *method* is a named sequence of statements. Other languages use the terms *function, subprogram,* or *procedure* to refer to a sequence of this kind. You can do two things with a method.

- **You can define the method.**

  When you define a method, Ruby doesn't execute the statements inside the method.

- **You can call a defined method.**

  When you call a method, Ruby executes the statements inside the method.

Listing 5-11 has some examples.

Listing 5-11: Don't Move! You're Surrounded.

```
# Method definitions...

def show_surrounded_alan
  puts "**Alan**"
end

def show_surrounded(param)
  puts "**#{param}**"
end

def surround(param)
  "**#{param}**"
end

def surrounding(param)
```

```
  yield("**#{param}**")
end

def surround_all(param_1, param_2, param_3)
  yield "**#{param_1}**", "**#{param_2}**",
    "**#{param_3}**"
end

def show_all_surrounded(*params_in)
  for param in params_in do
    puts "**#{param}**"
  end
end

# Method calls...

show_surrounded_alan

show_surrounded("Barry")
show_surrounded "Barry"

your_string = surround("Chris")
puts your_string

surrounding("Eddie") { |x| puts x }

surround_all("Frank", "George",
  "Harriet") { |x, y, z| puts x, y, z }

show_all_surrounded("Irene", "Jennie", "Karen")
```

Figure 5-8 shows a run of the code in Listing 5-11. The code defines six methods. Each method adds asterisks (in one way or another) to a string of characters.

```
Problems | RI | Console
<terminated> my_method.r
**Alan**
**Barry**
**Barry**
**Chris**
**Eddie**
**Frank**
**George**
**Harriet**
**Irene**
**Jennie**
**Karen**
```

Figure 5-8: How to choose a name for your baby.

Methods, methods everywhere

This section takes a closer look at each of the methods in Listing 5-11.

A method with no parameters

The `show_surrounded_alan` method is the simplest method in Listing 5-11. This method takes no parameters. When you call the method, the method's `puts` call displays `**Alan**`.

Later in Listing 5-11, a line containing the name `show_surrounded_alan` calls this method into action.

A method that displays a value

The next method in Listing 5-11 (the `show_surrounded` method) takes one parameter. The method's `puts` call displays that parameter surrounded with asterisks.

In Listing 5-11, I call the `show_surrounded` method twice — once with parentheses around the parameter `"Barry"` and once without parentheses. In Ruby, parentheses around parameter lists are optional.

A method that returns a value

The `surround` method's definition contains an expression (`"**#{param}**"`). When you call the method, Ruby evaluates this expression. At first the act of evaluating doesn't do anything. Nothing changes as a result of the evaluation.

But a Ruby method returns the result of its last expression evaluation. So in Listing 5-11, a call to the `surround` method returns the result `"**Chris**"`. Ruby assigns this result to `your_string` and displays `**Chris**` in the RadRails Console view.

The idea about a method's returning the value of its last expression is really important. The idea is worth repeating. So . . .

A Ruby method returns the result of its last expression evaluation. There. I repeated it.

A method call with a block

Putting curly braces around a statement (or a bunch of statements) turns the statement into a *block*.

In Listing 5-11, the call to the `surrounding` method has both a parameter and a block. The parameter is `"Eddie"`, and the block is `{ |x| puts x }`. (You can also create a block using the words `do` and `end`. See the explanation in Chapter 6.)

The definition of the `surrounding` method contains a `yield` statement. The word `yield` is a Ruby keyword. When the Ruby interpreter encounters a `yield` statement, the interpreter temporarily yields control to the block of statements following the method call. (See Figure 5-9.)

To make things even more interesting, a block may contain its own parameters. When you create a block, you enclose the block's parameters in pipe symbols (| |). For example, in Listing 5-11, the call to the `surrounding` method has a block with parameter `x`. In the same listing, the call to the `surround_all` method has a block with parameters `x`, `y`, and `z`.

So many different things have parameters! A method has parameters; a block has parameters. What else has parameters?

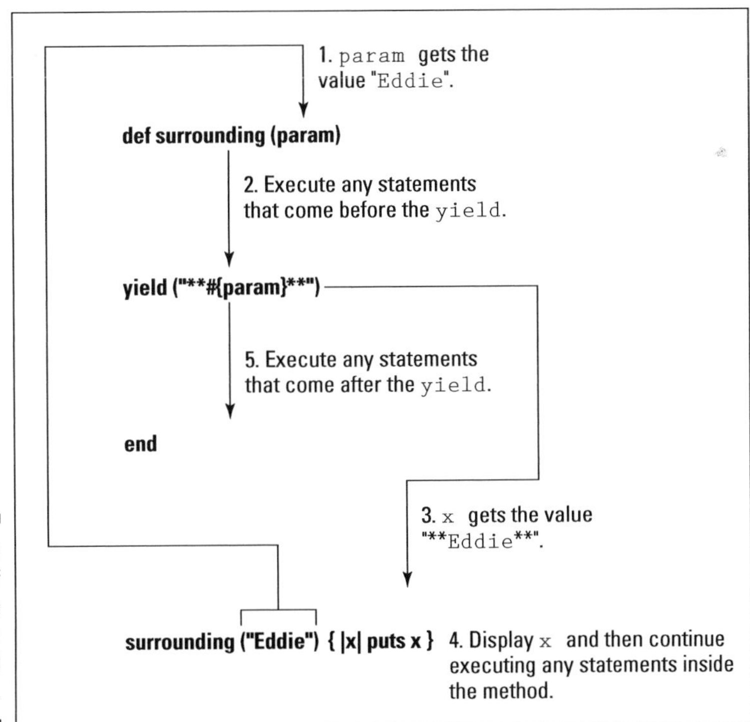
1. param gets the value "Eddie".
def surrounding (param)
2. Execute any statements that come before the yield.
yield ("**#{param}**")
5. Execute any statements that come after the yield.
end
3. x gets the value "**Eddie**".
surrounding ("Eddie") { |x| puts x }
4. Display x and then continue executing any statements inside the method.

Figure 5-9: The flow of execution when a method call has a block.

In Listing 5-11, the yield statement in the surrounding method's definition has a parameter! Ruby passes this parameter ("**Eddie**") to the method call's block. The call's block displays the parameter in the RadRails Console view.

A block with three parameters

The surround_all method does almost the same thing as the surrounding method. But the surround_all method takes three parameters (param_1, param_2, param_3). And the surround_all method's yield statement has three parameters ("**#{param_1}**", "**#{param_2}**", "**#{param_3}**").

To be in step with the method definition, the call to surround_all in Listing 5-11 has three parameters ("Frank", "George", "Harriet"). And the block following the call has three parameters of its own (x, y, z). When Ruby executes the yield statement, the block's x parameter becomes "**Frank**", the block's y parameter becomes "**George**", and the block's z parameter becomes "**Harriet**". The block displays these three values in the RadRails Console view.

A method with a variable number of parameters

In the show_all_surrounded method's definition, the parameter contains an asterisk (*). The asterisk before params_in tells Ruby that params_in may stand for more than one value.

Indeed, the last line of Listing 5-11 has three values in its call to show_all_surrounded. In the definition of show_all_surrounded, a for loop steps through the three params_in values. Each time through the loop, the code displays a name surrounded by asterisks.

If your method definition contains more than one parameter name, you can put an asterisk before the last of the names. You can't put an asterisk before any of the other parameter names.

Please pass the hash

A previous section describes Ruby hashes — lists of key/value pairs. In Ruby on Rails code, you often see a hash being passed as a parameter to a method. Listing 5-12 has an example.

Listing 5-12: Passing a Hash to a Method

```
def display(price_of)
  for first_thing, second_thing in price_of
    printf("%s\t$%5.2f\n", first_thing, second_thing)
  end
end

display( 'Book' => 20.00, 'Shirt' => 15.00,
                              'Cup' => 10.00 )
```

On first glance, the call to the `display` method in Listing 5-12 has three parameters. But the `display` method's definition has only one parameter. So what's going on?

In the call, the three things in parentheses form a single hash (a hash with three entries). If you do what you did in this chapter's "Hashes" section — that is, you surround the three entries with curly braces — the stuff in the method call looks more like a hash. But if you omit the curly braces, Ruby scratches its virtual head and figures out that these three things form a hash.

If you're not convinced that the parameter `price_of` represents a hash, add the statement `puts price_of.class` to the code inside the `display` method's definition. The output of the `puts` call is the word `Hash`.

A run of the code in Listing 5-12 is shown in Figure 5-10.

```
Problems  Ri  Consol
<terminated> hash_pass
Shirt   $15.00
Cup     $10.00
Book    $20.00
```

Figure 5-10: Displaying items and their prices.

What's the symbolism?

Twenty-five centuries ago, the Greek philosopher Democritus said that everything is made of atoms. In Democritus's view, each atom is indivisible. An atom has no characteristics. It's a point with no shape. It's a black hole with no hair. (Stephen Hawking would be pleased.)

Like a Democritus atom, a Ruby *symbol* has no characteristics. (Well, a symbol has a few characteristics, but not many.) You might ask, “What good is a thing with no characteristics?” You can’t display this thing’s parts because it has no parts. You can’t combine two of these things because if you did, the new thing would have internal parts.

Fortunately, you can distinguish one Ruby symbol from another, and that’s what makes symbols worth using. What’s more, a symbol without parts has no baggage; so symbols are efficient and easy to use.

Ruby on Rails code passes symbols around as if they were chips in a poker game. So symbols are worth investigating. Listing 5-13 begins the investigation.

Listing 5-13: Passing Symbols from Place to Place

```
def decide_about(thing)
  puts "Executing decide_about..."
  print thing, " is "
  puts "the 'b' symbol." if thing == :book
  puts "the 's' symbol." if thing == :shirt
  puts "a string."       if thing == "book"
  puts
end

def show_hash(my_hash)
  puts "Executing show_hash..."
  puts my_hash[:book], my_hash[:shirt]
  puts "$$$" if my_hash[:book] == 'costly'
  puts
end

def show_hash_again(my_hash)
  puts "Executing show_hash_again..."
  for entry in my_hash
    puts entry
  end
  puts
end

decide_about :book
show_hash :book => 'costly', :shirt => 'cheap'
show_hash_again :book => 'costly', :shirt => 'cheap'
```

The code in Listing 5-13 calls three methods — `decide_about`, `show_hash`, and `show_hash_again`.

Comparing and displaying symbols

In Listing 5-13, the `decide_about` method does what little you can do with symbols. You can compare them with other values, and you can display their names.

- The `decide_about` method compares its parameter with the symbols `:book` and `:shirt`. The only positive match is with `:book`. (See Figure 5-11.) Ruby distinguishes atoms with different names from one another. The `:book` atom isn't the same as the `:shirt` atom.
- The `decide_about` method compares its parameter with the string `"book"`. The match isn't positive. (Again, see Figure 5-11.) Atoms aren't strings. The `:book` atom isn't the same as the `"book"` string.
- When the `decide_about` method displays its `thing` variable (with value `:book`), the RadRails Console displays the word `book`. Each symbol has a name, and Ruby knows how to display a symbol's name.

```
Problems  RI  Console  Tasks
<terminated> use_symbol.rb [Ruby Applic
Executing decide_about...
book is the 'b' symbol.

Executing show_hash...
costly
cheap
$$$

Executing show_hash_again...
book
costly
shirt
cheap
```

Figure 5-11: How things look after a run of the code in Listing 5-13.

A string has many more characteristics than an atom. You can insert new characters into a string. You can find substrings within a string. You can capitalize the letters in a string. But you can't do any of these things with a symbol. A symbol is a symbol is a symbol. That's all there is to it. You can call a symbol's `to_s` method to derive a string from the symbol, but why bother?

Using symbols as hash keys

The second and third methods in Listing 5-13 deal with symbols as the keys for hash entries. Ruby on Rails code does this all the time. When you write your own Rails code, you may call a method with hash parameter `:book => 'costly', :shirt => 'cheap'`. In many cases, the method you call is part of the Rails library, so you don't have easy access to the method's code.

In one way or another, the Rails method's code looks like the `show_hash` method's code in Listing 5-13. With expressions such as `my_hash[:book]` and `my_hash[:shirt]`, the code distinguishes one hash entry from another. Then with the value of `my_hash[:book]`, the code forms a condition and makes a decision based on the condition's truth or falsehood.

The last method in Listing 5-13 (the `show_hash_again` method) steps through the hash's entries. But unlike the `show_hash` method, this `show_hash_again` method doesn't separate the keys from the values.

Chapter 6

Ruby Two's Day

In This Chapter

- Discovering object-oriented programming in 25 pages or fewer
- Using Ruby's iterators
- Gathering code into modules

Think about something tiny — a tiny icon on a computer's screen. Magnify the icon's image by a factor of 7 or more. What do you see?

You see dots. You see jagged edges and blurs. If you magnify by a sufficiently large factor, you don't even see the original image. What once looked like a picture of a file folder becomes a meaningless field of light and dark pixels.

If you look at an image too closely and you ignore the big picture, you're likely to miss something important. A similar thing happens when you write computer programs. If you concentrate too much on each little statement and ignore the way statements are organized into larger units, you miss some important concepts.

Objects and Classes

An *object* is a single thing. Here's an `employee` object. The `employee` object has a name (`"Barry Burd"`), a hire date (`2006-06-21`), and a salary (`1000000.00`). And here's a second `employee` object. This second object has a different name (`"Harriet Ritter"`), a different hire date (`2006-06-25`), and a different salary (`50000.00`).

A *class* is a blueprint. The blueprint describes each one of a bunch of similar things. The `Employee` class says that each employee object has a name, a hire date, and a salary. The `Employee` class doesn't contain any particular name (such as `"Barry Burd"` or `"Harriet Ritter"`). The `Employee` class doesn't contain any particular hire date or salary. Instead, the `Employee` class is an ethereal outline, a prediction of things to come when some `employee` objects are eventually created.

Each object forged from a class is called an *instance* of that class. The employee object whose name is `"Barry Burd"` is an instance of the `Employee` class. The employee object with name `"Harriet Ritter"` is another instance of the `Employee` class. After defining the `Employee` class, you can create as few or as many instances as you want. (See Listing 6-1 and the run in Figure 6-1.)

Listing 6-1: Defining and Using an Employee Class

```
require 'date'

class Employee
  attr_reader :name, :hiredate, :salary
  attr_writer :salary
  def initialize(n, h, s)
    @name = n
    @hiredate = h
    @salary = s
  end
end

a_date = Date.new(2006, 6, 21)
me = Employee.new("Barry Burd", a_date, 1000000.00)

a_date = Date.new(2006, 6, 25)
you = Employee.new("Harriet Ritter", a_date, 50000.00)

print me.name
printf("\t%s\t%5.2f\n", me.hiredate, me.salary)

print you.name
printf("\t%s\t%5.2f\n", you.hiredate, you.salary)

me.salary += 1000.00
print me.name
printf("\t%s\t%5.2f\n", me.hiredate, me.salary)
```

Listing 6-1 defines an `Employee` class. The `Employee` class has three *instance variables* — `@name`, `@hiredate`, and `@salary`. As the term "instance variable" suggests, each instance of the `Employee` class has its own `@name`, `@hiredate`, and `@salary`.

A variable that starts with a single at-sign (`@`) is an instance variable.

```
Problems  RI  Console  Tasks  RegExp
<terminated> employee.rb [Ruby Application] Ruby C:\ruby\bin\ruby.e
Barry Burd        2006-06-21      1000000.00
Harriet Ritter    2006-06-25      50000.00
Barry Burd        2006-06-21      1001000.00
```

Figure 6-1: Barry earns more money.

In Listing 6-1, the line `attr_reader :name, :hiredate, :salary` makes the instance variables' values visible to code outside the class definition. For example, the statement `print me.name` isn't inside the `Employee` class definition. So if you remove `attr_reader :name` from Listing 6-1, the statement `print me.name` is no longer allowed.

The method named `attr_writer` allows code outside the class definition to change one or more of the instance variables' values. Without the `attr_writer` call in Listing 6-1, the statement `me.salary += 1000.00` is no longer allowed.

Creating objects

After defining a class, you can create an instance of the class by calling the class's `new` method. Listing 6-1 creates two instances of the `Employee` class. In the first case, the listing assigns `Employee.new` to the `me` variable. In the second case, the listing assigns `Employee.new` to the `you` variable. So the variable `me` refers to one instance, and the variable `you` refers to another instance.

When you create an instance, you may include parameters along with the call to `new`. For example, in Listing 6-1, the first call to `Employee.new` has parameters `"Barry Burd"`, `a_date`, and `1000000.00`. The call to the `new` method triggers the execution of the `Employee` class's `initialize` method. In turn, the `initialize` method assigns these parameter values to the three instance variables — `@name`, `@hiredate`, and `@salary`.

A call to a `new` method triggers the execution of a class's `initialize` method. This relationship between two method names, such as `new` and `initialize`, is an irregular occurrence in Ruby. In most cases, a method call triggers execution of a method of the same name. For example, if you call `my_string.chomp`, Ruby looks for a method whose definition begins with `def chomp`.

An object stands in a "has a" relationship with each of its instance variables. An employee object *has a* `name`, *has a* `hiredate`, and *has a* `salary`.

Adding another file's code to your own file's code

Listing 6-1 defines the `Employee` class but not the `Date` class. The `Date` class is defined in a file named `date.rb` — a file that comes standard with the Ruby interpreter. When you fire up the Ruby interpreter, the interpreter loads only the stuff you need in order to run your code. If you don't put the statement `require 'date'` in your program, the interpreter doesn't load the `date.rb` code. In that case, the interpreter doesn't know what `Date.new(2006, 6, 25)` means.

If you put a file (call it `orphan.rb`) in some arbitrary directory on your hard drive, the chance that the Ruby interpreter responds to a `require 'orphan'` request is very small. A file such as `date.rb` or `orphan.rb` can't live in any old directory on your computer's hard drive. For the interpreter to find a file, the file must be somewhere in the interpreter's *load path.*

The load path is an array of directory names. When the interpreter encounters a `require` call, the interpreter searches this array's directories for a file whose name matches the name in the `require` call.

Ruby follows the UNIX shell tradition of using brief, cryptic combinations of characters to represent some important system variables. If you want to see the directory names in the load path, do you think of adding `puts $:` to your program's code? Sure, you do. Because in a Ruby program, `$:` stands for the load path. Go figure!

Classes, objects, and database tables

Database tables resemble classes and objects.

- **A class is like the collection of column names in a database table.**

  An `employees` table may have a `name` column, a `hiredate` column, and a `salary` column. The corresponding `Employee` class definition decrees that each of its instances has a `name`, a `hiredate`, and a `salary`.

- **An object is like a row in a database table.**

  The `employees` table may have a row with name `"Barry Burd"`, hire date `2006-06-21`, and salary `1000000.00`. The corresponding Ruby code may, at one time or another, have an `employee` object with name `"Barry Burd"`, hire date `2006-06-21`, and salary `1000000.00`.

- **A class is also like the collection of all rows in a database table.**

  An `employees` table may have 100 rows — one row for each of the company's 100 employees. You might find it useful to think of the `Employee` class as a bunch of employees (100 employees, all packed into a crowded room).

Comparing classes and objects with database tables might help you understand object-oriented programming (OOP) concepts. But the comparison isn't only metaphorical. Rich functionality arises when you connect objects to database table rows. For more information, see the material about *object-relational mapping* (ORM) in Chapter 9.

Objects Have Methods

An object can have methods. You may define the object's methods when you define the object's class. If you do, you tap into one of the central ideas in object-oriented programming. Listing 6-2 has an example.

Listing 6-2: Defining Methods within a Class

```
class Account
  attr_reader :name, :balance

  def initialize(n, b)
    @name = n
    @balance = b
  end

  def add_interest(rate)
    @balance += @balance * rate / 100
  end

  def display
    printf("%s, you have $%5.2f in your account.\n",
           @name, @balance)
  end
end

my_account = Account.new("Barry", 10.00)
my_account.add_interest(5.0)
my_account.display

your_account = Account.new("Harriet", 100.00)
your_account.add_interest(7.0)
your_account.display
```

The `Account` class in Listing 6-2 defines an `add_interest` method and a `display` method. The `add_interest` method takes a parameter (`rate`) and uses the `rate` to change the value of an instance's `@balance`. The `display` method takes no parameters. But the `display` method writes a sentence containing the instance's `@name` and `@balance`. A run of the code in Listing 6-2 is shown in Figure 6-2.

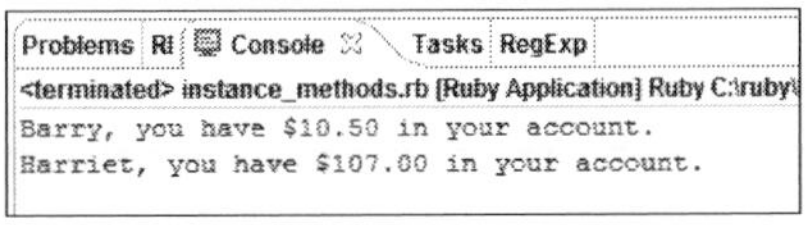

Problems | RI | Console | Tasks | RegExp

<terminated> instance_methods.rb [Ruby Application] Ruby C:\ruby\

```
Barry, you have $10.50 in your account.
Harriet, you have $107.00 in your account.
```

Figure 6-2: Barry must have spent all the money he earned in Figure 6-1.

The code in Listing 6-2 creates an instance of the `Account` class and assigns this instance to the `my_account` variable. Then the code calls the `my_account` instance's `add_interest` method. To state this a bit more precisely, the code *sends the* `add_interest(5.0)` *message* to the `my_account` object. When the `my_account` object receives the message, the object executes its `add_interest` method, adding 50 cents to my depleted account.

Next, the code sends a `display` message to the `my_account` object. In response, the `my_account` object executes its `display` method, writing my name and account balance in the RadRails Console view.

To call an instance's method, you follow a reference to the instance by a dot, then by the name of the method, and finally by any parameters to be sent along with the method call.

Like other authors, I use the words "call a method," even though in Ruby, the correct terminology is to "send a message." The differences between method calling and message sending are subtle. Most importantly, a call is an action (a verb), and a message is a thing (a noun). When you send a message, you send a thing of some kind to an object. The object can store that thing, analyze the thing, modify the thing, and so on. In this book, you don't have to sweat about the difference between method calling and message sending. But if you delve deeper into Ruby, you'll see how message sending works to your advantage.

Ruby's handy iterators

The whole is more than the sum of its parts. When you combine an instance method with a code block, you get an iterator — a super-duper Ruby programming technique.

An *iterator* method belongs to a collection (to an array or a hash). The iterator steps through the collection, from one element to another, doing something with each element. Different iterators do different things with the collection's elements.

The term "iterator" isn't baked into the Ruby programming language. The word `iterator` isn't a Ruby keyword. You don't declare a particular method to be an iterator. Instead, the word "iterator" describes certain kinds of methods. Thinking of certain methods as iterators helps you to understand how your program works.

Listing 6-3 makes use of my favorite iterator Ruby's `each` method.

Listing 6-3: The Truth about Iterators

```
class Account
  attr_reader :name, :balance

  def initialize(n, b)
    @name = n
    @balance = b
  end

  def add_interest(rate)
    @balance += @balance * rate / 100
  end

  def display
    printf("%s, you have $%5.2f in your account.\n",
            @name, @balance)
  end
end

my_account = Account.new("Barry", 10.00)
your_account = Account.new("Harriet", 100.00)
their_account = Account.new("Sam & Jen", 7836.00)

an_array = [my_account, your_account, their_account]

puts "ARRAY"
puts "an_array.each ..."
an_array.each { |e| e.display }
puts

a_hash = { :me => my_account, :you => your_account,
           :them => their_account }

puts "HASH"
puts "a_hash.each using |k, v| ..."
a_hash.each { |k, v| v.display }
puts

puts "a_hash.each_value ..."
a_hash.each_value { |v| v.display }
puts

puts "a_hash.each using |e| ..."
a_hash.each { |e| e[1].display }
puts

class Array
  def each_plus_interest(rate)
    for acct in self
```

(continued)

Listing 6-3 *(continued)*

```
        acct.add_interest(rate)
        yield acct
      end
    end
  end

  puts "ARRAY"
  puts "an_array.each_plus_interest ..."
  an_array.each_plus_interest(5.0) { |e| e.display }
  puts
```

Listing 6-3 begins by defining the `Account` class. (To keep things simple, I define identical `Account` classes in Listings 6-2 and 6-3.) After creating three accounts (mine, yours, and theirs), Listing 6-3 combines the accounts into an array (actually, into `an_array`).

A call to `an_array.each` sets interesting things into motion. Behind the scenes, Ruby's `each` method makes three `yield` calls — one call for each of the three array elements. With every `yield` call, Ruby executes the `{ |e| e.display }` block. During the first `yield` call, the variable `e` stands for the `"Barry"` account. So Ruby executes the `"Barry"` instance's `display` method. During the second `yield` call, Ruby displays the `"Harriet"` instance. And during the third `yield` call, Ruby reveals Sam and Jen's finances. (See Figure 6-3.)

```
Problems  RI  Console  Tasks  RegExp
<terminated> use_each.rb [Ruby Application] Ruby C:\ruby\bin\ruby.exe : u
ARRAY
an_array.each ...
Barry, you have $10.00 in your account.
Harriet, you have $100.00 in your account.
Sam & Jen, you have $7836.00 in your account.

HASH
a_hash.each using |k, v| ...
Sam & Jen, you have $7836.00 in your account.
Barry, you have $10.00 in your account.
Harriet, you have $100.00 in your account.

a_hash.each_value ...
Sam & Jen, you have $7836.00 in your account.
Barry, you have $10.00 in your account.
Harriet, you have $100.00 in your account.

a_hash.each using |e| ...
Sam & Jen, you have $7836.00 in your account.
Barry, you have $10.00 in your account.
Harriet, you have $100.00 in your account.

ARRAY
an_array.each_plus_interest ...
Barry, you have $10.50 in your account.
Harriet, you have $105.00 in your account.
Sam & Jen, you have $8227.80 in your account.
```

Figure 6-3: Running the code in Listing 6-3.

After calling `an_array.each`, Listing 6-3 repeats the process using a hash. In fact, Listing 6-3 repeats the process three times using the same hash.

- The first time, in a call to `a_hash.each`, Ruby distinguishes between each entry's key and value (each entry's `k` and `v`). Each value is an account, and Ruby calls the value's `display` method.
- The second time, Listing 6-3 calls `a_hash.each_value`. Ruby's `each_value` method works only with hashes. When you call `each_value`, the block's parameter becomes a hash entry's value (not an entire hash entry).

  In Listing 6-3, the variable `v` becomes an account, so the call `v.display` makes sense.
- The third time, Listing 6-3 calls `a_hash.each`. In this call, the block has only one parameter (the variable `e`). So the variable `e` stands for an entire hash entry (such as `:me => my_account`).

  To isolate an account from an entire entry, the code calls `e[1].display`. (For a hash entry `e`, the expression `e[0]` stands for the entry's key, and the expression `e[1]` stands for the entry's value. Isn't that convenient?)

Ruby iterators aren't mysterious. In fact, you can write your own iterators. For help, see this chapter's "Open classes" section.

Finding iterators where you least expect them

A listing in Chapter 5 contains this code:

```
3.times do
  # execute some statements
end
```

The code is so easy to read that you don't pay much attention to it. But, in fact, the code uses some nifty Ruby tricks.

For one thing, Ruby doesn't have a special `times` loop. The word `times` is the name of a method. When Ruby executes `3.times`, the interpreter sends a message to an object. In particular, the interpreter sends the `times` message to the `3` object.

In Ruby, a number such as `3` is an object. Like other whole numbers, the number `3` is an instance of Ruby's `Integer` class. And objects have methods. Every `Integer` instance (such as the number `3`) has a `times` method.

In Ruby, you can form blocks using curly braces. (Refer to Listing 6-3.) But you can also form blocks using the words do and end. When you write 3.times do, Ruby does the same kind of thing that it does in Listing 6-3. Namely, Ruby sends the times iterator message to the 3 object. In responding to the message, the times method yields repeatedly to the do ... end block's code.

Consider an example. You can display the word Ruby three times using either curly braces or do and end.

```
3.times do
  puts "Ruby"
end

3.times { puts "Ruby" }
```

You can even create a do ... end block with one or more parameters.

```
3.times do |x|
  print x, " "
end
```

When the times iterator performs a yield, the iterator passes a count (starting with 0) to the applicable block. So the output of this 3.times do |x| code is 0 1 2.

In most cases, you can flip a coin to decide how to create a block. "Heads, I use curly braces; tails, I use do and end." But a block enclosed in curly braces isn't exactly the same as a block created with the words do and end. The difference has to do with parameters — the parameters of the method to which the block applies. If you don't want to worry about the difference between curly braces and do/end blocks, always enclose the method call's parameter list in parentheses. If you use parentheses, curly braces are the same as do and end.

Enhancing Classes

If classes were fixed, inflexible things, object-oriented programming would be a momentary fad. No one would see the need to use classes and objects.

But classes are very flexible. After creating a class, you can use, reuse, and re-reuse the class. You can also modify the class in many useful ways. This section describes only two such ways. (Object-oriented programming has many more tricks up its virtual sleeve; but in this section, I cover only two.)

Open classes

Ruby has open classes. An *open* class is a class that obeys the old adage, "It ain't over 'til it's over."

Take, for example, Ruby's built-in `Array` class. The `Array` class has many methods — methods such as `insert`, `delete`, `fill`, and `length`. But the `Array` class has no built-in `each_plus_interest` method. So Listing 6-3 adds its own `each_plus_interest` method to the `Array` class's methods. An open class, even a class that's part of Ruby's standard library, is always "open for additional definitions."

The `each_plus_interest` method in Listing 6-3 is an iterator. The method calls `yield` for each account in the array. Each `yield` call defers temporarily to an `{|e| e.display }` block, and the block displays an account with interest added.

Being selfish

In the `each_plus_interest` method's definition (Listing 6-3), the word `self` refers to `an_array`. The word `self` (a Ruby keyword) refers to an instance of the class in which the word appears. (What does that mean? Read the next paragraph.)

In Listing 6-3, the word `self` refers to the array that receives the `each_plus_interest` call. Imagine having ten arrays. Name them `an_array`, `another_array`, `yet_another_array`, and so on. (Make up any names you want. It doesn't matter much.) When you call `an_array.each_plus_interest`, the word `self` refers to `an_array`. Later in the code, if you call `another_array.each_plus_interest`, the word `self` refers to `another_array`. And so on.

At first, you might find the word `self` confusing. But if you think about it, the word `self` in Ruby is very much like the word "self" in English. When I say "self," I refer to "Barry Burd." When you say "self," you refer to yourself (whoever you are). Everyone who says "self" refers to a different person. And in Ruby, every call to a method containing the word `self` refers to a different instance of a particular class. It's hard to imagine how you'd write the `each_plus_interest` method's definition without using something like the keyword `self`.

Defining subclasses

After defining a class, you can make things more specific by defining a *subclass.* Consider the Employee class in Listing 6-1. A subclass of Employee may be named FacultyMember. Another subclass of Employee may be named StaffMember. The Employee class is the *superclass* of both the FacultyMember and StaffMember classes.

In addition to having a name, a hiredate, and a salary, each FacultyMember instance has rank and research_specialty values. In addition to having a name, a hiredate, and a salary, each StaffMember has a sick_days value. In the language of object-oriented programming, the FacultyMember subclass *inherits* having a name, a hiredate, and a salary from its parent class (from the Employee class). Similarly, the StaffMember class inherits having a name, a hiredate, and a salary from the Employee class.

A class stands in an "is a" relationship with its superclass. A FacultyMember *is an* Employee. A StaffMember *is an* Employee.

Inheritance is important. With inheritance, the person who writes the FacultyMember code doesn't have to write any code dealing with a name, a hiredate, or a salary. The person writing the FacultyMember code writes only the rank and research_specialty code. The FacultyMember code inherits all the name, hiredate, and salary code from the parent Employee class. Listing 6-4 has an example.

Listing 6-4: A Tale of Two Subclasses

```
require 'date'

class Employee
  def initialize(n, h, s)
    @name = n
    @hiredate = h
    @salary = s
  end

  def display
    printf("%s\t%s\t$%5.2f", @name, @hiredate, @salary)
  end
end

class FacultyMember < Employee
  def initialize(n, h, s, ra, rs)
    super(n, h, s)
    @rank = ra
```

```
    @research_specialty = rs
  end

  def display
    puts "Faculty member:"
    super
    printf("\t%s\t%s", @rank, @research_specialty)
  end
end

class StaffMember < Employee
  def initialize(n, h, s, si)
    super(n, h, s)
    @sick_days = si
  end

  def display
    puts "Staff member:"
    super
    printf("\t%s", @sick_days)
  end
end

hire_date = Date.new(2004, 10, 12)
employee =
  Employee.new("Buddy Burd", hire_date, 2500.26)

hire_date = Date.new(1995, 3, 18)
faculty =
  FacultyMember.new("Bumper Burd", hire_date,
                    4125.01, "Assistant Professor",
                    "Computer Science")

hire_date = Date.new(2006, 1, 1)
staff =
  StaffMember.new("Binky Burd", hire_date, 1000.00, 24)

employee.display
print "\n\n"
faculty.display
print "\n\n"
staff.display
```

The less-than sign in `FacultyMember < Employee` means "is a subclass of." So in Listing 6-4, the `FacultyMember` class effortlessly inherits the instance variables `@name`, `@hiredate`, and `@salary` from the `Employee` class. You don't write code to handle these variables in the `FacultyMember` class. You simply use the variables with your newly created `FacultyMember` class.

Creating an instance of a subclass

In Listing 6-4, the call to `FacultyMember.new` has five parameters. The first three parameters match the inherited `Employee` variables, and the last two parameters match the `FacultyMember` class's own variables. To give values to all these variables, the `FacultyMember` class's `initialize` method does two things:

- **The `FacultyMember` class's `initialize` method calls `super(n, h, s)`.**

  The word `super` is a Ruby keyword. When you write `super` on its own, Ruby calls a method in the superclass. (Ruby calls a superclass method with the same name as the method containing the `super` keyword.) So in Listing 6-4, the call `super(n, h, s)` triggers execution of the `Employee` class's `initialize` method. In turn, the `Employee` class's `initialize` method assigns values to the variables `@name`, `@hiredate`, and `@salary`.

- **The `FacultyMember` class's own `initialize` method assigns values to `@rank` and to `@research_specialty`.**

  A plain old `Employee` instance doesn't have a `@rank` or a `@research_specialty`. So the `FacultyMember` class itself assigns values to these variables.

What is true of `initialize` methods is also true of the `StaffMember` class. The only difference is that the `StaffMember` class has `@name`, `@hiredate`, `@salary`, and `@sick_days` variables.

Using a subclass's method

Each class in Listing 6-4 has its own `display` method. The `faculty` variable refers to a `FacultyMember` instance. So when you call `faculty.display`, Ruby executes the `FacultyMember` class's `display` method.

When you call `staff.display`, Ruby executes the `StaffMember` class's `display` method. And the plain old `Employee` class doesn't go away. When you call `employee.display`, Ruby executes the original `Employee` class's `display` method. As proof, see Figure 6-4.

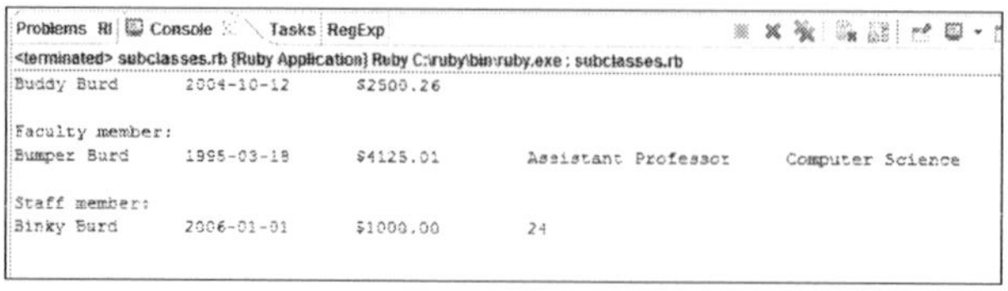

```
Problems RI  Console  Tasks  RegExp
<terminated> subclasses.rb [Ruby Application] Ruby C:\ruby\bin\ruby.exe : subclasses.rb
Buddy Burd      2004-10-12      $2500.26

Faculty member:
Bumper Burd     1995-03-18      $4125.01        Assistant Professor     Computer Science

Staff member:
Binky Burd      2006-01-01      $1000.00        24
```

Figure 6-4: Running the code in Listing 6-4.

Creating a Module

Each programming language provides ways of grouping code. Grouping is important because, without grouping, a large programming project is a large mess. In Ruby, you group code into *modules*. Listing 6-5 has an example.

Listing 6-5: Creating a Module

```
# This is human_resources.rb
require 'date'

module HumanResources
  Today = Date.today;

  class Employee
    def initialize(n, h, s)
      @name = n
      @hiredate = h
      @salary = s
    end

    def display
      printf("%s\t%s\t$%5.2f", @name, @hiredate, @salary)
    end
  end

end
```

The so-called "group of code" in Listing 6-5 consists of only two things — a `Today` constant and an `Employee` class. After defining this module, you can use the module's definitions in code outside of the module. Listing 6-6 shows you how. (A run of the code in Listing 6-6 is shown in Figure 6-5.)

Listing 6-6: Using the Things Defined in a Module

```
require 'human_resources'

class FacultyMember < HumanResources::Employee
  def initialize(n, h, s, ra, rs)
    super(n, h, s)
    @rank = ra
    @research_specialty = rs
  end

  def display
```

(continued)

Listing 6-6 ***(continued)***

```
    puts "Faculty member:"
    super
    printf("\t%s\t%s", @rank, @research_specialty)
  end
end


faculty =
  FacultyMember.new("Bumper Burd",
                    HumanResources::Today,
                    4125.01, "Assistant Professor",
                    "Computer Science")

faculty.display
```

```
Problems  Ri  Console  Tasks  RegExp
<terminated> use_module.rb [Ruby Application] Ruby C:\ruby\bin\ruby.exe : use_module.rb
Faculty member:
Bumper Burd     2006-10-02     $4125.01        Assistant Professor     Computer Science
```

Figure 6-5: Bumper rides again.

You can download Listings 6-5 and 6-6 from this book's Web site. But if you retype this code from scratch, put the code from Listing 6-5 in a file named `human_resources.rb`. Also, put the code from both listings in the same RadRails project.

Listing 6-6 begins with a `require` call. The call grabs the `human_resources.rb` file's code (the code in Listing 6-5). You can consider all the code in the `human_resources.rb` file to be resting soundly at the top of Listing 6-6.

With the `HumanResources` module's code at the top of Listing 6-6, the rest of Listing 6-6 may use anything defined inside the `HumanResources` module. The only caveat is that the code in Listing 6-6 must contain fully qualified names. Instead of `Employee` and `Today`, you must write `HumanResources::Employee` and `HumanResources::Today`.

If your fingers tire easily, you can avoid having to retype fully qualified names. Type the line `include HumanResources` immediately below the `require` call in Listing 6-6. If you do, Ruby assumes that `HumanResources::` belongs before any applicable names in the code.

Chapter 7

Weaving the Web

In This Chapter

- Understanding the Hypertext Transfer Protocol
- Coding basic Web pages
- Coding Web forms

What do the initials WWW mean to you? Wee Willie Winkie? Which way, Wanda? Where's Walter's wife? World Wide Web? If your answer is "World Wide Web," you've opened to the right chapter. This chapter describes the secrets behind Web pages. The chapter emphasizes secrets that pertain to Ruby on Rails developers.

The Working of the Web

What happens when you browse the Web? You sit in front of a computer, which is called the *client computer.* The client computer runs a piece of software (a *Web browser*). Because your browser runs on the client computer, your browser is called the *client program* (or simply, the *client*).

With your keyboard and mouse, you issue commands to the browser. You're called the *visitor* because you visit a Web site. Another name for you is the *user,* because you use the Web's services.

Whatever you call yourself, the Web browser turns each of your commands into a *request* and sends this request over the Internet to another computer somewhere else in the world. The computer that receives the request is called the *server computer.* The server computer runs a program called a *Web server.* The server program analyzes the request and sends back a *response.* (See Figure 7-1.) This response is typically a document known as a *Web page.*

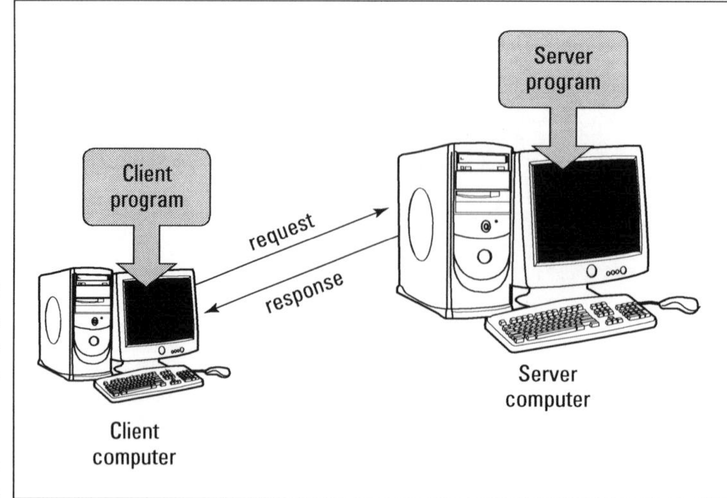

Figure 7-1: Communication between a client and a server.

Some Web pages are real documents. They sit on the server's hard drive, waiting to be sent along the Internet. They have filenames, such as `index.html`. A page of this kind (a page that's fully composed before a visitor makes a request) is called a *static* Web page.

In contrast, many Web pages aren't real documents. These pages don't exist until the server receives a visitor's request. When the server receives a request, the server composes one of these documents on-the-fly. A page of this kind is called a *dynamic* Web page.

The Web developer's point of view

The previous section describes the process from the visitor's point of view. Now look at it from the developer's point of view.

The developer works on the *local computer* — the computer on his or her desk. The developer creates and tests a Web page on the local computer. During this testing phase, the local computer runs both the client software and the server software. The flow of data is shown in Figure 7-2.

After testing a Web page, the developer *deploys* the page. The developer copies (that is, *uploads*) the page from his or her local computer to a *host computer.* The host computer's server accepts requests from clients all over the world. The page is finally "on the Internet." This scenario applies to both static and dynamic Web pages.

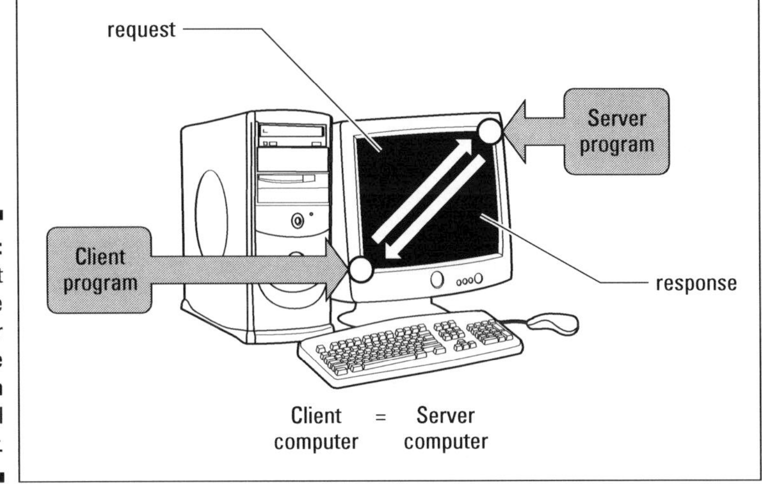

Figure 7-2: Client software and server software are both on one local computer.

The Hypertext Transfer Protocol

When you click a link, your computer's Web browser sends a request out over the Internet. The server interprets your request and prepares a response. The server tosses the response back over the Internet. After a brief delay, the response ends up at your computer (the client), where your Web browser displays a page. The entire exchange — one request followed by a response — is called a *transaction.*

The whole process depends on one important thing: The client and server computers must share some common languages. The client needs to compose a request that can be interpreted by the server, and the server must compose a response that can be interpreted by the client. The Internet uses dozens of shared languages, but the two most important ones are HTTP and HTML. If you compare these languages with paper mail, HTTP is a language for addressing envelopes, and HTML is a language for writing letters (the letters inside the envelopes).

The acronym *HTTP* stands for *Hypertext Transfer Protocol.* Imagine a room with no computers in it. The room has two whiteboards and a person standing at each board. The person on the left side of the room writes the following text on her board:

```
GET /pages/hello.htm
```

The person on the other side of the room reads this text, thinks for a minute, and then writes the following text on her whiteboard:

```
HTTP/1.0 200 OK
Last-Modified: Mon, 18 Dec 2006 14:35:52 GMT
Content-Type: text/html
Content-Length: 14

<h1>Hello</h1>
```

Words such as `GET`, `OK`, and `Content-Type` are words in the HTTP language. So these two people are communicating using the Hypertext Transfer Protocol.

The point of the story is that HTTP is a language. Like many other languages, the medium used for communication is not cast in stone. It's hard to imagine using HTTP for anything but communication between computers over a network, but other scenarios (using whiteboards, carrier pigeons, or whatever) are certainly possible.

Web pages

The previous section refers to two languages — HTTP and HTML. A small HTML document is shown in Listing 7-1.

Listing 7-1: The HTML Code in a Simple Web Page

```
<center>
  <h1>Welcome to Burd Brain Consulting</h1>
  <img src="family1.jpg"><img src="family2.jpg"<br><br>
  <i>"A Proud Family Tradition Since 2006"</i>
</center>
```

Your browser receives this text, interprets the text, and displays a nicely arranged layout of words and images on your screen. The resulting display, as it's interpreted and rendered by your browser, is shown in Figure 7-3.

The document in Listing 7-1 describes the look and content of a page. The user's Web browser interprets the document, formulates a layout for the page, and displays the formatted content on a user's screen. The part of a browser that does all this is called a *layout engine*. Each browser's layout engine works a bit differently, and the variations in displays from one browser to another can plague a Web designer.

Figure 7-3: How your browser displays the code from Listing 7-1.

Figure 7-4 illustrates the role of a layout engine in the processing of a response document. To emphasize the difference between the response document and the layout engine's display, we say that the browser creates its own *display* on the user's screen.

Figure 7-4: The role of the layout engine in processing a response document.

Your HTML Starter Kit

Listing 7-2 contains a basic Web page. The page's code uses 10 or 20 of my favorite HTML features.

Listing 7-2: A Page Filled with Tags

```
<html>

  <head>
    <title>This text appears in the
      browser's title bar</title>
  </head>

  <body>
    <!-- This is a comment. A comment does
      not appear in the browser window. -->

    <h1>This is a level 1 heading.</h1>

    <h2>This is a level 2 heading.</h2>

    <h3>This is a level 3 heading.</h3>

    <b>This is bold <i>and this is both
      bold and italic</i>.</b>

    <p>This is a paragraph of normal text.</p><p>Most
      browsers separate paragraphs from one another by
      putting a blank line between them.</p>

    <p>Link to <a href="http://www.burdbrain.com">Barry
      Burd's Web site</a>.</p>

    This paragraph ends with a paragraph tag.
      (In many cases, Web browsers don't care if your
      start tags and end tags don't come in pairs.)<p>

    Here's a sentence.
      This sentence appears on the same line as the
      previous sentence!<p>

    Here's a sentence.<br>This sentence appears
      on the line beneath the previous sentence.<p>

    42 &lt; 55 and 59 &gt; 41<p>

    &copy; 2006 Wiley Publishing, Inc.
```

```
  </body>

</html>
```

You can find out how your Web browser displays the text in Listing 7-2. Here's how:

1. **Save the code in Listing 7-2 in a file on your computer's hard drive.**

   Call the file `whatever-you-want.html`.

2. **Find the file in your system's file explorer.**

   In Windows, use My Computer or Windows Explorer.

3. **Double-click the file's icon.**

   Presto! Your Web browser opens, and you see the page in Figure 7-5.

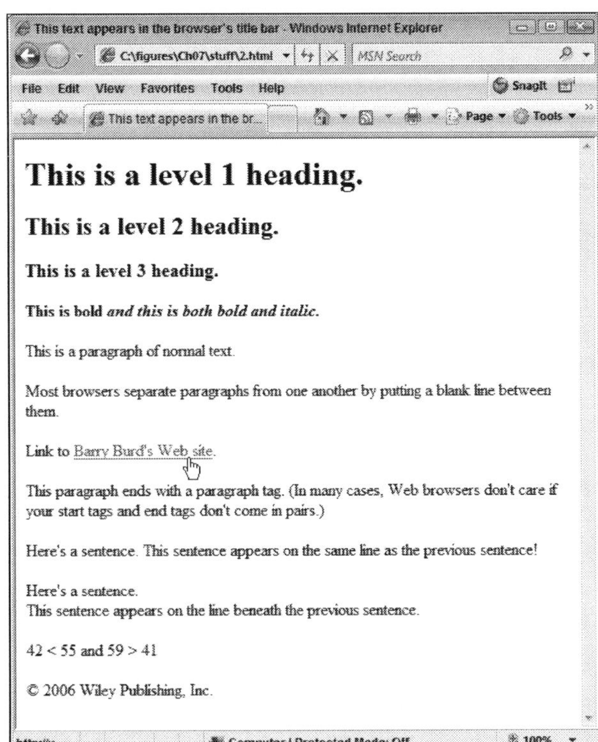

Figure 7-5: Testing the code in Listing 7-2.

You can also work in the other direction. That is, you can view the code that your browser receives when the browser displays any Web page. To do so, follow these steps:

1. **Open your browser to almost any Web page.**
2. **Right-click a neutral place on the page (a place without an image or a hyperlink).**

   If you're a Macintosh user and, therefore, have no right mouse button, click the View menu at the top of the screen.
3. **In the resulting contextual menu, select View Source (or View Page Source, or something like that).**

   Whichever Web browser you use, conjuring up a page's source shows you something like the text in Listing 7-2.

When your Web browser receives a page, the browser receives a bunch of text. Much of this text is ordinary words (the text in a paragraph, for example), but some of the text consists of *elements* — instructions telling the browser how to display the ordinary words. These elements belong to the HyperText Markup Language (HTML).

An HTML element consists of one or two *tags*. Each tag consists of some text enclosed in angle-brackets (< >). An HTML document may have four kinds of tags — start tags, end tags, comments, and declarations. The next few sections contain the details on these tags.

Start tags

A start tag has the form <*tagname attribute attribute . . .* >.

Listing 7-2 has several start tags, such as <html>, <p>, and <a href="http://www.burdbrain.com">. Each start tag consists of a tagname (such as html, p, or a) followed optionally by *attributes*.

An attribute gives specifics about the nature of the tag. For example, the tag <a href="http://www.burdbrain.com"> is called an *anchor start tag* (because the tagname, a, stands for the word "anchor"). Taken together, the anchor start tag and its *anchor end tag* (</a>) form an *anchor element*. An anchor element designates a link on a Web page, and the attribute href="http://www.burdbrain.com" specifies the URL of the link's target. (If you click the link, your Web browser visits the target page.)

The anchor tag's href attribute follows a familiar pattern. This attribute has the form *key*="*value*" (where the key is href, and the value is http://www.burdbrain.com). But other tags' attributes may have different forms. For examples, see the section "Using an option selector" in this chapter.

End tags, empty tags, and paired tags

An *end tag* has the form </*tagname*>.

Listing 7-2 has several end tags, such as </title>, </h1>, </p>, and so on. As you might expect, an end tag denotes the end of something (the end of the title, the end of a level 1 heading, the end of a paragraph, or the end of something else). An end tag has no attributes.

An end tags ends whatever a start tag starts. For example, in Listing 7-2, the big level 1 heading starts with the <h1> start tag and ends with the </h1> end tag. So start tags and end tags frequently come in pairs.

But a start tag without an end tag is like a man without a tuxedo. Some have them, and some don't. In the lower half of Listing 7-2, you find some start tags (<p> and <br>) without corresponding end tags. A start tag without a corresponding end tag is sometimes called an *empty tag.*

You rarely see an end tag without a corresponding start tag. But if you make the mistake of putting a lonely, orphan end tag in your document, chances are good that the Web browser will display something sensible. That's how HTML is supposed to work. If you make a mistake, the Web browser recovers gracefully.

Taken together, a start tag, its end tag, and all the stuff in between are called an *element.* For example, in Listing 7-2, the text starting with <b> and ending with </b> is an element.

```
<b>This is bold <i>and this is both
  bold and italic</i>.</b>
```

In addition, the portion of this text from the start tag <i> to the end tag </i> is an element. An element within another element is called a *nested element.* In Listing 7-2, the <i>. . .</i> element is nested inside the <b>. . . </b> element.

You can overlap elements without nesting them, as in the following code:

```
<b>This is bold <i>and this is both
  bold and italic</b>, but this is
  only italic.</i>
```

But this non-nested overlapping isn't good form. To achieve a scattered mix of bold and italic, use nested tags as follows:

```
<b>This is bold <i>and this is both
  bold and italic</i></b>, <i>but this is
  only italic.</i>
```

The stuff between a start tag and its end tag, not including the tags themselves, is called *content.* In Listing 7-2, the <i> element's content consists of the words and this is both bold and italic.

If it feels good, do it

The HTML philosophy is loose as a goose. If your code contains errors, the Web browser tries to live peacefully with them. Tagnames aren't case-sensitive, and the quotation marks surrounding attribute values are optional. (That is, the quotation marks are optional unless the attribute value contains blank spaces or other weird characters. The safest course is always to use quotation marks.)

If you misspell a tagname or you mismatch angle brackets, the Web browser doesn't display any error messages. Instead, the browser may ignore the improper tag and treat any mismatched brackets as normal text. For example, have a look at the following bad HTML code:

```
<italick>This is text.</italic>> This is more text.
```

When a browser receives this code, the browser displays the following line:

```
This is text.> This is more text.
```

The browser ignores the misspelled <italick> start tag and displays the extra greater-than sign (>) in the browser window.

The permissiveness of HTML is intentional. After all, a Web pages travels from continent to continent. I might know 1 percent of the people whose Web sites I visit (or maybe fewer). If someone in Australia makes a mistake on his or her Web page, I shouldn't get an error message on my screen in New Jersey, USA. Let my Web browser deal with it. If I can read the text in spite of the HTML errors, I might get whatever I need from the Web page.

Entities

Listing 7-2 contains three HTML *entities.* The entities are the codes <, >, and ©. Each entity stands for something whose display on a Web page is problematic. For example, the © entity stands for a copyright symbol ©. (Refer to Figure 7-5.) The < and > entities stand for the less-than and greater-than characters (< and >). Imagine not using the < and > entities and putting the following bad code in your document:

```
b=12 and 2<b and b>10
```

The Web browser displays the following unwanted line of text.

```
b=12 and 210
```

The browser interprets <b and b> to be an HTML bold tag. (It's a bold tag with an and attribute and a b attribute. The browser ignores the two meaningless attributes.) The browser doesn't display any text inside the tag. Instead, the browser displays the number 10 in bold.

The HTML standard defines plenty of useful entities. For more information, visit www.w3.org/MarkUp.

Comments and declarations

An HTML *comment* begins with the characters <!-- and ends with the characters -->. A Web browser ignores any text within the comment. Comments are useful to people who read HTML code (because a comment tells the reader what the author of the page intends the code to do).

Another tag that you might see in an HTML document is a *declaration*. For example, at the top of an HTML document, you might see the following lines:

```
<!DOCTYPE HTML PUBLIC "-//W3C//DTD HTML 4.01//EN"
   "http://www.w3.org/TR/html4/strict.dtd">
```

These two lines form a DOCTYPE declaration. This declaration tells a Web browser that the document conforms to strict HTML version 4.01 standards. To this I sarcastically say, "Big deal!" Many HTML documents (including some Ruby on Rails documents) don't begin with a DOCTYPE declaration, and Web browsers display these documents with no difficulties.

The DOCTYPE declaration represents an effort to enforce standards for HTML documents. The effort is worthwhile, but many Web developers don't follow them. For now, the world and its Wide Web seem to be surviving with or without the use of these standards.

HTML Elements

The hypertext markup language has approximately 100 different kinds of elements, and a typical element has many variations. If you read about all these elements and variations, you'll be bored to tears. So this section covers the highlights — the 25 elements that are most useful to you as a novice Ruby on Rails developer.

Many of these useful elements appear frequently in the Web pages that Rails generates. Some of the elements don't appear in generated pages, but you probably want to use these elements to customize and enhance the generated pages.

Displaying images

An HTML *image element* is an empty tag. Listing 7-3 contains a one-line example:

Listing 7-3: An Image Tag

```
<img src="/images/mypic.jpg" alt="Picture of me">
```

Listing 7-3 tells the Web browser to find a file named `mypic.jpg` which supposedly contains image information. This image information is in the `jpg` format — one of many different formats for storing images. (Other commonly used Web image formats include `gif` and `png`.) If the file `mypic.jpg` isn't available, or if the file's content doesn't describe a displayable image, the browser displays a rectangle containing the words `Picture of me` (the *alternate* text).

Like other filenames, the names of image files are either relative or absolute. A *relative name* describes a file's location in terms of some other known location. It's like saying "Start where we're standing, then go 2 miles north, and then go 1 mile west. That's where you'll find the file." Of course, in an HTML document you don't go 2 miles north. Instead, you may go down one level from a known starting directory to a subdirectory named `images`. That's what the image tag in Listing 7-3 tells the browser to do.

The known starting directory may vary from one server to another. Normally, this starting directory is a directory on the Web server's hard drive. But your mileage may vary. If you view a Web page as I suggest in the section "Your HTML Starter Kit" (in this chapter), the starting directory is the directory containing your `.html` document.

Instead of specifying a relative name, you can specify a file's *absolute name*. A tourist asks, "How do you get to Carnegie Hall?" And the old codger replies "No matter where on earth you start, go to latitude 40.76477°N and longitude 73.97988°W."

If you view a page as I suggest in this chapter's "Your HTML Starter Kit" section, an absolute name may be `c:\Pictures\family_smiling_and_waving.jpg`. For an image on a Web server, the absolute name may be `http://www.burdbrain.com/book_cover.gif`. One way or another, an absolute name points to a file's location without reference to any particular starting point.

In many cases, relative names are better than absolute names. Imagine you need more space on your c: drive. To free up some space, you move all your Web pages and image files from the c: drive to the d: drive. (See Figure 7-6.) Now, an absolute name, such as `c:\myproject\public\images\mypic.jpg`, is no longer correct. (The absolute name points to the old c: drive.)

But a relative name, such as `/images/mypic.jpg` points from the Web site's new location (the new starting point in Figure 7-6) to the location of the `mypic.jpg` file. That's good!

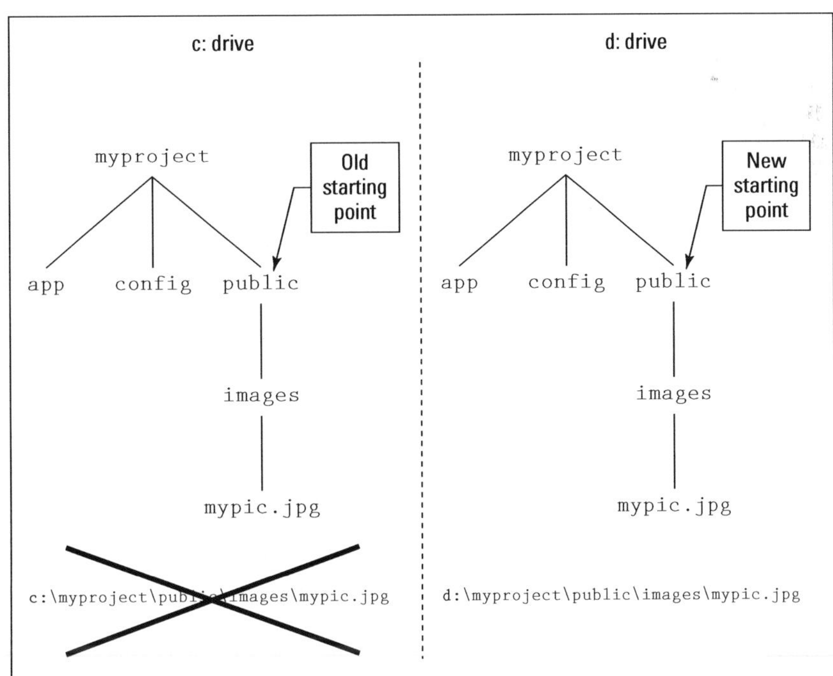

Figure 7-6: Moving Web pages from one disk drive to another.

Using tables to align things

If you're a statistician or some other strange person, you think of a table as a grid containing numbers. The grid's visible border separates one cell from another.

To a Web designer, however, a table is a place to align visual elements — any elements at all. And nine times out of ten, a visible border adds an unwanted, techie look. So Web designers often make their table borders invisible. Listing 7-4 has an example.

Listing 7-4: An HTML Table

```
<table>

  <tr>
    <th>Item</th>
    <th>Cost</th>
    <th>Feeling</th>
  </tr>

  <tr>
    <td>Tuition</td>
    <td>$20,000</td>
    <td><img src="frown.jpg"></td>
  </tr>

  <tr>
    <td>Books</td>
    <td>$500</td>
    <td><img src="frown.jpg"></td>
  </tr>

  <tr>
    <td>Room and board</td>
    <td>$6,000</td>
    <td><img src="frown.jpg"></td>
  </tr>

  <tr>
    <td>Peace and quiet</td>
    <td>Priceless</td>
    <td><img src="smile.jpg"></td>
  </tr>

</table>
```

The page resulting from the code in Listing 7-4 is shown in Figure 7-7. The page contains a table with five rows and three columns. Accordingly, the code in Listing 7-4 has five *table row* elements (`<tr>. . .</tr>`). Each table row element (except the first) contains three *table data* elements (`<td>. . .</td>`).

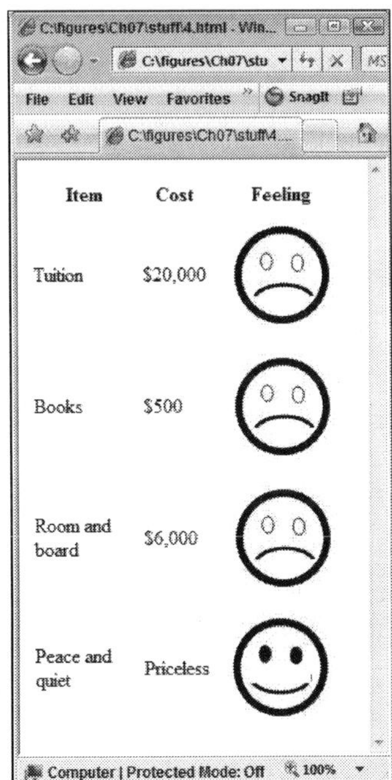

Figure 7-7: The table defined by the code in Listing 7-4.

The first row of the table contains three *table header* elements (`<th>. . . </th>`). A table header is like a piece of table data, but a header's format is a bit different. Most Web browsers display headers in bold and centered text.

If you want, you can restore visible borders to a table on a Web page. To make a table's border visible, add a `border` attribute to the table's start tag.

```
<table border="2">
```

The larger you make the attribute's number, the thicker the border.

Creating an HTML form

Many Web pages contain forms. A form consists of some input fields and a button. When you click the button, your browser sends the input fields' data to a Web server. Listing 7-5 contains the code for a simple form. Figures 7-8, 7-9, and 7-10 show you what happens when a user fills in the text field and clicks the Search button on this form.

Listing 7-5: A Form with a Text Field

```
<form action="http://www.google.com/codesearch">
  <label for="terms_field">Google Code Search</label>

  <input type="text" id="terms_field" name="q"
    size="55" maxlength="2048"
    value="Type your search terms here."><br>

  <input type="submit" value="Search">
</form>
```

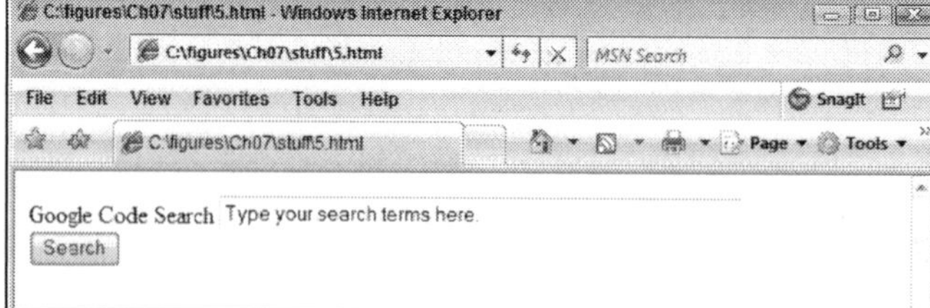

Figure 7-8: The form as it initially appears.

Listing 7-5 consists of a single HTML `form` element. The start form tag contains an `action` attribute — a URL pointing to the place on the Web that receives all the form's data. When you click the button on the form, your browser sends the form's data to the place designated by the URL of its action attribute. In return, a Web server sends a new HTML document to your browser.

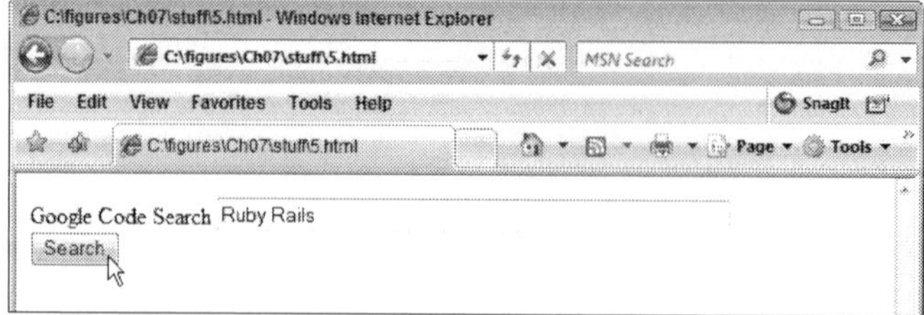

Figure 7-9: The visitor fills in the form's text field.

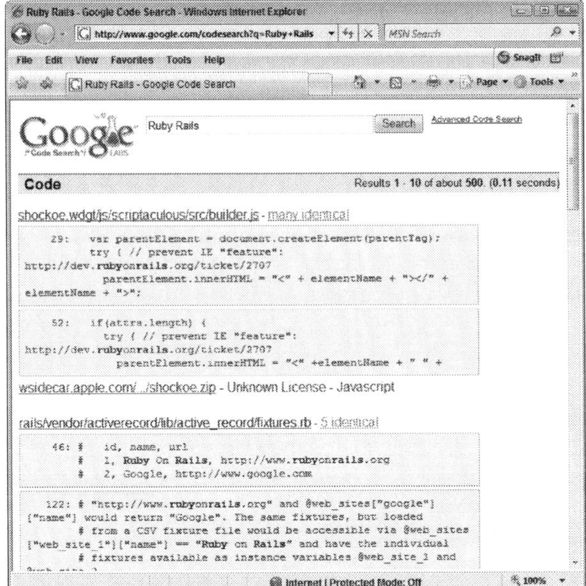

Figure 7-10: Google's Web server responds.

What I describe as the "place on the Web" that receives a form's data is actually a piece of code on a Web server. In Listing 7-5, the server belongs to Google (Thanks, Google!) and the piece of code is a specialized search engine. (The specialized search engine is Google's Code Search engine. The engine finds computer programs that match your search terms. Nice, huh?)

If you work from the bottom of Listing 7-5 upward, you see an `input` tag with attribute `type="submit"` that represents a button. (Refer to Figure 7-8.) The tag's `value` attribute contains whatever text the browser displays on the face of the button.

An input tag with attribute `type="text"` represents a text field. (Again, refer to Figure 7-8.) The tag's `size` attribute contains a number. The browser displays a text field whose width is large enough to display that number of characters all at once.

The text field tag's `maxlength` attribute also contains a number. The browser allows a user to type up to that number of characters in the text field.

The text field tag in Listing 7-5 has id and name attributes.

- **The id attribute allows other HTML code to refer to the text field.**

  For example, Listing 7-5 contains an HTML label element. This label element's for attribute has value terms_field. And whadaya' know? The <input type="text" . . . tag has attribute id with value terms_field. Is that a coincidence, or what?

  Of course, it's no coincidence. The matching of terms_field values tells a Web browser that a particular label is *for* a particular field. In other words, "Browser, this label is supposed to be a label for that text field. So do me a favor, and display the label near the text field. Thank you, browser."

- **The name attribute allows a Web server to identify the text field's data.**

  When you click the button shown in Figure 7-9, your browser sends a request to Google's Web server. The request looks something like this:

  ```
  http://www.google.com/codesearch?q=Ruby+Rails
  ```

  You can see this request in the address field near the top of Figure 7-10. The first part of the request (up to but not including the question mark) comes from the action attribute in the form's start tag. (Refer to Listing 7-5.) The second part of the request (starting with the question mark) comes from the stuff you type in the form's text field. In Figure 7-9, a user types Ruby Rails, so the Web browser appends ?q=Ruby+Rails to the end of the request.

  The name q comes from the name attribute in the text field's input tag. (Refer to Listing 7-5.) But in a sense, the name q originates in some cubicle in an office building at Google. The people who developed Google's Code Search page decreed that they'd search for anything in a request that comes after this name q. So when I created Listing 7-5, I named my text field q.

  The q=Ruby+Rails part of the request is called a *parameter.* Like many other things in this book, a parameter consists of a *name* and a *value.* In the parameter q=Ruby+Rails, the name is q, and the value is Ruby+Rails.

  The more fields a form has, the more parameters you find in the form's request. A question mark (?) signals the start of the parameter list. In a request containing several parameters, the parameters are separated by ampersands (&). For example, a request containing two parameters may look like this:

  ```
  http://www.google.com/search?hl=en&lr=&q=Rails
  ```

Using form elements

Listing 7-5 contains a form with a text field. That fine, but there's more to life than text fields. Forms may also include text areas, check boxes, and other goodies.

Creating a text area

Nothing on a Web page can ever be quite as welcoming as a big, fat text area. If the area could talk, it would say "Type your thoughts here. I'm a *tabula rasa.* Fill me with whatever happens to be on your mind."

Maybe you don't romanticize text areas the way I do. One way or another, you can examine the code that creates a text area. The code is in Listing 7-6, and the display resulting from the code is shown in Figure 7-11.

Listing 7-6: Creating a Text Area

```
<form action="http://chapter9photos.com" method="post">
  <label for="my_area"><b>Chapter 9 Photos</b></label>

  <br>

  <textarea id="my_area" name="description"
    rows="5" cols="40">Describe your photo here.
  </textarea>

  <br>

  <input type="submit">
</form>
```

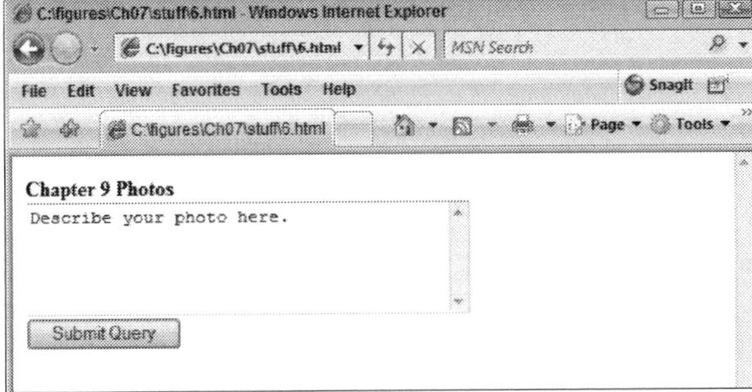

Figure 7-11: A browser renders the text area of Listing 7-6.

On a Web page, text areas and text fields look almost the same. But in an HTML document, `textarea` elements and text field `input` elements are very different. A `textarea` element has both start and end tags. In contrast, a text field's `input` element has no end tag. (See Listing 7-5.) The content of a `textarea` element (the stuff between the start and end tags) is whatever text is to be displayed initially in the text area.

Getting and posting

In your Web travels, you may notice a form tag with a `method="post"` attribute. The HTTP protocol has several *methods* — methods named `get`, `post`, `delete`, `checkout`, and so on. In practice, most Web developers use only the `get` and `post` methods. And because the default for an HTML form is the `get` method, you seldom see the `method="get"` attribute in an HTML form tag.

Each method represents a slight variation on the response expected of a Web server. In general, you use the `get` method to retrieve a page or other resource from a Web site, and you use the `post` method to send data to a Web site. For example, the form in Listing 7-5 uses the `get` method. The user retrieves a page of search hits from Google's server. In the process, no information is added to Google's server.

Now imagine entering comments in a text area labeled "Tell us in 25 words or fewer. . . ." Your little essay becomes part of the server's database. In this case, the form containing the text area probably uses the `post` method.

The `get` and `post` methods differ in several other ways. A `get` form's parameters appear as part of a URL. (See the address field near the top of Figure 7-10. The address field contains the parameter `?q=Ruby+Rails`.) In contrast, a form using `method="post"` sends its parameter information separately from the URL (actually, in a big glob of text following the URL). So with a `get` request, a form's parameters are more visible. A casual passer-by can see how you filled out a form by examining the text in the browser's address field.

As a corollary from the previous paragraph, forms with long-winded parameters tend to use `post` rather than `get`. Imagine creating a `get` form as part of an essay contest. With an essay in a URL, the URL may look something like this:

```
http://www.chapter9photos.com
    /?essay=It%27s+three+in+th
    e+morning.+I%
27m+dreaming+about+the+histor
    y+course+that+I+failed+in+
    high+school.+
The+teacher+is+yelling+at+me%
    2C+%22You+have+two+days+to
    +study+for+th
e+final+exam%2C+but+you+won%2
    7t+remember+to+study.+You%
    27ll+forget+a
nd+feel+guilty%2C+guilty%2C+g
    uilty.%22%0D%0ASuddenly%2C
    +the+phone+ri
ngs . . .
```

That's a cumbersome URL, so Web developers tend to avoid such things.

Another difference between `get` and `post` is *idempotence*. My aunt has a habit of saying things several times. She doesn't think you hear her, so she repeats the same sentence over and over again. "Become a bookkeeper. Do you hear me? Bookkeepers make money. Become a bookkeeper." And a few minutes later, "Become a bookkeeper." What my aunt doesn't realize is that her career advice is idempotent.

The word *idempotent* applies to any operation for which repeated applications have the same effect as one application. The first time my aunt says "Become a bookkeeper," everyone gets the message. But the second time she says it, no one gets any new information. The same holds true of the third time, the fourth, the fifth, and so on.

The `get` method is meant to be idempotent, and the `post` method is not. If I ask the Google Code Search engine once, twice, or ten times to search for `Ruby Rails`, the Google server doesn't care. As far as the Google server is concerned, one request to search `Ruby Rails` is the same as ten requests. The server composes a page of hits and then sends the page to the user.

But successive `post` requests tend to accumulate. Think about an online credit card transaction. You click the Submit button once to purchase a product. The page warns you not to click twice, but you become impatient and you ignore this advice. You click a second time, and then a third time. Lo and behold! Your credit card statement shows three separate purchases, and you receive three specially bred hypoallergenic cats in the mail! The online form sent `post` requests to the e-commerce server, and the `post` operation isn't idempotent. Unlike my aunt's commands, the second and third button clicks have measurable effects.

Using an option selector

Every HTML element has a personality. If text areas are welcoming, option selectors are demanding. An option selector says "Hey, stop stalling and make a decision!" Listing 7-7 illustrates the use of an option selector.

Listing 7-7: Defining an Option Selector

```
<form action="http://chapter9photos.com/">
  <label for="choices"><h2>Your answer:</h2></label><br>

  <select id="choices" name="answer">
    <option value="1">Purple</option>
    <option value="2">Dogs and cats</option>
    <option value="3">Bowling at midnight</option>
    <option value="4">America in the 1950s</option>
  </select>

  <input type="submit" value="Submit">
</form>
```

An HTML `select` element creates an option selector on a Web page. (See Figure 7-12.) The `select` element contains one or more `option` elements. Each `option` element describes an item that the user may choose.

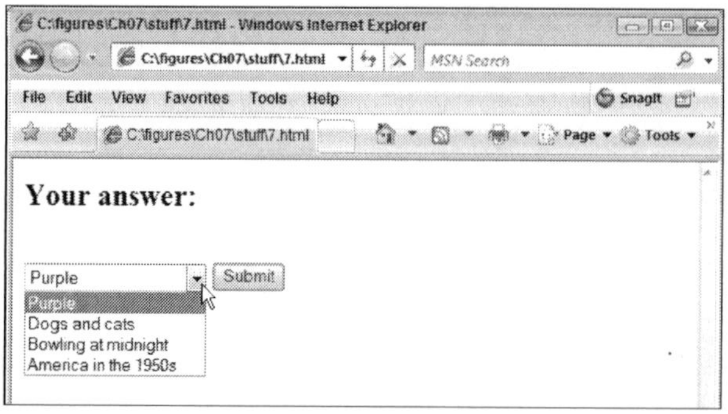

Figure 7-12: Take your pick.

In Listing 7-7, each `option` element has a `value` attribute. When you click the form's Submit button, the Web browser sends the value of one of the options to the server. For example, if you select Purple in Figure 7-12, the browser sends the following request to the Chapter9Photos server:

```
http://chapter9photos.com/?answer=1
```

With the selector in Listing 7-7, a user can select only one item at a time. If you want users to be able to select several items at once, add the word `multiple` to the form's start tag.

```
<select id="choices" name="answer" multiple>
```

This added word `multiple` creates a selector like the one in Figure 7-13. When you click the Submit button on the form, the Web browser sends the value(s) of one or more options to the server. For example, if you select the two options highlighted in Figure 7-13, the browser sends the following request to the Chapter9Photos server:

```
http://chapter9photos.com/?answer=1&answer=3
```

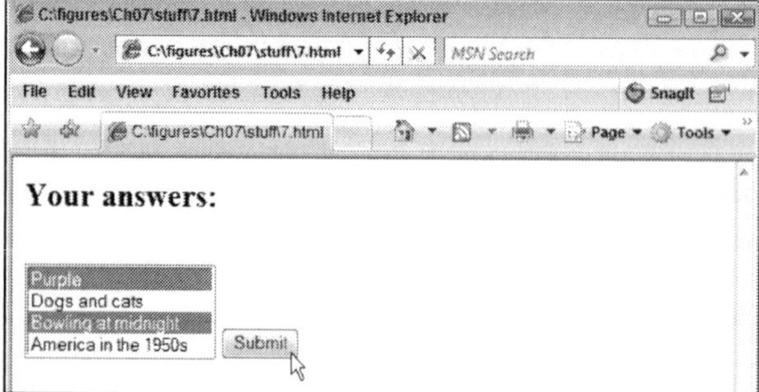

Figure 7-13: Take your picks (as many as you want).

Creating check boxes

A check box is a handy form element. Check the box when you want to say "yes"; uncheck the box when you want to say "no." How convenient! This section is about check boxes. Listing 7-8 has an example.

Listing 7-8: Can You Repeat the Question, Please?

```
<form action="http://chapter9photos.com/">
  <h2>Your answers:</h2>

  <input type="checkbox" name="A" value="1">
  Purple<br>
  <input type="checkbox" name="B" value="1">
  Dogs and cats<br>
  <input type="checkbox" name="C" value="1">
  Bowling at midnight<br>
  <input type="checkbox" name="D" value="1">
  America in the 1950s<p>

  <input type="submit" value="Submit">
</form>
```

Figure 7-14 shows you the check boxes you see when you visit the page in Listing 7-8.

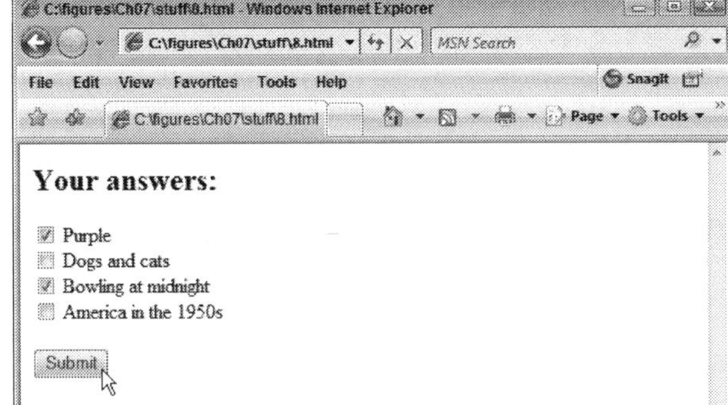

Figure 7-14: Check a box, or two, or three, or four (or none).

In Listing 7-8, each `<input type="checkbox"` element has a start tag with no end tag. Each start tag has a `name` and a `value`. If the user checks the boxes with names `A` and `C` (as in Figure 7-14), the server receives a request in the following form:

```
http://chapter9photos.com/?A=1&C=1
```

Mining for hidden fields

A Web page may have invisible elements — secret gremlins that lurk beyond your view. Listing 7-9 unveils one of these *hidden fields.*

Listing 7-9: What You Don't See . . .

```
<form action="http://chapter9photos.com/">
  <h2>Your answers:</h2>

  <input type="checkbox" name="A" value="1">
  Purple<br>
  <input type="checkbox" name="B" value="1">
  Dogs and cats<br>
  <input type="checkbox" name="C" value="1">
  Bowling at midnight<br>
  <input type="checkbox" name="D" value="1">
  America in the 1950s<p>

  <input type="hidden" name="user's blood type"
         value="Bpos">

  <input type="submit" value="Submit">
</form>
```

When a Web browser receives the form in Listing 7-9, the browser displays the form as you see it in Figure 7-14. In other words, the displays of Listings 7-8 and 7-9 are identical. But behind the scenes, the form in Listing 7-9 sends an additional parameter to the Web server. If the user checks the first of the four boxes, the request sent to the Web server looks like this:

```
http://chapter9photos.com/?A=1&user%27s+blood+type=Bpos
```

The request contains two parameters — one for the checked box, and another for the hidden field.

In the URL with the hidden field's parameter, the field's name uses *URL encoding.* In a URL, a real apostrophe character (`'`) may be mistaken for the start of a quoted string. But in Listing 7-9, the apostrophe is just an apostrophe. (The name of the field contains the word *user's* — a possessive noun.) To avoid confusion, the Web browser encodes the apostrophe as `%27`. The number 27 is the hexadecimal value of the ASCII code for an apostrophe character.

On most reputable Web sites, the use of hidden fields is a legitimate practice. A hidden field stores useful information that's of no interest to the user. Of course, the same is not true of disreputable Web sites. On a malicious Web page, a tag such as `<input type="hidden" name="sucker number" value="18272938">` stores nothing but bad news.

Part III

Real Rails

"Yes, I know how to query information from the program, but what if I just want to leak it instead?"

In this part . . .

In Parts I and II, you might have become tired of all the preliminaries. You want to dig in, get your hands dirty, and put all those preliminaries to good use.

If that's how you feel, you've opened to the right page! Part III presents several working Web applications using Ruby on Rails. You can download the code and run them on your computer. You can tweak them, customize them, or rewrite them completely to build an application that suits your needs.

Hey, you bought the book, so let your imagination soar. Go crazy with this stuff!

(If you borrowed the book or bought it at a heavily discounted price, don't go too crazy. Try to be a bit restrained. Thanks.)

Chapter 8

Action-Packed Adventures

In This Chapter

- Watching the controller interact with the view
- Passing information between the controller and the view
- Dividing a task into several different files

The material back in Chapter 3 involves a lot of magic. When you click a Finish button, Rails creates 35 folders and 45 files. Later in the process, Rails creates Web forms and updates databases. And to get all this functionality, you write only five lines of code.

So what's the trick? What does Rails do behind your back to make all this wizardry happen?

This chapter reveals one part of the magic; namely, the interaction between a controller and its view.

Model/View/Controller

Imagine that you chair a committee whose members are writing a big report. How do you divide the work? There are good ways and bad ways to assign tasks.

As committee chair, you can decide to do all the work yourself. This saves you the headache of having to delegate tasks. Committee members don't have to contact one another to coordinate their work and check the consistency of their contributions. In the end, no one has to paste parts of the report together. But writing the entire report might overwhelm you. You might have trouble keeping all the facts in your head while you juggle sections 6, 7, 10, and 20 in the huge volume of material.

Another approach is to divide the report into words. The committee has three members, so have each member write every third word. This is definitely a bad idea. If the Gettysburg address had been written this way, Lincoln would have written "Four," "seven," and "our" himself. His speechwriter would have written "score," "years," and "fathers," and his wife, Mary Todd, would come up with the words "and," "ago," and "brought." Not a good situation.

In matters related to computing, the situation is even more complicated. The old days when a program was one monolithic chunk of code are gone forever. These days, you have a database in California, an accounting department in New York, and users all over the world. What's the best way to partition the system?

In the late 1970s, the Smalltalk team at Xerox PARC developed the Model/View/Controller (MVC) concept. The idea is to separate an application's data from the presentation of the data. The code to display the data doesn't mix with the code to compute the data.

I've seen this principle in action in my very own home. When my son was in fifth grade, he started writing school reports by using Microsoft Word. I'd watch him type a sentence and then adjust the margins. Then he'd prepare to center the next sentence and fish around for a fancier font. By the time he found the right formatting menus, he'd forgotten what he wanted to say. With this mixing of formatting and content, he couldn't devote full attention to the ideas he was trying to express. I advised him to separate the content and presentation tasks — that is, to write the words first and then go back to format the paragraphs in the report.

In MVC terms, an application's data is called the *model,* and the presentation of the data is called the *view.* The model belongs in one part of the code, and the view belongs in another. For a very large project, one team of programmers writes code to develop the model, and another team writes code to develop the view. Each team applies its expertise to the task. More importantly, each team worries about its specific problems. The team that computes the millionth digit of pi doesn't worry about the font used to display that digit. And the team that shapes a neon tube into the digit 1 doesn't worry about the formula used to calculate that millionth digit of pi. When a company modernizes its equipment (going from an old neon sign to a modern LED display), the calculation team doesn't want to compute the digits of pi all over again. The millionth digit doesn't change, no matter how the company chooses to display that digit. So questions about the calculation of the data and the display of the data should be separate from one another.

Models and views are passive things. Each of these things sits around waiting for someone to request its services. So to do anything useful, you need more than a model and a view. You need something that says, "I just got a request to display today's weather forecast. I'll get the forecast from the model and tell the view to display the forecast." The thing that says all this is called a *controller.* A controller is the mover and shaker in the MVC architecture.

The controller waits for a user request (a button click, or something like that). When a request arrives, the controller gets some required data from the model or tells the model to modify some data. Then the controller fires up the view. The view displays the data in a way that keeps the user happy.

This chapter sets the model aside and focuses heavily on the controller and the view. The controller and view go hand in hand, like Gilbert and Sullivan, or Rimsky and Korsakov. So intimate is the controller-view relationship that Rails combines the two into one component: the *Action Pack.*

Creating a controller and a view

I searched far and wide for the simplest example to illustrate the relationship between a controller and a view. After decades of research, traveling on foot across several continents, I found a nice, little, Ruby on Rails example. The example doesn't do anything astounding. (It displays the words `Your Shopping Cart` in a Web browser. Wow!) But the example illustrates how controllers and views cooperate to form an application.

To see the example, follow these steps:

1. **Create a Rails project named `myproject`.**

   For details on creating a Rails project, see Chapter 3.

2. **In the Generators view of RadRails, generate a controller named `ShoppingCart` with an action named `show`. (See Figure 8-1.)**

   As in Figure 8-1, make the following choices:

   - In the Generators view's drop-down list, select Controller.
   - Among the radio buttons, select Create.
   - In the text field, type **ShoppingCart show**.

     The controller's name is `ShoppingCart`, and the controller defines an action named `show`. An *action* is something that a controller can do. For example, the controller in Chapter 3 (the scaffold) has many actions — actions named `new`, `list`, `show`, `destroy`, and some others.

   - Leave the check boxes deselected.

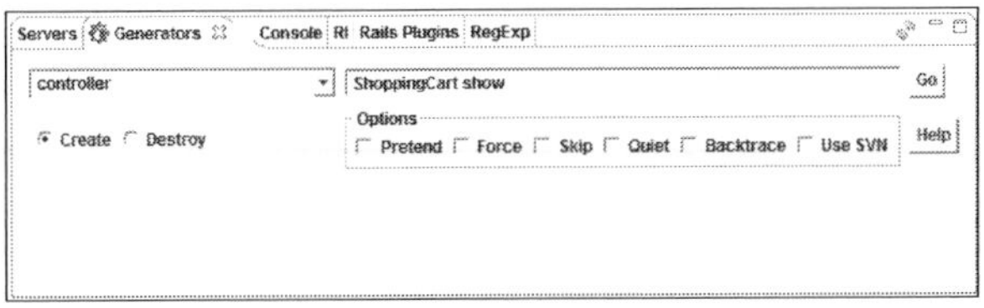

Figure 8-1: Generating a controller.

When you click Go, RadRails creates a new file named `shopping_cart_controller.rb`. For more details on generating a controller, see Chapter 4.

3. **Open the `myproject\app\controllers\shopping_cart_controller.rb` file in a RadRails editor.**

   For details about opening a file for editing, see Chapter 4.

   RadRails displays the code inside the new controller. (See Figure 8-2.) Notice the words `def show` in the controller code. These words (along with some other stuff) make it possible for a user to visit `http://localhost:300x/shopping_cart/show`.

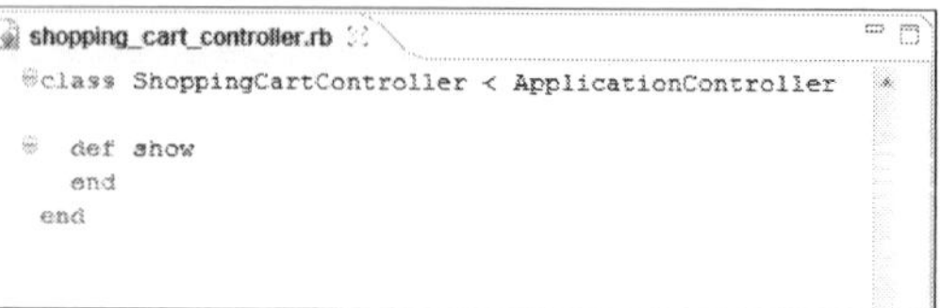

shopping_cart_controller.rb
class ShoppingCartController < ApplicationController
def show
end
end

Figure 8-2: A new controller.

When I write `localhost:300x`, the *x* stands for a digit. For the Web server in your first Rails project, the URL contains `localhost:3000`. For the Web server in your second Rails project, the URL contains `localhost:3001`. RadRails adds 1 to the port number for every newly created Web server.

4. **Open the `myproject\app\views\shopping_cart\show.rhtml` file in a RadRails editor.**

   Again, for details about opening a file for editing, see Chapter 4.

   You might be accustomed to seeing `html` files but not `rhtml` files. The `r` in `rhtml` isn't a typo. After all, this is a Ruby book. You can expect a few extra *R*s here and there.

5. **In the `show.rhtml` file, type** <h1>Your Shopping Cart</h1>**, as shown in Figure 8-3.**

   If you're familiar with HTML (HyperText Markup Language), you recognize the `<h1> </h1>` tags as a pair of "heading level 1" tags. This is one of the basic building blocks for all Web pages.

6. **Save your changes in the `show.rhtml` file.**

   For details on saving an edited file, see Chapter 4.

```
show.rhtml
<h1>Your Shopping Cart</h1>
```

Figure 8-3: A very simple view.

7. **Visit `http://localhost:300x/shopping_cart/show`.**

   For details on visiting a URL in RadRails, see Chapter 4.

   In the browser window, you see the display shown in Figure 8-4.

Figure 8-4: The page presented by a controller and a view.

I admit — you've done a lot of work just to display `Your Shopping Cart` in a browser window. Without Rails and with a modest Web development tool, you can generate the same display in just a few steps. In fact, if you're not fussy about the display medium, you can write "Your Shopping Cart" on paper in two seconds!

Good technology can turn an easy task into a difficult task. Imagine living in the suburbs and trying to visit your neighbor's house. You can walk there in less than a minute. Or you can look for your car keys, start up the car, back out of your driveway, pull into your neighbor's driveway, and remember to lock the car door as you head for your neighbor's front door. What a hassle! A car represents good technology, but a car is overkill if you're performing a very small transportation task. In the same way, Rails is great technology. But Rails is overkill for developing a simple, unchanging Web page.

Wait! I shouldn't be complaining about how useless this example is! This first example offers a first insight into the relationship between a controller and a view. The second insight (and the third, the fourth, and so on) comes in the remainder of this chapter.

Why you shouldn't rename files

In this section's example, you find out more about the view/controller partnership. In particular, you discover how the names of the files affect that partnership.

You don't create a cool Web application by following the section's steps. On the contrary, you intentionally change something and watch your application stop working. All Rails developers make mistakes and do things that break their applications. I figure you should break at least one application while you read this book.

Try the following experiment:

1. **If you haven't already done so, create the `ShoppingCart` controller by following the steps in the preceding section.**
2. **In the Rails Navigator view, right-click the `myproject\app\controllers\shopping_cart_controller.rb` branch.**
3. **In the resulting contextual menu, choose Rename.**
4. **Make a minor change in the name of the `shopping_cart_controller.rb` file.**

   For example, add a letter `x` so that the name becomes `xshopping_cart_controller.rb`.
5. **Press the Refresh button in the RadRails Web browser.**

   The Refresh button is on the browser's toolbar, which is shown in Figure 8-5.

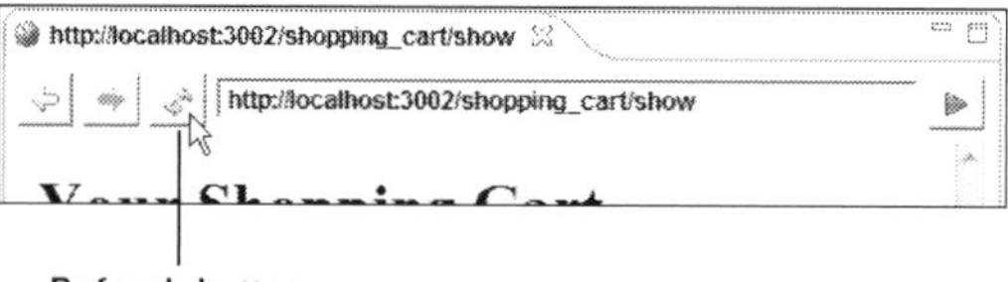

Figure 8-5: The RadRails browser's toolbar.

After pressing the refresh button, you no longer see the friendly "Your Shopping Cart" page. Instead, you see an error message like the one shown in Figure 8-6. Without a file named `shopping_cart_controller.rb`, Rails can't find the controller. And without the controller, you can't visit `http://localhost:300x/shopping_cart/show`.

Figure 8-6: Up a creek without a controller.

6. **Repeat Steps 2–4, changing the file back to its original `shopping_cart_controller.rb` name.**
7. **Press the Refresh button in the RadRails Web browser.**

   After you restore the file's original name, the browser displays the nice Web page in Figure 8-4.

You can redo the entire experiment and rename the `myproject\app\views\shopping_cart\show.rhtml` file. The results aren't as drastic, but you still don't get the nice page of Figure 8-4. (Try it!)

The Rails Way of Life

The earlier "Creating a controller and a view" section's experiment illustrates two key features of Ruby on Rails.

Convention over configuration

In the experiment, several similar-but-not-exactly-identical names are related to one another. Something named `ShoppingCart` is defined inside a file named `shopping_cart_controller.rb`. You use the `ShoppingCart` code when you visit a URL containing the name `shopping_cart` (the URL `http://localhost:300x/shopping_cart/`).

In addition, the controller contains `def show` (which defines an action named `show`). The action's view is in a file named `show.rhtml`, and you use the `show` action when you visit `http://localhost:300x/shopping_cart/show`.

In many non-Rails frameworks, the names you choose for these things are meaningless. The non-Rails system doesn't assume that something named `ShoppingCart` has anything to do with a URL containing the characters `/shopping_cart/`. To tell a non-Rails system how all these names are related, you have to create a configuration file. The file might look something like Listing 8-1.

Listing 8-1: A Non-Rails Configuration File

```
<?xml version="1.0" encoding="UTF-8"?>
<!-- You don't do this in Rails -->
<controller name="ShoppingCart"
        file_name="shopping_cart_controller.rb"
        url_mapping="/shopping_cart/">
    <action name="show" url_mapping="/show">
        <view file_name="show.rhtml"/>
    </action>
</controller>
```

The file in Listing 8-1 looks very official, but it's really a big bag of wind. Forcing the developer to write this configuration file is a bad idea. For one thing, configuration files can become very complicated. A typical Web application can involve dozens of configurable items, and if all the items aren't specified correctly, the application doesn't work at all.

Besides that, having a big, hairy configuration file isn't usually necessary. If Rails can figure out on its own that `ShoppingCart` handles a visit to any `/shopping_cart/` Web page, there's no reason for having a configuration file to help connect the dots.

Rails shuns configuration files in favor of naming conventions. If you name a controller `ShoppingCart` and put the controller's code in a file named `shopping_cart_controller.rb`, Rails connects the controller with Web pages whose names include `/shopping_cart/`. Similarly, if you name a controller `TheBoss` (in a file named `the_boss_controller.rb`), Rails connects the controller with Web pages whose names include `/the_boss/`. If you define an action named `show` (by writing `def show` inside a controller's code), Rails connects the action with Web pages whose names include `/show`. Then Rails looks for a file named `show.rhtml`. With Rails, you don't have to configure these relationships. They're all created automatically with the Rails naming conventions.

In certain situations, you might not have the luxury of using all the Rails naming conventions. You might be working with someone else's rotten old code (also called *legacy code*), and in that old code, names like George for the controller and Gracie for the Web page are cast in stone. In that case, Rails gives you the option of overriding its naming conventions, and manually configuring the way things like controllers connect to things like Web pages. For details, see this book's Web site.

Don't Repeat Yourself (DRY)

Look again at the non-Rails configuration file in Listing 8-1 of the preceding section. Assume that you've written `ShoppingCart` controller code and that you put this code inside a `shopping_cart_controller.rb` file. A line in the configuration file

```
file_name="shopping_cart_controller.rb"
```

connects the `ShoppingCart` controller with the `shopping_cart_controller.rb` filename.

Then, if you want to change the filename, you have to do two things:

- Perform renaming steps, such as Steps 2–4 in the "Why you shouldn't rename files" section.
- Edit the configuration file to reflect the filename's change.

There's plenty of room for error, because one piece of information is stored in two different places. The controller file's name is stored in your computer's file system, and the name is duplicated inside a configuration file. If you change a name in one place, you have to remember all the other places where the name is stored, and you must change all those other places without introducing new errors. It's like changing your phone number and having to call everyone who has your old number. No matter how careful you are, someone's going to lose track of you (and, of course, it won't be a telemarketer).

The trouble starts when one piece of information is repeated in two or more places. With the name `shopping_cart_controller.rb` in your computer's file system and with the same `shopping_cart_controller.rb` name in a configuration file, you're repeating yourself unnecessarily. This repetition leads to errors. So the Rails philosophy is *Don't Repeat Yourself* (abbreviated DRY). Any information that the system can deduce from naming conventions should be settled once and for all by using naming conventions. The developer shouldn't have to make up new names for all the related Ruby code, files, and URLs.

Writing What You Want Where You Want It

In the next several sections, you play tricks with a Rails application's output. These tricks turn out to be useful for designing Web sites.

Sending text to the console

The controller and the view can display messages. Often, these messages help you understand how these two components work. Here's how you get the controller and view to display information:

1. **If you haven't already done so, create the `ShoppingCart` controller by following the steps in this chapter's "Creating a controller and a view" section.**
2. **Add** puts 'I am the controller.' **to the `show` action in `shopping_cart_controller.rb`.**

   Repeat Steps 4–6 in the "Creating a controller and a view" section. But this time, open the `myproject\app\controllers\shopping_cart_controller.rb` file in a RadRails editor and add the new line of code immediately after the `def show` line, as follows:

   ```
   def show
     puts 'I am the controller.'
   end
   ```

3. **Add** <% puts 'I am the view.' %> **to the `myproject\app\views\shopping_cart\show.rhtml` file.**

   If you add this line to the `<h1>Your Shopping Cart</h1>` line from the "Creating a controller and a view" section, the `show.rhtml` file now contains the following text:

   ```
   <h1>Your Shopping Cart</h1>
   <% puts 'I am the view.' %>
   ```

4. **Press the Refresh button in the RadRails Web browser.**

   At this point, pressing the refresh button is uneventful. The browser repaints itself, showing the same `Your Shopping Cart` message. Where did all that `puts 'I am'` text go?

5. **Look at the Console view (see Figure 8-7).**

   The Console view logs the Web server's activity. In addition, the Console view displays the result of the controller's and view's `puts` commands. The `puts` commands supply information to whoever administers the server — not to the person who visits the Web site.

   This step deals with two (unrelated) things named "views." The Console view is part of the RadRails IDE. But the view in Step 3 (the view containing a `puts` command) is a Ruby on Rails component.

```
Servers  Generators  Console  RI  Rails Plugins  RegExp
myproject - WEBrick Server - (Jul 17, 2006 2:13:28 AM)
http://localhost:3002/ -> /javascripts/effects.js
127.0.0.1 - - [16/Jul/2006:23:14:32 Eastern Daylight Time] "GET /images/rails.png HTT
http://localhost:3002/ -> /images/rails.png
I am the controller.
I am the view.
127.0.0.1 - - [16/Jul/2006:23:14:41 Eastern Daylight Time] "GET /shopping_cart/show HT
- -> /shopping_cart/show
```

Figure 8-7: The Console view responds to Ruby puts commands.

Ruby's `puts` command sends a line of output to a console of some sort. In this case, the lowercase word *console* stands for a place that displays plain text, often a place that displays log messages and error messages. Depending on what you're doing, the RadRails Console view or your systems command window qualify as consoles of one sort or another.

In its essence, the `shopping_cart_controller.rb` file contains an ordinary Ruby program. So in `shopping_cart_controller.rb`, the `puts` command is happy to send text to the RadRails Console view.

But, in the case of the `show.rhtml` file, the situation is a bit different. Like any other Web document, the `show.rhtml` file normally sends stuff to a Web browser's screen. However in this example, you want `I am the view` to go to the RadRails Console.

So you need a way of saying "Execute this `puts` command as an ordinary Ruby command. Do whatever `puts 'I am the view.'` would do in an ordinary Ruby program." That's what the `<% %>` characters say in the `show.rhtml` file. (See Step 3.) Putting `<% %>` around `puts 'I am the view.'` says "Don't display the words `puts 'I am the view.'` in the Web page. Instead, interpret `puts 'I am the view.'` as a Ruby command. Do whatever you'd do if you encountered this `puts` command inside a Ruby program." And indeed, in Step 5, you see that the words `I am the view` appear inside the RadRails Console view.

These `<% %>` characters are part of *ERb,* which is a kind of *Embedded Ruby.* Using ERb (or other kinds of Embedded Ruby), you can mix Ruby commands with assorted HTML tags. For more about ERb, see the section entitled "The Controller Shakes Hands with the View" in this chapter.

The art of Web server redirection

You can make a Web server jump from one action to another action. Here's how:

1. **If you haven't already done so, create the `ShoppingCart` controller by following the steps in this chapter's "Creating a controller and a view" section.**
2. **Using a RadRails editor, add a new action named `display_cart` to the controller's code.**

   Add the `display_cart` action as follows:

   ```
   class ShoppingCartController < ApplicationController
     def show
     end

     def display_cart
       puts 'I am the display_cart action'
       redirect_to :action => "show"
     end
   end
   ```
3. **Visit `http://localhost:300x/shopping_cart/display_cart`.**

   The server plops the words `I am the display_cart action` into the RadRails Console view. After that, the server calls the `show` action. In the Web browser window, you see the show page (as shown earlier in Figure 8-4). And in the Web browser's address field, you see `/shopping_cart/show`. The server has shifted, thoroughly and completely, to the controller's `show` action.

Making the controller do the work

Rails supports two kinds of rendering:

- **Automatic rendering:** When the view renders something (as in the "Creating a controller and a view" section)
- **Manual rendering:** When the controller renders something

Without doing some extra work, you can't have both automatic and manual rendering. Whenever the controller renders something, the view remains completely dormant. This section's experiment brings the idea home.

1. **If you haven't already done so, create the `ShoppingCart` controller by following the steps in this chapter's "Creating a controller and a view" section.**
2. **Using a RadRails editor, add a line of code to the `show` action in `shopping_cart_controller.rb`.**

   Add the new line of code immediately after the `def show` line, as follows:

   ```
   def show
     render :text => '<h1>The controller rules!</h1>'
   end
   ```

   Again, for details about opening a file for editing, see Chapter 4.
3. **Press the Refresh button in the RadRails Web browser.**

   The browser repaints itself, showing `The controller rules!` as a big level 1 heading. But you no longer see the view's `Your Shopping Cart` heading. (See Figure 8-8.)

Figure 8-8: The controller does all the rendering.

If you followed the steps in the "Sending text to the console" section, you can check the Console view. After this section's experiment, the console still displays `I am the controller`, but the console no longer displays `I am the view`.

The Controller Shakes Hands with the View

This section shows you how to pass values from a controller to a view and from a view to a controller.

1. **If you haven't already done so, create the `ShoppingCart` controller by following the steps in this chapter's "Creating a controller and a view" section.**
2. **Using a RadRails editor, add two lines of code to the `show` action in `shopping_cart_controller.rb`, placing them between `def show` and `end`, like so:**

```
def show
  @item = "Book: Ruby on Rails For Dummies"
  @price = 20.00
end
```

3. **Add one line of code to the `myproject\app\views\shopping_cart\show.rhtml` file.**

   It doesn't matter where you put the new line, but the most cosmetically pleasing place to put the line is after the level 1 heading.

```
<h1>Your Shopping Cart</h1>
<%= @item %><br><%= number_to_currency(@price) %>
```

4. **Press the Refresh button in the RadRails Web browser.**

   The browser repaints itself, showing an item's name and price. (See Figure 8-9.)

Figure 8-9: It would be cheap at twice the price.

This section's example involves some cryptic-looking symbols. But the basic idea isn't mysterious. The controller defines two variables named `@item` and `@price`. The controller also assigns values to these variables. Then the view uses these values inside `<%= %>` symbols.

The `<%= %>` symbols are a variation on the `<% %>` symbols from this chapter's "Sending text to the console" section. (Like the `<% %>` symbols in the "Sending text to the console" section, these new `<%= %>` symbols are part of ERb.) The added equal sign in `<%= %>` says "Evaluate the stuff between `<%=` and `%>` as if all that stuff is part of a Ruby program. Then replace this entire `<%= %>` business with that stuff's value."

So, in the code of Step 3, the server does the following:

- **Substitutes `@item` with its value, and substitutes `@price` with its value:** So effectively, the second line in Step 3 becomes

  ```
  <%= "Book: Ruby on Rails For Dummies" %><br>
  <%= number_to_currency(20.00) %>
  ```

- **Interprets `number_to_currency(20.00)` as meaning `"20.00"` instead of "20", `"20.0"`, or `"20.00000"`:** After all, US currency has two digits to the right of the decimal point. Effectively, the second line in Step 3 becomes

  ```
  <%= "Book: Ruby on Rails For Dummies" %><br>
  <%= "20.00" %>
  ```

- **Replaces each `<%= %>` tag with the value between the `<%= %>` symbols:** So effectively, the second line in Step 3 becomes

  ```
  Book: Ruby on Rails For Dummies<br>20.00
  ```

The line Book: Ruby on Rails For Dummies
20.00 can be part of any ordinary Web page — Rails or no Rails. Any Web browser interprets this as an instruction to display Book: Ruby on Rails For Dummies, then break to the next line (with the <br> tag), and then display 20.00. (For more information, see Chapter 7.)

After all the substitutions, the `<%= %>` tag fizzles into nothing but plain old HTML code. That's good because the server sends this code to people's Web browsers, and Web browsers deal with plain old HTML code.

Here's an FAQ with only one question in it: Why do you need the `<%= %>` symbols at all? Why can't you write

```
@item<br>number_to_currency(@price)
```

in the `show.rhtml` file? (Okay, that's two questions. But the second question clarifies the first question.)

Here's the answer: If you omit the `<%= %>` symbols, then, when you visit the Web page, you see the stuff in Figure 8-10. The Web server doesn't treat `@item` and `number_to_currency(@price)` as Ruby program expressions. Instead, the server takes each of these things at its face value, displaying the text @item and number_to_currency(@price) on the Web page. The only time any evaluating happens is when your Web browser interprets <br>. All Web browsers interpret <br> tags as forced line breaks.

Figure 8-10: Oops! That's not what you want.

Using parameters

In this section, you make the shopping cart example a bit more like a real Web page. The section's code uses a Ruby hash — a structure created with curly braces and funny-looking arrows (=>).

If you feel queasy about Ruby hashes, be sure to read the section on hashes in Chapter 5. (I'd explain that stuff here, but I don't want to "rehash" all the material from Chapter 5!)

1. **If you haven't already done so, follow the steps in this chapter's "The Controller Shakes Hands with the View" section.**
2. **Using a RadRails editor, modify the `show` action in the `shopping_cart_controller.rb` file as follows:**

```
def show
  @item = params[:item]

  price_of =
   {'Book' => 20.00, 'Shirt' => 15.00, 'Cup' => 10.00}
  @price = price_of[@item] || 0.00
end
```

3. **Visit `http://localhost:300x/shopping_cart/show?item=Book`.**

   The Web browser displays a page like the one shown in Figure 8-9.

4. **Visit `http://localhost:300x/shopping_cart/show?item=Shirt`.**

   The Web browser displays a page like the one shown in Figure 8-9. But this time, the text on the page is `Shirt $15.00` instead of `Book $20.00`.

5. **Visit `http://localhost:300x/shopping_cart/show?item=Cat`.**

   The Web browser displays a page like the one shown in Figure 8-9. But this time, the text on the page is `Cat $0.00` instead of `Book $20.00`. (Cats are free.)

This section's example relies on two kinds of tricks — the covert (behind-the-scenes) kind of trick and the overt (you-see-all-the-code) kind of trick.

- **The covert trick involves parameters.** A parameter is an old-fashioned Web page trick — a way of sending information on the fly as part of a request for a Web page. If you look at your browser's address field after searching for Rails, you might see

  ```
  http://www.google.com/search?hl=en&q=Rails
  ```

  The URL has two parameters — one for the language (`hl=en`) and another for the query (`q=Rails`). For more about parameters, refer to Chapter 7.

  In the URL of Step 3 of the "Using parameters" example, the text `?item=Book` creates one parameter. Rails takes this single parameter and uses it to create a Ruby hash. Rails sends the new hash to the controller's `show` action. It's as if someone types

  ```
  params = {:item => 'Book'}
  ```

  except that the server builds the `params` hash behind the scenes. (See Figure 8-11.) So the expression `params[:item]` stands for the value `'Book'`.

  When the server builds the `params` hash, the server executes code that's a bit more complicated than `params = {:item => 'Book'}`. But that's not worth worrying about here.

- **The overt trick in this section's example is the substitution of values in the code of Step 2 of the "Using parameters" example.** The substitution story is illustrated in Figure 8-12. The expression `params[:item]` has the value `'Book'`, so `@item` has the value `'Book'`, and `price_of[@item]` has the value `20.00`.

  When all is said and done, `@item` has the value `'Book'` and `@price` has the value `20.00`. This brings you back to where you were in Step 2 of this chapter's "The Controller Shakes Hands with the View" section. From that point on, the view displays `Book` and `20.00`, as it does in Figure 8-9.

The only loose end in this example is the `|| 0.00` stuff of the code in Step 2 of the "Using parameters" example. This is the way a Ruby programmer makes 0.00 be a default value. The two bars (||) stand for the "or" operation. So the statement

```
@price = price_of[@item] || 0.00
```

says the following: "Make `@price` be `price_of[@item]` or, if the `@item` is a `Cat` and there's no `price_of['Cat']`, make `@price` be `0.00`." For more details, see Chapter 5.

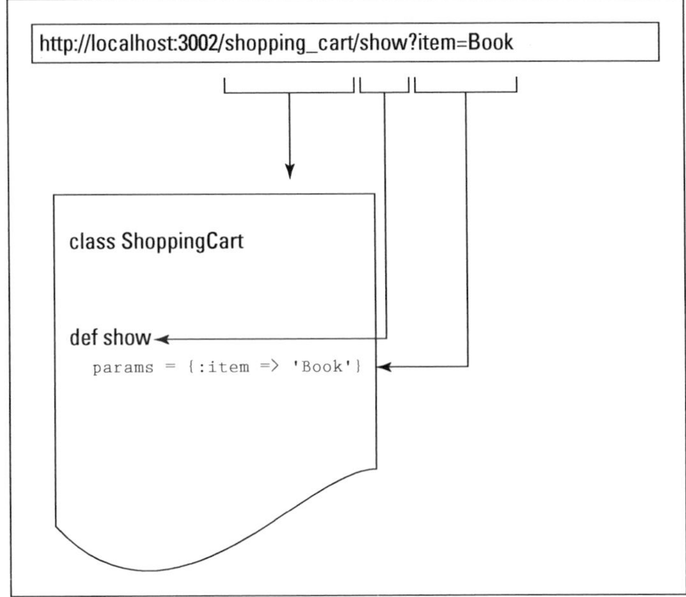

Figure 8-11: The server builds the `params` hash.

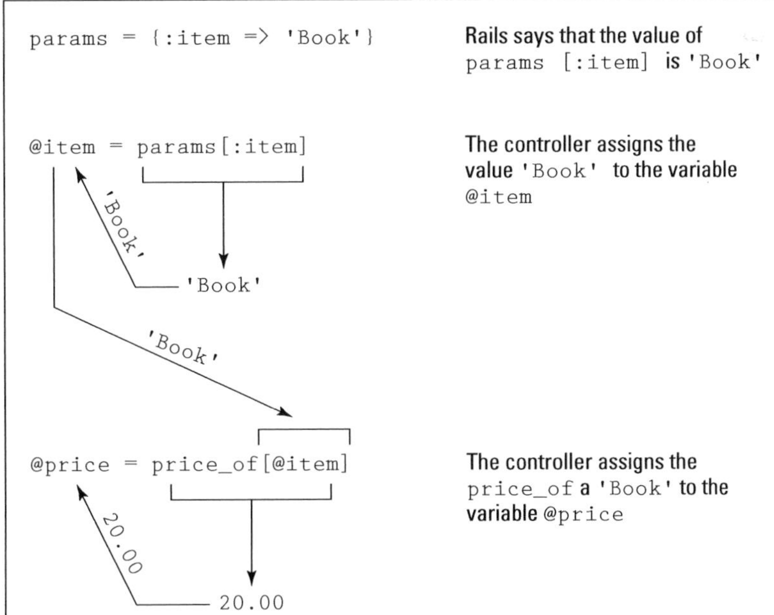

Figure 8-12: How @item gets to be 'Book' and @price gets to be 20.00.

Getting parameters from a form

I really like the preceding section. But in all honesty, I have to admit something. No one in his or her right mind wants to type `?item=Book` in a Web browser's address field. Typing `?item=Book` defeats the whole purpose of having Web pages. Besides, the less a user knows about a page's parameters, the less chance you have of someone's making malicious use of those parameters. So what do you do to avoid having the user type `?item=Book`? Here's what you do:

1. **If you haven't already done so, follow the steps in this chapter's "Using parameters" section.**
2. **With the `myproject\app\controllers\shopping_cart_controller.rb` file open in a RadRails editor, add the following two lines of code:**

   ```
   def ask to show
   end
   ```

   These lines create a brand-new action named `ask_to_show`. In the next step, you create a corresponding view.
3. **In the `myproject\app\views\shopping_cart` directory, create a file named `ask_to_show.rhtml`.**

   To create this file, follow the steps in Chapter 4 to create a new Ruby Class. But this time, change a few parts of the procedure:

   a. Start by selecting the `myproject\app\views\shopping_cart` directory in the Rails Navigator view.

   b. When the old Select a Wizard dialog box appears, expand the General branch of the tree and select File within that branch.

   c. When you're prompted for a filename, type **ask_to_show.rhtml**.
4. **Edit the new `ask_to_show.rhtml` file by typing the following code in the file:**

   ```
   <form action="/shopping_cart/show">
     Item <input type="text" name="item" size="30"><p>
     <input type="submit">
   </form>
   ```

   The stuff that you type is old-fashioned HTML code. You can find code like this in an ordinary Web page — a page whose author never heard of Ruby on Rails. The code creates the form shown in Figure 8-13.

   For more information about this step's HTML code, see Chapter 7.
5. **Visit `http://localhost:300x/shopping_cart/ask_to_show`.**

   The cool thing about the form in Figure 8-13 is that when the user types a word like *Book* and presses the form's Submit Query button, the form generates a particular URL. It's the URL in Step 3 of the "Using parameters" section.

```
http://localhost:300x/shopping_cart/show?item=Book
```

The URL includes the extra `?item=Book` parameter. So give it a try. . . .

6. **Type** Book **in the Item field and then press the Submit Query button.**

   In the "Using parameters" section, the user types a clumsy-looking URL. But in this section, just typing the word **Book** and clicking the form's Submit Query button does the trick. The browser displays a book's price as in Figure 8-9.

   And if you like hideous URLs, you can still see one. After pressing the Submit Query button, you see the big, nasty `?item=Book` URL in the browser's Address field. How comforting! Clicking Submit Query creates the same URL that you create in the "Using parameters" section.

   That settles it. You must be doing something right.

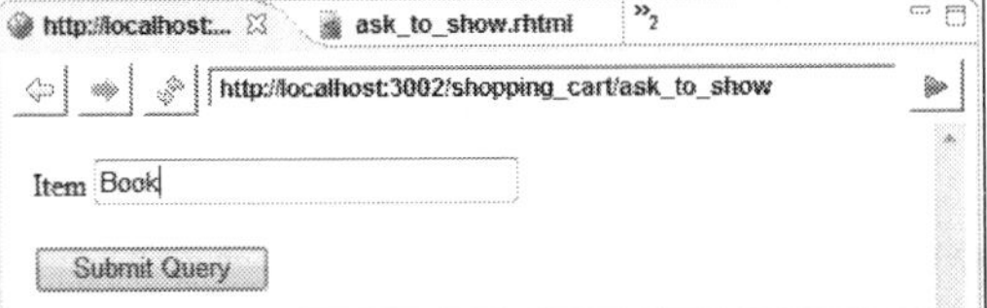

Figure 8-13: Typing the word *Book* in a text field.

Dividing the Work of the View

Pity the poor view! It works all day with little help from its friends. Occasionally, you find the view doing some calculations. But the view is supposed to concentrate only on the data's presentation. A view shouldn't dirty its hands with ugly calculations.

Well, in this section, you put some of the view's friends to work. The first friend is called a *layout.* It gives you a good way to put one piece of content on each of your Web site's pages.

1. **If you haven't already done so, follow the steps in this chapter's "Creating a controller and a view" section.**

   If you've already marched on and followed the steps in any of the subsequent sections, that's fine too.

2. **In the `myproject\app\views\layouts` directory, create a file named `shopping_cart.rhtml`.**

   To create this file, use a wizard as you do in Chapter 4.

3. **Using a RadRails editor, add two lines of code to the `shopping_cart.rhtml` file.**

   The lines of code are

   ```
   <%= @content_for_layout %><p>
   &copy; 2006 Burd Brain Consulting
   ```

   These are the only lines in the `shopping_cart.rhtml` file.

4. **Visit a `shopping_cart` page.**

   Depending on which section's steps you've already followed, you might visit `http://localhost:300x/shopping_cart/show`, `http://localhost:300x/shopping_cart/show?item=Book`, or even `http://localhost:300x/shopping_cart/ask_to_show`. One way or another, you see a page like the one in Figure 8-14. The page begins with some familiar content and ends with a handy copyright message.

Figure 8-14: A copyright message at the bottom of every page.

When you visit any of our example's `shopping_cart` controller's pages, Rails looks in the layout directory for a file named `shopping_cart.rhtml`. If Rails finds such a file, the browser window shows you the result of following the instructions in that file.

In this example, the `<%= @content_for_layout %>` tag tells Rails to display whatever it would normally display. For instance, in the "Creating a controller and a view" section, Rails normally displays only a Your Shopping Cart heading. In the "Using parameters" section, Rails normally displays an item and a price below the Your Shopping Cart heading.

After the `<%= @content_for_layout %>` tag comes the `<p>` tag. The `<p>` tag is called paragraph tag. The tag tells your Web browser to go to a new paragraph. For most Web browsers, "going to a new paragraph" means skipping a line before moving to the next line.

Finally, the additional `© 2006 Burd Brain Consulting` line tells Rails to display a copyright message. The `©` thing is part of standard HTML. It's called an HTML entity. When the `©` entity appears in an HTML file, your Web browser displays a copyright symbol.

Creating and using a partial (a partial what?)

Among people in the Ruby on Rails community, the word *partial* is a noun. A *partial* is a part of a Web page. It's not an entire Web page — just a piece to be inserted into a larger page. Here's how it works:

1. **If you haven't already done so, follow the steps in this chapter's "Using parameters" section.**

   If you've already marched on and followed the steps in any of the subsequent sections, that's fine too.

2. **In the `myproject\app\views\shopping_cart` directory, create a file named `_item_and_price.rhtml`.**

   To create this file, use a wizard as you do in Chapter 4.

   The filename contains three underscore (_) characters. The initial underscore is part of the Rails naming conventions. (See the "Convention over configuration" section in this chapter.)

3. **Using a RadRails editor, cut the `<%= @item %><br><%= number_to_currency(@price) %>` line of code from the `app\views\shopping_cart\show.rhtml` file and then paste the line into the new `app\views\shopping_cart\_item_and_price.rhtml` file.**

4. **Using a RadRails editor, add `<%= render :partial => 'item_and_price' %>` as one line of code to the `app\views\shopping_cart\show.rhtml` file.**

   After adding the line, the `show.rhtml` file contains the following two lines of code:

   ```
   <h1>Your Shopping Cart</h1>
   <%= render :partial => 'item_and_price' %>
   ```

   The new `render` command tells the view to look for a partial and to insert that partial's code into the view's own code. In the meantime, the string `'item_and_price'` tells Rails to look for the partial in a file named `_item_and_price.rhtml`.

5. **Visit `http://localhost:300x/shopping_cart/ask_to_show` or `http://localhost:300x/shopping_cart/show?item=Book`.**

   Either way, you see the page displayed in Figure 8-9. When the view gets a line from the partial, the view becomes just like the code in Step 3 of the "Controller Shakes Hands with the View" section.

Partials are nice because they share the responsibility. They help you keep clear in your mind what duties belong inside the view and what other duties belong outside the view. The only thing wrong with a partial is the name. Hey folks, how about calling it a "partial page" or a "partial document"?

A view's little helper

In the preceding section, you create a Web page (okay, a *partial* Web page) to take some of the computing burden off of the view. In this section, you do almost the same thing. But instead of creating part of a Web page, you create part of a Ruby program. One way or another, it's all about putting each piece of code in the most appropriate place.

1. **If you haven't already done so, follow the steps in the preceding section.**
2. **In the Rails Navigator view, find the `myproject\app\helpers\shopping_cart_helper.rb` file.**

   This file is created automatically when you generate the `ShoppingCart` controller.
3. **Using a RadRails editor, type the following code (the three bold lines) in the `shopping_cart_helper.rb` file:**

   ```
   module ShoppingCartHelper
     def price_with_tax(percent)
       @price * (1.0 + percent * 0.01)
     end
   end
   ```

   The code defines a `price_with_tax` method. The method takes a percentage (such as 7.0) and returns the `@price` with the percentage increase. The method is inside a Ruby module. (For more information on Ruby modules, see Chapter 6.)
4. **Using a RadRails editor, modify the `_item_and_price.rhtml` file so that it contains the following code:**

   ```
   <%= @item %><br>
   <%= number_to_currency(price_with_tax(7.0)) %>
   ```

   The call to `price_with_tax` is the only change from the previous section's `_item_and_price.rhtml` file. Any methods defined in the helper module are available for use by a `shopping_cart` view. So this step's call to `price_with_tax` is permissible.
5. **Revisit `http://localhost:300x/shopping_cart/ask_to_show` or `http://localhost:300x/shopping_cart/show?item=Book`.**

   You see the page shown in Figure 8-9 with the price increased by 7 percent. Once again, you've partitioned the work between the view, the layout, and the helper. You've separated the tasks so that each part of the code performs a specific, targeted task.

Chapter 9

Some Things You Can Do with Models

In This Chapter

- Creating a Web site to store personal data
- Viewing and modifying a Rails model
- Programming for a model with Ruby

Here's a list of things that come in sets of three:

- **Stooges:** Curly, Larry, Moe
- **The number of strikes until you're out:** Strike one, Strike two, Strike three
- **Things that influence the price of a house:** Location, Location, Location
- **Monkeys:** See no evil, Hear no evil, Speak no evil
- **People involved in a love triangle:** Person 1, Person 2, Person 1's best friend
- **Books in the *Hitchhiker's Guide* "trilogy":** *Guide*, *Restaurant*, *Universe*, *Fish*, *Harmless*
- **Items that would be in this list, if the list were more concise:** Stooges, Strikes, Houses
- **Parts of the Rails framework:** Model, View, Controller

In case you missed it, the last item in the list is the most relevant. Chapter 5 deals with the view and the controller. This chapter covers the model — the supreme item in the Rails triumvirate.

To make the discussion concrete, this chapter uses one big example — a Web site that stores photographs.

A Web Site for Photos

Here's my completely unoriginal idea: Create a Web site that displays photos. Initially, each photo entry has its own `filename` and its own `description`. The `filename` refers to an image file on a hard drive. (For example, `niagara_falls.jpg` may be a `filename`.) The `description` tells you something about the photo. ("Alan beats me up on our trip to Niagara Falls with Mom and Dad watching in the background.")

Niagara Falls?

This chapter shows you how to start building the Photo Web site. The next two chapters add some important details (such as displaying photos, associating peoples' comments with photos, and so on).

To start building this Web site, follow the steps in Chapter 3. Just change a few names to protect the innocent.

1. **Create a new Rails project.**

   In this example, I name the project `album`.

2. **Create a new database.**

   Use MySQL Administrator as you do in Chapter 3. If you name your project `album`, the name of the database is `album_development`.

3. **Generate a model.**

   In this example, I name the model `Photo`. (See Figure 9-1.)

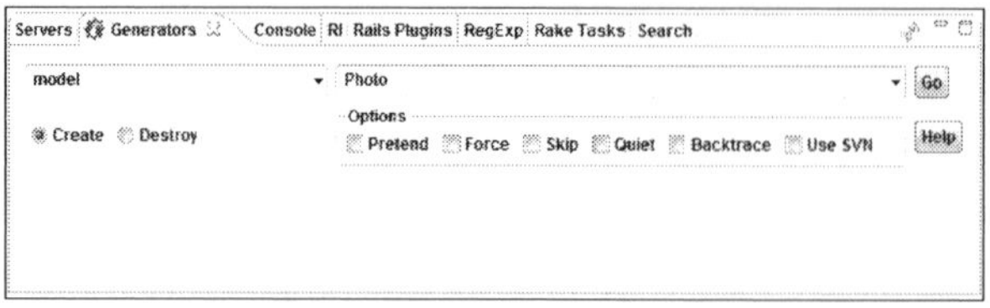

Figure 9-1: Generating the Photo model.

   Rails generates a `photo.rb` file in the project's `app\models` directory. The file contains only two lines of code:

```
class Photo < ActiveRecord::Base
end
```

   This terse piece of code defines an entire `Photo` model. How? The newly defined `Photo` class is a subclass of the Rails `ActiveRecord::Base` class. (For some good reading about subclasses, see Chapter 6.) As a subclass of `ActiveRecord::Base`, the `Photo` class inherits approximately 80 methods — methods such as `find`, `establish_connection`, `create`, `destroy`, and so on. You don't write code to define these methods yourself. You just use these with your newly created `Photo` class. That's the magic of subclasses and inheritance.

The `Photo` class's inherited methods are capable of performing CRUD operations on the `photos` database table. That's good because, according to Chapter 3, a model is some Ruby code that mirrors the data in a database table.

The acronym CRUD stands for the four fundamental database operations — Create, Read, Update, and Destroy. For details, see Chapter 3.

When you ask RadRails to generate a model, the system also generates a migration file — a file named `001_create_photos.rb`. In this example, the name of the model is `Photo`, so Rails automatically names the new table `photos`. (One of the lines in the `001_create_photos.rb` file is `create_table **:photos** do |t|`.)

A *migration* is a Ruby program that creates tables, adds columns to tables, and does other nice things to databases. For an introduction to migration files, see Chapter 3.

4. **Create a database table.**

   To create the database table, add two lines to the `001_create_photos.rb` migration code, as shown in Figure 9-2. (Listing 9-1 tells you which two lines are crucial here.)

```
001_create_photos.rb
class CreatePhotos < ActiveRecord::Migration
  def self.up
    create_table :photos do |t|
      t.column :filename, :string    #add this line
      t.column :description, :text   #add this line
    end
  end

  def self.down
    drop_table :photos
  end
end
```

Figure 9-2: Setting up columns in a database.

Listing 9-1: Creating the Database Table

```
class CreatePhotos < ActiveRecord::Migration
  def self.up
    create_table :photos do |t|
      t.column :filename, :string    #add this line
      t.column :description, :text  #add this line
    end
  end

  def self.down
    drop_table :photos
  end
end
```

The first `t.column` line creates a column to store the names of image files (names such as `myfirstphoto.jpg`). The second `t.column` line creates a column to store descriptions of the photos.

After adding these two lines to the `001_create_photos.rb` file, run the `db:migrate` task using the Rake Tasks view. (See Figure 9-3.)

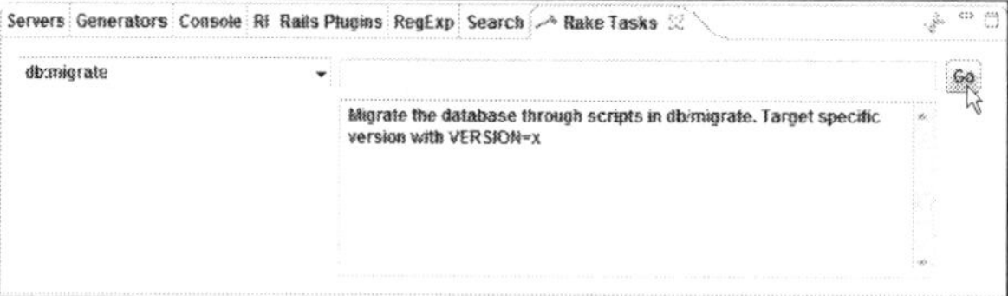

Figure 9-3: Running a migration.

In Figure 9-3, the thing on the left (containing the text `db:migrate`) is a drop-down list. Sometimes RadRails takes its good old time populating this drop-down list. When I click the list's downward-pointing triangle, I see an empty list. If this happens to you, wait a few seconds and then click the little triangle again. If a minute passes and you still don't see any list options, try leaving the triangle alone. Type **db:migrate** into the list and then click the Go button.

5. **Create a scaffold.**

   To create the scaffold, use the Generators view in RadRails. Select Scaffold from the drop-down list on the left and type the name **Photo** in the text field on the right. (See Figure 9-4.)

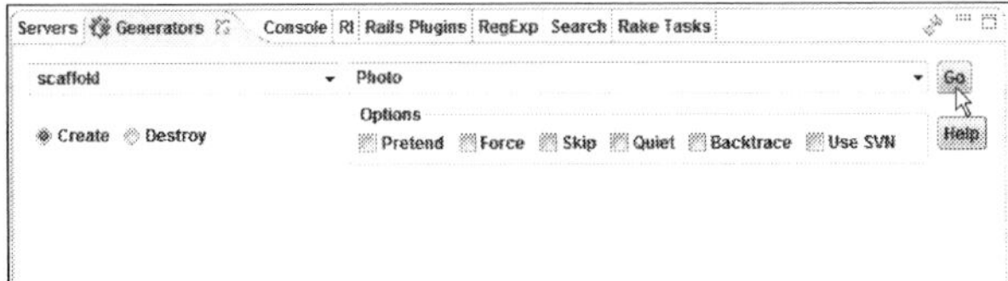

Figure 9-4: Generating the Photo scaffold.

Always look at the left side of the Generators view to make sure that the Create radio button is selected (unless, of course, you want to delete something that you created previously).

6. **Use the new Web interface.**

   When you visit `http://localhost:300x/photos/new`, you see the page shown in Figure 9-5.

Figure 9-5: Adding a new photo.

7. **Type some text into the fields on the New Photo page and then click the Create button. (See Figure 9-5.)**

   At this point, the stuff you type in the Filename field doesn't have to refer to any image file that's actually on your hard drive. Referring to real image files is discussed in Chapter 10.

8. **Repeat Step 7 a few times.**

   Each time you do, Rails sends your Web browser to a Listing Photos page. After adding a few photos, you can see a page like the one in Figure 9-6.

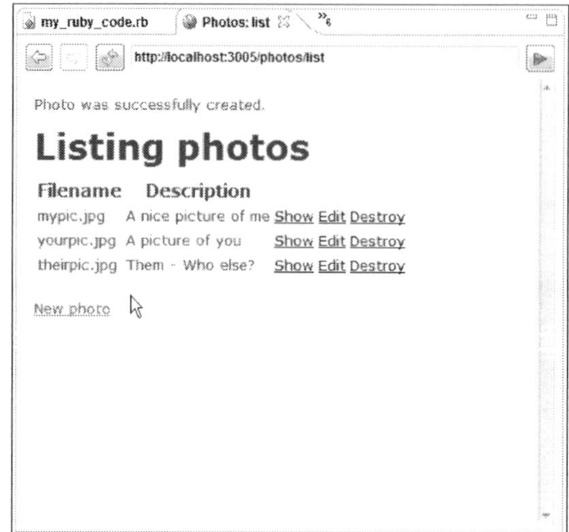

Figure 9-6: The Rails application lists some photos.

Programming with a Rails Model

The rest of this chapter is a brief detour (a fork in the Rails road). If I were a typical Ruby-on-Rails author, the rest of this chapter would embellish the previous section's Web pages. But instead, the chapter covers some pure Ruby code — code that's independent of any Web page.

This section's code connects to a database and retrieves the data from a database table. The code works with the preceding section's `Photo` model.

1. **Right-click the album project branch in the Rails Navigator view.**
2. **In the resulting contextual menu, choose New⇨File.**

   The New File dialog box appears.
3. **In the dialog box's File Name field, type a name that ends in** `.rb`**.**

   How about `my_ruby_code.rb`? That's a good name.
4. **Click Finish.**

   The empty `my_ruby_code.rb` file appears in the RadRails editor pane. In addition, the name `my_ruby_code.rb` shows up in the Rails Navigator view (near the bottom of the album project's tree).

5. **In the RadRails editor pane, type the code shown in Listing 9-2.**

Listing 9-2: Displaying the Rows in a Database

```
require_gem "activerecord"

class Photo < ActiveRecord::Base
end

Photo.establish_connection(
  :adapter => "mysql", :database => "album_development")

for column in Photo.columns
  print column.name, "\t"
end

puts
puts

for photo in Photo.find(:all)
  for column in Photo.columns
    print photo.send(column.name), "\t"
  end
  puts
end
```

Listing 9-2 contains two indispensable lines of code:

```
class Photo < ActiveRecord::Base
end
```

You might recognize these lines from Step 3 of this chapter's "A Web Site for Photos" section. As in Step 3, these two lines define a `Photo` model. With these lines and the call to `establish_connection` in Listing 9-2, the rest of the listing's code has access to the `photos` database table's values.

6. **Right-click the editor pane. Then, in the resulting contextual menu, choose Run As➪Ruby Application.**

   In response, the RadRails Console view displays a list of photos (the photos stored in the `photos` database table). See Figure 9-7.

Figure 9-7: A Ruby program lists the rows in a database.

The migration file in Listing 9-1 describes only two columns — `filename` and `description`. But according to Figure 9-7, the `photos` table in the `album_development` database has three columns — `id`, `filename`, and `description`. Why does the table have this extra `id` column? For an answer, see the section entitled "Using id numbers," later in this chapter.

The code in Listing 9-2 illustrates several important ideas. So the next few sections dissect the code in Listing 9-2.

Using Active Record

In Listing 9-2, two brief lines of code tell Ruby about the `photos` database table.

```
class Photo < ActiveRecord::Base
end
```

These lines say a lot. They say "Make the `Photo` class a subclass of the previously defined `ActiveRecord::Base` class." That's a real mouthful. The `ActiveRecord::Base` class comes standard with Rails. Any subclass of `ActiveRecord::Base` (the `Photo` class, for example) inherits dozens of methods from the `ActiveRecord::Base` class — methods named `find`, `create`, `establish_connection`, `delete`, and so on.

But wait! There's more. Active Record is a strange and wonderful thing! If it weren't for Active Record, you'd have to add more code to Listing 9-2.

- **You'd have to add the name `photos` somewhere in Listing 9-2.**

  This name would tell the code to look for a table named `photos` in the `album_development` database. Notice that, although the words `Photo` and `photo` (uppercase and lowercase) appear in Listing 9-2, the name `photos` appears nowhere in the listing.

- **You'd have to define `photos` table's contents.**

  You'd need a definition like the following: "Each row has a filename and a description. The filename is of type `string`, and the description has type `text`. Take it or leave it!"

And what would be so bad about adding that code to Listing 9-2? Some programmers love to write code. What's the big deal?

Well, remember the DRY (Don't Repeat Yourself) principle from Chapter 8? A characteristic of the database or its Web site should be declared in only one place. You should have no redundant declarations. Nothing that's defined in one place should have its definition repeated in any other place. If you follow the DRY principle, you won't risk introducing inconsistencies when you change a particular characteristic. (You can't make the mistake of changing the declaration in some, but not all, of the relevant places.)

So here's an indisputable fact:

> *The database itself (in this example, the `album_development` database on your computer's hard drive) is the ultimate authority on the nature of the columns in the `photos` table.*

Sure, you might have created the `filename` and `description` columns yesterday by running the migration code in Listing 9-1. But today that migration code might be obsolete. (Overnight, the boss might have told someone to use MySQL Administrator to add a `date_created` column to the table.) Your code must be able to deal with any change that comes about in the actual database table.

So Active Record does something very nice. When you run the code in Listing 9-2, Active Record deduces the table name (`photos`) and looks at the actual `photos` table in the database. From the table, Active Record deduces the number of columns, the names of the columns, and the types of the columns. You don't have to define the columns in Listing 9-2.

Requiring a gem

In Listing 9-2, the name `ActiveRecord` refers to a Ruby module that's defined inside another file. This `ActiveRecord` module belongs to a Ruby add-on (a Ruby *gem*) named `activerecord`. So before you can write `ActiveRecord::Base` anywhere in Listing 9-2, you have to write `require_gem "activerecord"`. That's why Listing 9-2 starts with `require_gem "activerecord"`.

To be brutally precise, calling `require_gem "activerecord"` adds the `activerecord` gem's directory to the Ruby load path and loads the gem into the current runtime. For a few words about the Ruby load path, see Chapter 6.

Connecting to the database

In Listing 9-2, the call to the `establish_connection` method does exactly what its name indicates. The call connects the `Photo` class to the `album_development` database (the database that you create in the first section of this chapter). Without this call, the code wouldn't be able to get rows from the `album_development` database.

In Listing 9-2, the `establish_connection` call specifies `:adapter` and `:database` values. In addition, the call can specify things such as `:host`, `:username`, and `:password`.

Heavily ORMed

If you've done some database programming, you might be familiar with two programming styles:

- Inserting procedural statements into the code
- Using object-relational mapping

The first style (the older of the two) involves direct instructions to the database. Get a row, change a value, add a row, and so on. The instructions may be SQL statements (`SELECT * FROM photos`) or they may be statements in some general-purpose programming language (`resultSet.updateString("filename", "myphoto.jpg")`). This manual handling of the database can be cumbersome, especially if you spread the database code across many parts of an application.

The newer *object-relational mapping* (ORM) style avoids having direct instructions in the code. Instead, the programmer declares the correspondence between a class and a database table. The declaration might look something like this:

```
<mapping>
    <table class="Photo" name="photos" database="album_
   development">
        <row field="filename" type="string" column="filename"/>
          <row field="description" type="text" column=
   "description"/>
    </table>
</mapping>
```

With this declaration, the system ties a class named `Photo` (a class in the programming language code) to a database table named `photos`. In a program, an instruction may assign a value to a variable

```
Photo.getInstance().filename = "disneyworld.jpg";
```

With this assignment, the system automatically modifies a row in the `photos` database table. The programmer doesn't have to dirty his or her hands with explicit database instructions. Instead, the programmer writes ordinary object-oriented code; and in response, the system automatically keeps the `photos` database table in sync with the `Photo` class's code.

Active Record is the heart and soul of Ruby on Rails. Active Record is an ORM framework, but Active Record takes ORM where no ORM has gone before. Active Record avoids the big `<mapping>. . .</mapping>` definition that you see earlier in this sidebar. Using Active Record, Rails creates a `<mapping>. . .</mapping>` definition automatically. Rails seeks out the most current version of the database in use, and then formulates a definition based on the shape of the database table. Using this formulated definition, Rails guides the flow of the model's data.

> Using Active Record with Rails, the programmer doesn't write explicit database instructions. Heck! The programmer doesn't even define the mapping between the class and the database. Does this mean that the programmer is a lazy bum? No. With all the database-mapping grunt work being done automatically by Rails, the programmer is free to concentrate on the important stuff — the database business logic. That's a very good thing.

The value `:host => "localhost"` should work nicely to specify a host (if the Ruby code lives on the same computer as the database).

The `establish_connection` method is a class method of the `ActiveRecord::Base` class. And, because of inheritance, `establish_connection` is a class method of the `Photo` class. Being a *class method* means that only one copy of the `establish_connection` method exists for the entire `Photo` class. If you create several instances of the `Photo` class or no instances of the `Photo` class, the `Photo` class still has one and only one `establish_connection` method. That's why, when you call the `establish_connection` method, you preface the call with the name of the class. You write `Photo.establish_connection`.

Displaying data

The part of Listing 9-2, from the first `for column` line downward, is the do-something-conspicuous part of the listing. This part displays column headings and the values in the `photos` table. The code contains some `for` loops (which isn't startling if you're used to computer programming). But the code also contains some useful *Rails-isms.*

- **The `Photo` class has a `columns` method (inherited from `ActiveRecord::Base`).**

  The `columns` method returns an array consisting of the columns in the `photos` database table. In this chapter's example, the `photos` table has three columns — `id`, `filename`, and `description`. (Refer to Figure 9-7.) So the line `for column in Photo.columns` iterates over these three columns.

  Each column is a Ruby object, and each of these objects has a `name`. So to be painfully precise, the first time through this loop, `column.name` has the value `'id'`. The second time through, `column.name` has the value `'filename'`. The third time, `column.name` has the value `'description'`. Each time through, the variable `column` contains a string of characters.

In Listing 9-2, you can replace column.name with column.human_name. A human_name looks friendlier than a plain old name. If column.name is description, then column.human_name is Description. If column.name is MAX_VALUE, then column.human_name is Max value.

- **The Photo class has a find method (also inherited from the ActiveRecord::Base class).**

  When you supply the :all argument to the find method, the method returns an array containing the data from all rows in the photos database table. In Listing 9-2, each time through the for photo in Photo.find(:all) loop, the variable photo refers to a row of the photos database table.

- **The send method is Ruby's way of turning a method's name into a method call.**

  This is a very subtle concept, and (for better or worse) Ruby on Rails uses the concept everywhere in its code.

  With seemingly infinite versatility, Active Record looks inside the photos table and creates three brand-new methods — methods named id, filename, and description. (For details, see the section entitled "Using Active Record," earlier in this chapter.) Each of these methods belongs to Photo instances. (That is, each object created from the Photo class has its own id, filename, and description methods.)

  So now you have a hurdle to overcome. Inside the loops of Listing 9-2, you have a photo — an instance of the Photo class. This photo has a method called filename. So you're free to write photo.filename and have Ruby display c:\myfolder\myphoto.jpg (or something like that).

  But the variable column stores the string 'filename', so you can't put photo.column in your code. That would be like putting photo.'filename' in your code. But then you'd be applying the 'filename' string of characters (not the filename method) to the photo object. Applying a string of characters is a no-no.

  Ruby solves this problem with the send method. The send method turns a string into a method call. When you write photo.send('filename'), Ruby calls photo.filename on your behalf. If you write photo.send(column.name), as done in Listing 9-2, and column.name happens to contain the string 'description', Ruby calls photo.description on your behalf. If the comic Yakov Smirnoff knew Ruby, he'd exclaim "What a language!"

  Oh, well! When all is said and done, the loops in Listing 9-2 display the values in all the columns of all the rows of the photos database table. (Again, refer to Figure 9-7.)

Modifying a Database

In this chapter's "Using Active Record" section, someone sneaks into your office overnight and adds a `date_created` column to your `photos` database table. How dare he (or she or it)! How did this nefarious person add a column?

The scoundrel might have used MySQL Administrator, but you can do the same thing with a Rails migration. Here's how:

1. **Follow the steps in the section entitled "A Web Site for Photos" (at the start of this chapter).**
2. **In the Rails Navigator view, select the `album` project (the project that you create at the beginning of this chapter).**
3. **In the Generators view, create a migration.**

   See Figure 9-8. In that figure, the rightmost text field contains the name `add_date_created`. This name reminds you that the purpose of your new migration is to add a `date_created` column. You can type any name in the rightmost text field, but a more informative name is better than a random, hastily-generated name.

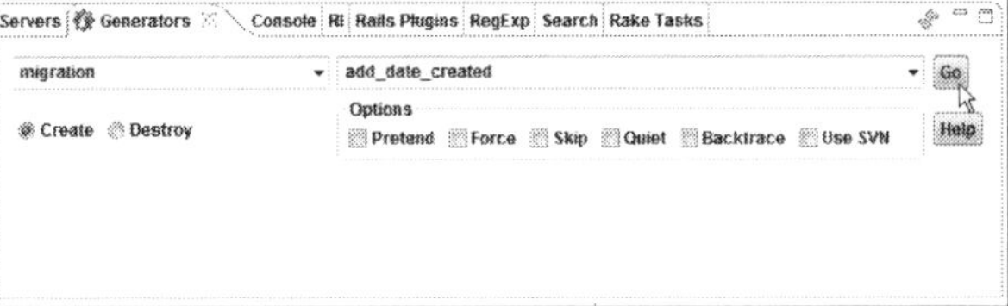

Figure 9-8: Generating a migration.

   When you press Go, Rails creates a file named `002_add_date_created.rb`.

   At this point, the album project has two migration files — `001_create_photos.rb` and `002_add_date_created.rb`. The numbers `001` and `002` are version numbers. For details, see the end of this section.

4. **Using a RadRails editor, add two lines of code to the `002_add_date_created.rb` file — a line in the `self.up` method, and another in the `self.down` method. (See Listing 9-3.)**

Listing 9-3: Your Hand-Made Migration

```
class AddDateCreated < ActiveRecord::Migration
  def self.up
    add_column :photos, :date_created, :date   #added
  end

  def self.down
    remove_column :photos, :date_created       #added
  end
end
```

The new code in the `self.up` method tells Rails to add a column to the `photos` database table. The column's name is `date_created`, and the values stored in the column are of type `date`.

The new code in the `self.down` method tells Rails to dispose of the `date_created` column. (To find out how and when you call the `self.down` method, see the end of this section.)

5. **Run the `db:migrate` task using the Rake Tasks view.**

   Refer to Figure 9-3.

6. **Rerun the code in Listing 9-3. (Repeat Step 6 of this chapter's "Programming with a Rails Model" section.)**

   You see the revised output shown in Figure 9-9. As promised, Active Record deduces the names of the columns in the database. Without changing a word of Listing 9-2, the new output contains a `date_created` column.

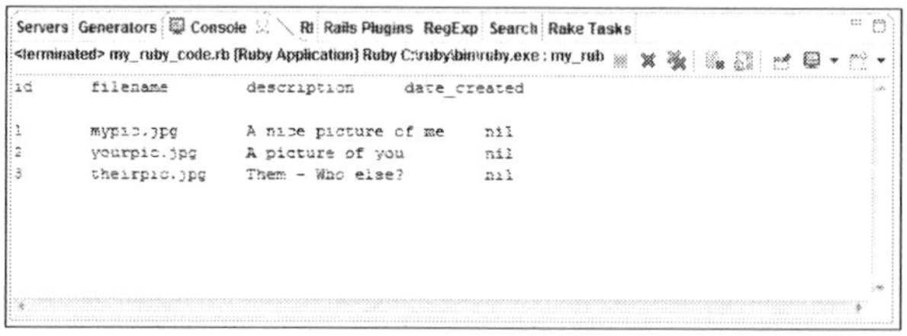

```
Servers Generators Console Rl Rails Plugins RegExp Search Rake Tasks
<terminated> my_ruby_code.rb [Ruby Application] Ruby C:\ruby\bin\ruby.exe : my_rub
id      filename        description             date_created

1       mypic.jpg       A nice picture of me    nil
2       yourpic.jpg     A picture of you        nil
3       theirpic.jpg    Them - Who else?        nil
```

Figure 9-9: Listing the rows in the modified database.

You haven't inserted values into the table since you added the `date_created` column, so the values in the new `date_created` column are all `nil`. You can remedy this situation by updating each row's values. Tips on updating values appear later in this chapter.

In the filename `002_add_date_created.rb`, the `002` is a migration version number. Rails keeps track of the order in which you apply migrations.

1. You start with an empty database. The empty database is version 0 (also known as version 000).

2. You generate and run 001_create_photos.rb. The run adds a photos table to the database. The database with this new photos table is version 1 (version 001).
3. You generate and run 002_add_date_created.rb. The run adds a date_created column to the photos table. The modified database, with the date_created column, is version 2 (version 002). And so on.

Rails stores each database's current version number in a table named schema_info. The schema_info table has only one row and one column. The column's name is version. You can see the schema_info table using MySQL Administrator.

Why keep track of all these version numbers? Well, if you ever change your mind and decide to return to an earlier version, you can use migration to go backwards.

Assume, for example, that this new date_created column makes you nervous. You decide to march back to version 1 of the database — a version without the date_created column. To revert, you run db:migrate with VERSION=1, as shown in Figure 9-10.

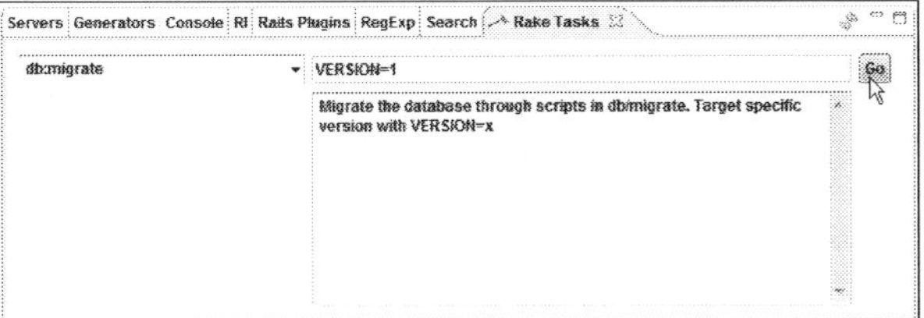

Figure 9-10: Migrating to a particular version of the database.

You can even trash the photos table and start all over again. To do this, run db:migrate with VERSION=0.

When you migrate from one version to another, Rails executes the appropriate sequence of self.up or self.down methods. For example, when you migrate from version 2 down to version 0, Rails calls the self.down method in the 002_*blah_blah*.rb file, and then calls the self.down method in the 001_*blabity_blah*.rb file. Later, if you decide to return from version 0 to version 2, Rails calls the self.up method in 001_*blabity_blah*.rb, and then calls the self.up method in 002_*blah_blah*.rb.

When you write your own migration file, the code inside the self.down method should undo whatever the code inside the self.up method does.

More Rails Programming Tricks

To put it bluntly, Listing 9-2 is a wimp. Listing 9-2 mollycoddles the `album_development` database. If you want to get tough with the database, you have to do more CRUD operations (more Creating, more Reading, more Updating, and more Deleting). This section shows you how.

But first, look at Listing 9-4. This listing continues to pamper the `album_development` database. (The listing defines some goodies that help with subsequent code in this chapter.)

Listing 9-4: Getting Ready

```
# ready_photos.rb

require_gem "activerecord"

class Photo < ActiveRecord::Base
  def show
    Photo.columns.each {|col| print send(col.name), "\t"}
  end

  def Photo.show_all
    find(:all).each { |photo| photo.show; puts }
  end
end

Photo.establish_connection(
  :adapter=> "mysql", :database => "album_development")
```

Listing 9-4 defines two handy methods. The `show` method displays the contents of a single photo, and the `show_all` method displays the contents of all photos. Both the `show` and `show_all` methods use Ruby's `each` iterator instead of `for` loops. For example, inside the `show_all` method, the code finds all instances of the `Photo` class (all rows in the `photos` table). To each of these instances (each instance temporarily named `photo`), the code applies the statements `photo.show; puts`.

In turn, the call to `photo.show` displays the instance's id, filename, and description. Then the call to `puts` forces the RadRails output console onto a brand-new line.

The choice between an iterator and a loop is purely cosmetic. (In Listing 9-4, I use iterators just to show off.)

In addition to defining `show` and `show_all`, Listing 9-4 forges a connection to the `album_development` database. That way, you don't have to connect in subsequent listings.

The comment at the top of Listing 9-4 reminds you that the listing's code belongs in a file named `ready_photos.rb`. This is important because, in subsequent listings, you refer to the file named `ready_photos.rb`. (Each listing begins with the line `require "ready_photos.rb"`.) You can change the file's name if you want, but when you change the file's name, you have to change the `require` references in the other listings. And remember, changing the comment at the top of Listing 9-4 does nothing. To change a file's name, you have to change the name as it appears in the Rails Navigator view.

Deleting rows

In Listing 9-5, you clear the deck. You remove any photos that might already be in the database.

Listing 9-5: Goodbye to All My Photos

```
require "ready_photos.rb"

Photo.destroy_all

puts "List of photos:"
Photo.show_all
puts "End of the list"
```

Listing 9-5 gives you a fresh start for the examples in the remainder of this chapter. So notice a few things about Listing 9-5:

- **The `require` call at the top of Listing 9-5 drags in all the code from Listing 9-4.**

  In particular, the `require` call makes the `show` and `show_all` methods available. The call also invokes the `establish_connection` method, so that a run of Listing 9-5 can communicate with the `album_development` database.

- **You don't have to define your own `destroy_all` method.**

  Rails defines the `destroy_all` method as part of the `ActiveRecord::Base` class. A call to `destroy_all` uses Active Record to remove all rows from the database table.

  Rails has a similar method named `delete_all`. A call to `delete_all` digs right into the database and removes all records from the database table. In doing so, `delete_all` bypasses some nice Active Record features. All in all, if you're not desperate to obliterate every trace of the database table, `destroy_all` is safer to use.

- **At the end of Listing 9-5, a call to `show_all` proves that the `photos` table contains no rows. (See Figure 9-11.)**

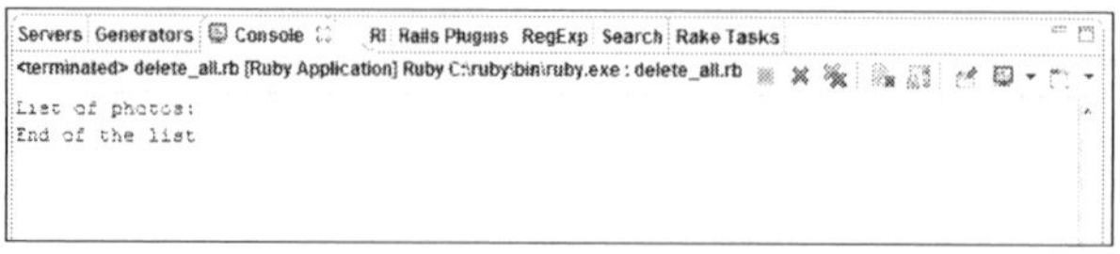

Figure 9-11: A run of the code in Listing 9-5.

Servers Generators Console RI Rails Plugins RegExp Search Rake Tasks

<terminated> delete_all.rb [Ruby Application] Ruby C:\ruby\bin\ruby.exe : delete_all.rb

List of photos:
End of the list

Adding rows

This section's code (see Listing 9-6) adds two rows to the `photos` database.

Listing 9-6: Nice Kitty

```
require "ready_photos.rb"

photo = Photo.new
photo.filename = 'willie.jpg'
photo.description = 'Our old cat Willie'
photo.save

Photo.create(:filename => 'kitten.jpg',
             :description => 'Our cat Boop')

Photo.show_all
puts '------------'

photo = Photo.find(:first,
             :conditions => "filename = 'kitten.jpg'")
photo.filename = 'boop.jpg'
photo.save

Photo.show_all
```

Listing 9-6 demonstrates a few things that Active Record can do with a database.

- **The `new` method makes a brand-new object.**

  In Listing 9-6, the statement

  ```
  photo = Photo.new
  ```

  makes an object whose `filename` and `description` have meaningless default values. It's up to the next two statements

  ```
  photo.filename = 'willie.jpg'
  photo.description = 'Our old cat Willie'
  ```

  to supply meaningful `filename` and `description` values.

If you want, you can combine the three statements into one big statement:

```
photo = Photo.new(:filename => 'willie.jpg',
          :description => 'Our old cat Willie')
```

How you choose to make an object is ultimately a matter of taste.

- **The `save` method takes an object (a mere Ruby program construct) and shoves that object's data into the database.**

  In Listing 9-6, the call to `save` adds a `willie.jpg` row to the `photos` table.

REMEMBER

  A call to `new` (without a follow-up call to `save`) has no effect on the database table.

- **The `create` method does the work of both `new` and `save`.**

  Listing 9-6 makes a new object with meaningful values and stores those values in the database, all with one call to `create`.

- **The `find` method locates a row (or several rows) in the database.**

  In Listing 9-6, the code

  ```
  Photo.find(:first,
        :conditions => "filename = 'kitten.jpg'")
  ```

  returns the earliest row in the database table whose `filename` column contains `kitten.jpg`.

  Active Record's `find` methods come in several delicious flavors. The `find(:all)` flavor appears in Listing 9-2, and the `find(:first)` flavor appears in Listing 9-6. Some other flavors appear later in this chapter.

- **Near the end of Listing 9-6, you change a value in one of the database table rows. (You change `'kitten.jpg'` to `'boop.jpg'`.)**

  The `save` method suffers from a split personality disorder. Near the start of Listing 9-6, you create a new instance of the `Photo` class. So, in that part of the code, `save` adds a brand-new row to the `photos` database table.

  But near the end of the listing, you find an existing row in the database table. So at that point, instead of adding a new row, `save` modifies the existing row.

- **A final call to `show_all` displays all rows of the database table.**

  The output of the code in Listing 9-6 appears in Figure 9-12.

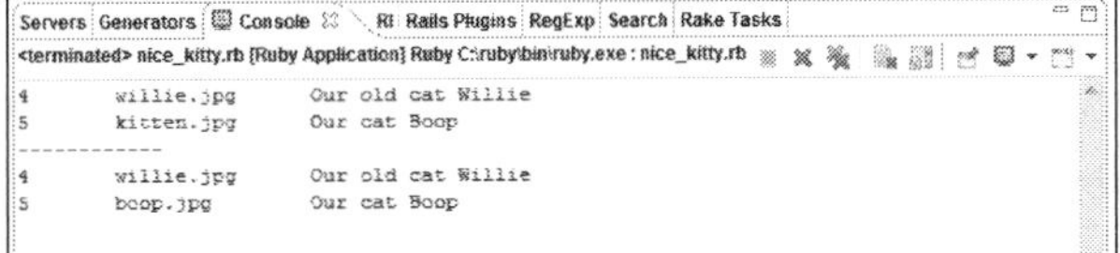
Servers Generators Console RI Rails Plugins RegExp Search Rake Tasks
<terminated> nice_kitty.rb [Ruby Application] Ruby C:\ruby\bin\ruby.exe : nice_kitty.rb
4 willie.jpg Our old cat Willie
5 kitten.jpg Our cat Boop
----
4 willie.jpg Our old cat Willie
5 boop.jpg Our cat Boop

Figure 9-12: A run of the code in Listing 9-6.

Finding rows

This section's example performs some acrobatics with the `find` method. An example is shown in Listing 9-7, and the output of a run appears in Figure 9-13.

Listing 9-7: Letting the Cat out of the Bag

```
require "ready_photos.rb"

Photo.create(:filename => 'kitty.jpg',
             :description => 'A big cat')

Photo.create(:filename => 'kitty.jpg',
             :description => 'A little cat')

Photo.create(:filename => 'calico.jpg',
             :description => 'Another little cat')

print "Enter a filename (without the .jpg extension): "
STDOUT.flush
f_name = gets.chomp + '.jpg'

print "Enter part of a description: "
STDOUT.flush
cat = '%' + gets.chomp + '%'

photo = Photo.find(:first, :conditions =>
  "filename = '#{f_name}' AND description LIKE '#{cat}'")
photo.filename = 'other_cat.jpg'
photo.save

Photo.show_all
```

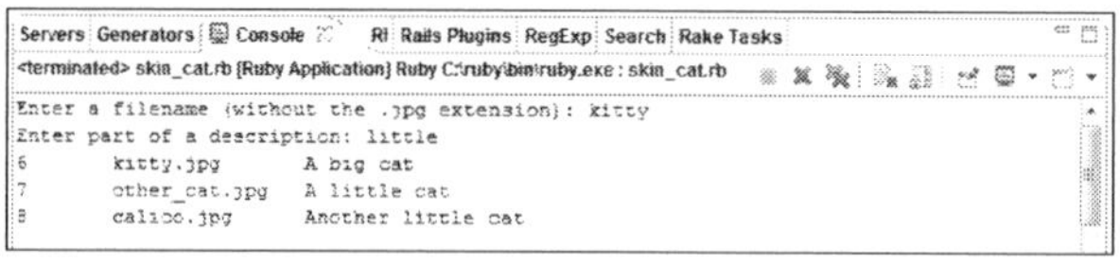

```
Servers Generators Console RI Rails Plugins RegExp Search Rake Tasks
<terminated> skin_cat.rb [Ruby Application] Ruby C:\ruby\bin\ruby.exe : skin_cat.rb
Enter a filename (without the .jpg extension): kitty
Enter part of a description: little
6       kitty.jpg       A big cat
7       other_cat.jpg   A little cat
8       calico.jpg      Another little cat
```

Figure 9-13: A run of the code in Listing 9-7.

Most of the tricks in Listing 9-7 are Ruby-ish or SQL-ish rather than Rails-ish.

- **With a `STDOUT.flush` call, the system displays a prompt before the user types a response.**

  Without `STDOUT.flush`, you might see the ugly run shown in Figure 9-14.

- **The `gets` method reads a line of input from the keyboard.**

For example, the first `gets` call in Figure 9-13 reads `kitty`*<Enter>* (the word `kitty` followed by an Enter key).

- **The `chomp` method removes the Enter key character.**

  The value of `f_name` becomes `kitty.jpg`, not `kitty`*<Enter>*`.jpg`.

- **The percent sign (%), an SQL wildcard, stands for any sequence of characters.**

  When the user types the word `little` in Figure 9-13, the value of `cat` becomes `%little%`. This `%little%` string is a pattern. In an SQL statement, the pattern `%little%` stands for any string or characters containing `little` anywhere inside it.

- **The pound sign (#) inside a double-quoted string represents Ruby *interpolation*.**

  At runtime, Ruby evaluates the expression after the pound sign. Ruby substitutes that value into the double-quoted string.

  For example, if the value of `f_name` is `kitty.jpg` and the value of `cat` is `%little%`, then the code

  ```
  "filename =
    '#{f_name}' AND description LIKE '#{cat}'"
  ```

  stands for the following SQL condition string:

  ```
  "filename =
    'kitty.jpg' AND description LIKE '%little%'"
  ```

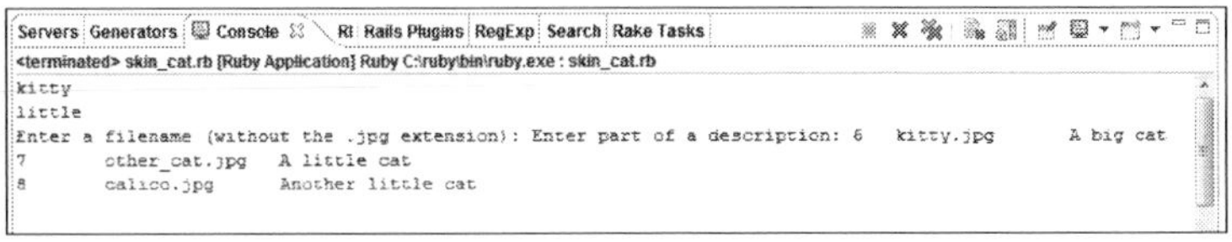

Figure 9-14: What can happen when you don't call STDOUT.flush.

Using SQL

Do me a favor. Run the code in Listing 9-6 a few times. When you do, you see output of the kind shown in Figure 9-15.


```
9       willie.jpg      Our old cat Willie
10      boop.jpg        Our cat Boop
11      willie.jpg      Our old cat Willie
12      boop.jpg        Our cat Boop
13      willie.jpg      Our old cat Willie
14      kitten.jpg      Our cat Boop
------------
9       willie.jpg      Our old cat Willie
10      boop.jpg        Our cat Boop
11      willie.jpg      Our old cat Willie
12      boop.jpg        Our cat Boop
13      willie.jpg      Our old cat Willie
14      boop.jpg        Our cat Boop
```

Figure 9-15: The third run of the code in Listing 9-6.

After three runs of the code in Listing 9-6, the `photos` table contains six rows — three Willie rows and three Boop rows.

Now what if you want to pick out all the Willie rows using a good, old-fashioned SQL statement? No sweat! You can use `find_by_sql` as in Listing 9-8.

Listing 9-8: Where's Willie?

```
require "ready_photos.rb"

Photo.find_by_sql("SELECT * FROM photos
  WHERE filename = 'willie.jpg'").each {|p| p.show; puts}
```

Active Record's `find_by_sql` method brings all the functionality of SQL to your Ruby programs. Just write your SQL command and plop it into the `find_by_sql` method.

Listing 9-8 takes each object that `find_by_sql` returns and displays that object's data on the RadRails Console.

SQL accepts single- or double-quoted strings, and so does Ruby. In fact, Ruby accepts all kinds of strange string literals. In Ruby, you can write `find_by_sql(`**`%q/`**`SELECT * FROM photos WHERE filename = "willie.jpg"`**`/`**`)`. You should, however, avoid using the same character in one call for both the Ruby string and the SQL string. For example, the Ruby interpreter flags the following code (with too many double-quote marks) as a syntax error: `find_by_sql("SELECT * FROM photos WHERE filename = "willie.jpg"")`.

Using id numbers

When you use `db:migrate` to create a database table, Rails creates whatever table columns you specify. In addition, Rails creates an additional column — a column named `id`. This `id` column stores an *auto-incremented* integer value. When you create the first row, the row's `id` value automatically becomes 1. When you create a second row, the row's `id` value automatically becomes 2. And so on. Even if you get rid of the first row, when you create a third row, the third row's `id` value automatically becomes 3.

Rails provides a convenient way for you to avoid dealing with the `id` column. In Listing 9-2, change both occurrences of `Photo.columns` to `Photo.content_columns`. This causes Rails to skip the `id` column and to display only the `filename` and `description` columns.

As a Ruby-on-Rails programmer, you seldom have to deal with explicit `id` values. When you modify a particular row, you don't care whether that row's `id` value is 2 or 2240948. You can write the code shown in Listing 9-9, but chances are, you never will.

Listing 9-9: Dealing Explicitly with id Numbers

```
require "ready_photos.rb"

Photo.delete(170)
Photo.find(172).show
```

An id number's actual value doesn't matter. In the United States, we have things called debit cards. I use my debit card to pay for groceries. After tallying all my purchases, the store employee runs my debit card through an electronic sensor. Then the employee asks me to type my PIN (my personal id number).

A computer (located thousands of miles from the grocery store) checks the number I type against the number associated with the debit card. Like the id number in a database table row, my actual id number is of no concern to the store employee. The employee just wants to be sure that whatever number I type matches the number associated with my debit card.

Listing 9-10 (an admittedly lame example) illustrates this concept using a database table's id numbers.

Listing 9-10: Dealing Implicitly with an id Number

```
require "ready_photos.rb"

target = Photo.find(:first,
           :conditions => "filename = 'calico.jpg'")

Photo.find(target.id).show unless not target
```

Listing 9-10 is indeed lame. Why write `Photo.find(target.id).show`, when a simple `target.show` does the job? Listing 9-10 doesn't solve the problem efficiently. But the listing illustrates the way a row's id number can be passed from place to place without ever being seen by the programmer or the user.

In Rails, id numbers are passed all the time. A controller's action passes an id to a view. In turn, the view passes the id to another of the controller's actions. That's how Rails remembers that it's updating a particular row. For a more concrete view of the process in Rails, see Chapter 10.

If you're not a seasoned Ruby programmer, you might be confused by the word `unless` in Listing 9-10. The `find` method looks for a row whose `filename` is `calico.jpg`. If such a row doesn't exist, the `find` call returns `nil`, and variable `target` gets this `nil` value. But in a Ruby condition, `nil` is the same as `false`. So in that case, `unless not target` is true.

In a Ruby condition, everything that's not `nil` or `false` is true. Among other things, this means that both `0` and `1` are true. If you're a C++ programmer, having `0` represent `true` might be upsetting. On behalf of the Ruby community, I apologize for any loss of sleep this might cause.

Chapter 10

I've Been Working on the Rails Code

In This Chapter

- Displaying images
- Adding new images to your Rails project
- Using the RadRails Import Wizard

Chapter 9 demonstrates the creation of a photo album Web site. The site's managers (the folks at Chapter9Photos.com, Inc.) have hired a marketing team to promote the Web site. Here's an excerpt from the team's proposed marketing blurb:

> *Visit Chapter 9 Photos online! See the filename and description of your favorite photo! Enter any filename you want — correct or incorrect. It doesn't matter, because the Web site doesn't even display your photo!*

How appealing! I can't wait to visit the site!

Displaying an Image

When I was a child, my family was so poor that we couldn't afford photos. All we could afford were the filenames of photos. That's why we created Chapter9Photos.com.

But these days, kids are spoiled. When they visit a photo album Web site, they expect to see photos, not just filenames! So this chapter adds visible photos to the site in Chapter 9.

Creating code

You can add images to a Web site with only a few lines of code. Here's how:

1. **If you haven't already done so, create a simple photo album Web site.**

   Follow Steps 1 through 5 in the first section of Chapter 9.

2. **In the Rails Navigator view, find the project's `public\images` branch.**

   The `public\images` directory contains a file named `rails.png`. See Figure 10-1.

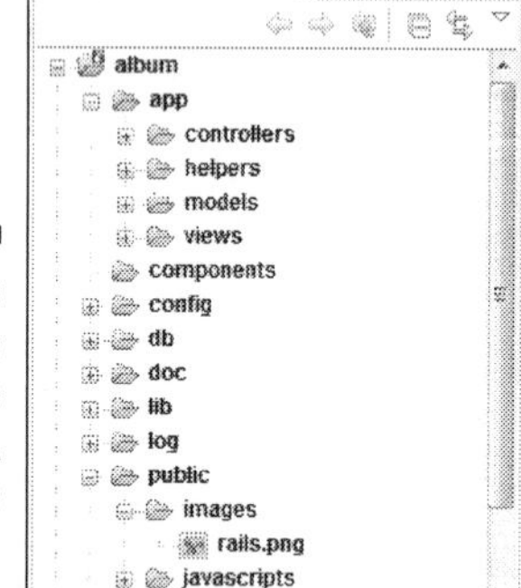

Figure 10-1: A Rails project's public\images directory.

Between the time I write this book and the time you read this book, the name of the file inside the `public\images` directory may change. If the file's name isn't `rails.png`, jot down the name of whatever file you find in the `public\images` directory. If you find more than one file, choose one of the names arbitrarily. If you don't find any files in the `public\images` directory, then panic! (No, don't panic. Check this book's Web site for updates.)

3. **In your Rails project, open the `app\views\photos\show.rhtml` file.**

   For details on opening files, see Chapter 4.

4. **Using a RadRails editor, add the code in Listing 10-1 to the `show.rhtml` file.**

Listing 10-1: Adding Code to show.rhtml

```
<% fname = @photo.filename %>
<%= image_tag(fname,
  { :size => "100", :border => "1" }) %><p/>
```

5. **Visit `http://localhost:300x/photos/new`.**

   The New Photo page appears. (See Figure 10-2.)

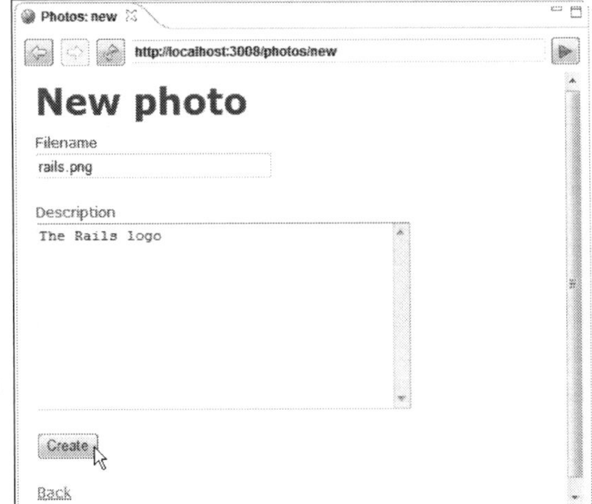

Figure 10-2: The New Photo page.

In `localhost:300x`, the letter *x* doesn't stand for the letter x! Instead, the letter *x* stands for a digit. In fact, `0x` may stand for `23`! For details, see Chapter 8.

6. **Fill in the fields in the New Photo page.**

   In Figure 10-2, you type **rails.png** in the Filename field and **The Rails logo** in the Description field.

   The name you type in the Filename field must be the same as the name of a file in your project's `public\images` directory.

7. **Click Create at the bottom of the New Photo page.**

   After clicking Create, your browser lands on the Listing Photos page. The list on the page includes your newly added photo. (See Figure 10-3.)

Figure 10-3: The Listing Photos page.

8. **On the Listing Photos page, click the Show link.**

   The resulting page displays your photo. (See Figure 10-4.)

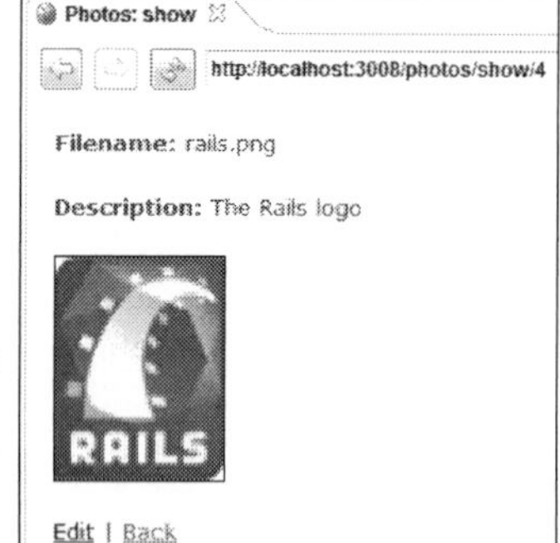

Figure 10-4: The Show page.

This paragraph is more a confession than a tip. I doctored the page shown earlier in Figure 10-2. When I first took the screenshot, the Description text area was too big. So later, to bring the Description text area down to a reasonable number of rows, I edited my project's `app\views\photos\_form.rhtml` file. I changed `<%= text_area 'photo', 'description' %>` to `<%= text_area 'photo', 'description', **'rows' => 10** %>`.

Understanding the code

Listing 10-1 offers a lot more than meets the eye. But you can comprehend Listing 10-1 on any level, ranging from the very shallow to the very deep.

The shallow version

Listing 10-1 makes Rails compose an HTML element known as an *image tag* — a portion of a Web page — an instruction that looks something like this:

```
<img alt="Rails" border="1"
  src="/images/rails.png?1157938513" width="100" />
```

Web browsers recognize this image tag as an instruction to display a picture — a picture named `rails.png` stored in a directory named `images`. (Rails takes the directory named `public` for granted.) The border around the display is 1 pixel wide. Any browser that can't display the image shows a less satisfying alternative — the word `Rails` inside a little box.

No matter the size of the original image, the display created by this image tag is 100 pixels wide. For a sufficiently large image, this crude hack turns the image into a kind of "thumbnail." To display a full-size image, remove `:size => "100"` from Listing 10-1.

Rails composes a Web page containing the image tag and sends the page to the Web browser. (Refer to Figure 10-4.)

Diving into the depths

The next several paragraphs contain more detail about the code in Listing 10-1.

- **Listing 10-1 uses ERb tags. (See Chapter 8.) The first ERb tag executes a Ruby assignment statement:**

  ```
  fname = @photo.filename
  ```

  See Figure 10-5.

- **The expression `@photo.filename` stands for `rails.png`.**

  Again, see Figure 10-5. The variable `@photo` refers to a photo in the project's database. Each photo has a filename and a description. (See Listing 9-1.) So in Listing 10-1, the expression `@photo.filename` stands for a photo's filename (in this example, the name `rails.png`).

  If you're curious about the value of an expression in an `rhtml` file, you can display the value in the Web browser's window. For example, to see the value of `@photo.filename`, add `<%= @photo.filename %>` to the code inside the `rhtml` file. (Don't forget to remove this extra code before making your Web site available to the public! And please don't tell any professional Rails programmers about this tip. If you do, they'll criticize me for including the tip in my book. They'll also tell you to ignore my tip and use a fancy automated debugger instead.)

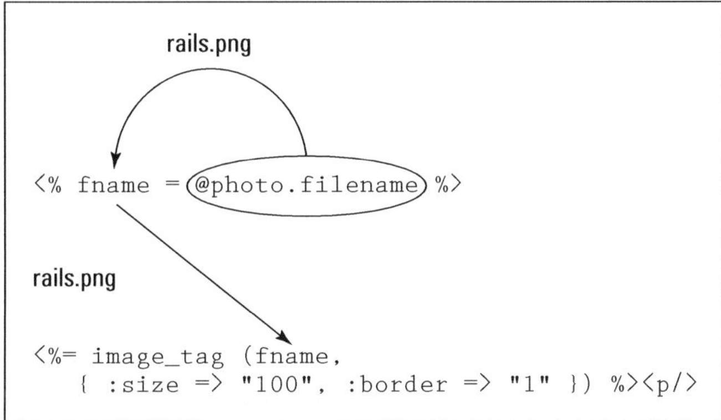

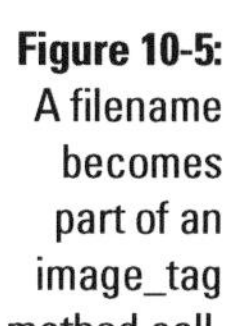

Figure 10-5: A filename becomes part of an image_tag method call.

- **Ultimately, the first line in Listing 10-1 makes `fname` stand for `rails.png`.**
- **The second and third lines in Listing 10-1 contain another kind of ERb tag.**

  Rails executes the Ruby code inside the `<%= %>` tag. This Ruby code is an expression whose value is a string of characters. Rails substitutes this string of characters in place of the entire `<%= %>` tag. (For details about the `<%= %>` tag, see Chapter 8.)
- **The value of the code inside the `<%= %>` is an HTML image tag.**

  As in the previous section (the "shallow" explanation), the image tag looks something like this:

  ```
  <img alt="Rails" border="1"
    src="/images/rails.png?1157938513" width="100" />
  ```

  Rails manufactures this image tag by executing some Ruby code in Listing 10-1.

  ```
  image_tag(fname, { :size => "100", :border => "1" })
  ```

  This Ruby code is actually a method call. It's a call to the Rails `image_tag` method.

  The `image_tag` method bites off a name (such as `rails.png`) and some options (such as `{ :size => "100", :border => "1" }`). When it finishes chewing, the `image_tag` method spits out the `<img alt="Rails" . . .` stuff. (See Figure 10-6.)

  The `image_tag` method doesn't perform any magic. The method simply takes some values (`rails.png`, `:size => "100"`, and so on) and uses those values to compose a piece of text (the `<img alt="Rails" ...` stuff).

Rails manufactures an HTML image tag by executing the code in Listing 10-1. You can see this tag (and other tags that Rails creates) by right-clicking anywhere inside the Rails browser. In the resulting contextual menu, select View Source. (And don't worry. You can tell professional Rails programmers that this tip is in my book.)

The `image_tag` method is one of approximately 50 Rails methods that help you create HTML tags. Other such methods include `text_field_tag`, `start_form_tag`, `submit_tag`, `password_field_tag`, and `link_to`. Each of these HTML methods lives in one of the Rails `ActionView::Helpers` modules. For example, the `image_tag` method lives in the `ActionView::Helpers::AssetTagHelper` module. For details, visit `http://api.rubyonrails.org`.

- **The HTML image tag becomes part of a Web page — the page sent to your Web browser.**

  When rendered by your browser, this page displays the Rails logo image. (Refer to Figure 10-4.)

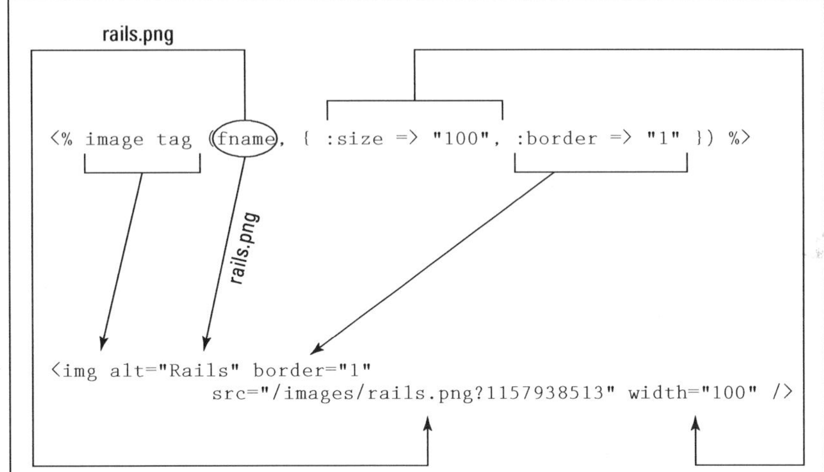

Figure 10-6: A Rails image_tag method call composes an HTML image tag.

Passing photos from place to place

I quote from the previous section:

> *[In Listing 10-1] the variable `@photo` refers to a photo in the project's database.*

Of all the concepts that authors tend to gloss over, the concept in this quotation is the murkiest. How does `@photo` get its value? How does Rails remember which photo you want to show? Rails cycles among the Web site's pages (Listing Photos, New Photo, Show, and so on) without forgetting which photo is the one of interest. At any given moment, how does Rails keep track of a particular photo?

To understand what's going on, start by examining the code that links to Listing 10-1. The code is a snippet from `app\views\photos\list.rhtml`, the code Ruby created when you generated a `Photo` scaffold. This section introduces that snippet, and the next few sections describe how the snippet helps Rails keep track of a particular photo. The snippet is shown in Listing 10-2.

Listing 10-2: Some Code from the list.rhtml File

```
<% for photo in @photos %>
  <tr>
  <% for column in Photo.content_columns %>
    <td><%=h photo.send(column.name) %></td>
  <% end %>
    <td><%= link_to 'Show',
          :action => 'show', :id => photo %></td>
    <td><%= link_to 'Edit',
          :action => 'edit', :id => photo %></td>
    <td><%= link_to 'Destroy',
          { :action => 'destroy', :id => photo },
          :confirm => 'Are you sure?', :post => true %>
    </td>
  </tr>
<% end %>
```

Like most ERb code, the code in Listing 10-2 generates part of a Web page. For your reading enjoyment, I put an excerpt from the generated Web page in Listing 10-3.

Listing 10-3: Rails Converts the Listing 10-2 Code into HTML Tags

```
<tr>

  <td>rails.png</td>

  <td>rails</td>

  <td><a href="/photos/show/9">Show</a></td>
  <td><a href="/photos/edit/9">Edit</a></td>
  <td><a href="/photos/destroy/9"
        onclick="if (confirm('Are you sure?'))
        { var f = document.createElement('form');
        this.parentNode.appendChild(f);
        f.method = 'POST'; f.action = this.href;
        f.submit(); };return false;">Destroy</a>
  </td>
</tr>
```

You can see the code in Listing 10-3 by right-clicking anywhere inside the Rails browser on the project's Listing Photos page. In the resulting contextual menu, select View Source.

The next three sections describe the code from Listings 10-2 and 10-3 in detail.

A link_to method creates an anchor element

Listing 10-2 contains three calls to the `link_to` method. Like the `image_tag` method in Listing 10-1, the `link_to` method creates an HTML element. In the `link_to` case, the resulting HTML element is an *anchor element,* which creates a link on a Web page.

```
<a href="/photos/show/9">Show</a>
```

Practice safe HTML

In Listing 10-2, the extra letter `h` in `<%=h photo.send(column.name) %>` is a call to a Ruby method. (This method belongs to Ruby's ERb library.) Some people refer to this method as the *HTML-safe* method because it makes text safe for insertion into an HTML document.

Imagine a goofy situation in which someone selects the name `hue-<h1>` for a database table's column. (Sure, it's unlikely. But in real-world applications, unlikely things happen.) Your code includes the following lines:

```
<% column_name = 'hue-<h1>' %>
<%= column_name %><br>
...the fine print
```

Then the Web browser receives the following HTML code:

```
hue-<h1><br>
...the fine print
```

As a result, the browser interprets `<h1>` as an HTML tag, and displays the phrase `the fine print` as a big, bold, level-1 heading. That's not what you want. But add a call to the HTML-safe (`h`) method:

```
<% column_name = 'hue-<h1>' %>
<%=h column_name %><br>
...the fine print
```

The HTML-safe method changes the less-than sign (<) in `'hue-<h1>'` to the `<` entity and changes the greater than sign (>) in `'hue-<h1>'` to the `>` entity. (For a look at HTML entities, see Chapter 7.) So after adding the `h` method call, the Web browser receives the following HTML code:

```
hue-&lt;h1&gt;<br>
...the fine print
```

As a result, the browser displays `hue-<h1>` (the correct column name) and doesn't display the phrase `the fine print` as a level-1 heading.

The anchor element consists of two tags, a start tag and an end tag. In this example, the start tag is `<a href="/photos/show/9">` and the end tag is `</a>`. Most people abuse the terminology, using the phrase *anchor tag* either for the start tag or for both the start and end tags. When I talk to people about such things, I abuse the terminology too. But when I write, I have to use the correct terminology. After all, I'm writing a book — a printed document whose pages will last until the end of time (or until the book goes out of print, whichever happens first).

The `link_to` method can take several parameters. In fact, the first `link_to` call in Listing 10-2 takes two parameters:

- **The first parameter (the string `'Show'`) becomes the link's text.**

  I copied lines from Listings 10-2 and 10-3 to create Figure 10-7. At the bottom of Figure 10-7, notice how the word `Show` becomes sandwiched between a start tag and its end tag.

  To find out how `Show` appears in the Web browser window, look at Figure 10-3.

- **The second parameter (the hash `:action => 'show', :id => photo`) determines the link's URL. (Again, see Figure 10-7.)**

  In Listing 10-3, the first link's URL is `/photos/show/9`. Each part of this URL comes directly or indirectly from the hash parameter.

  - The `/show` part comes from the hash's `:action` entry.
  - The number `9` comes (somewhat indirectly) from the hash's `:id` entry.

    The `for` loop at the top of Listing 10-2 makes the variable `photo` refer to a row in the database table. Each row has its own `id` value. (See Chapter 9.) In Listing 10-2, the entry `:id => photo` tells the `link_to` method to add the current row's id number to the newly formed link's URL.

    If the current row's id number happens to be 9, the link's URL ends with the number `9`. (See the bottom of Figure 10-7.)

    The next section has more details about the use of a row's `id` number.

  - The `/photos` part of the link's URL is a default. This particular default value stems from the fact that Listing 10-2 is on the `app\views\`**`photos`**`\list.rhtml` page.

When you call the `link_to` method, you type **:id => photo**, and not `:id => photo.id`. The `link_to` method knows that `:id => photo` involves a row's id number.

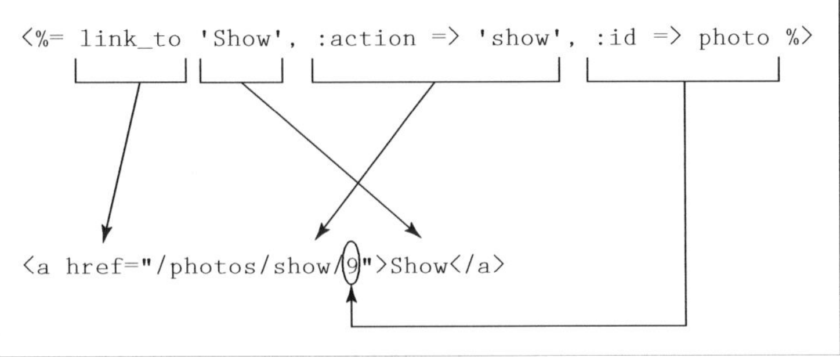

Figure 10-7: A Rails link_to method call composes an HTML anchor element.

In addition to the `:action` and `:id` entries, a `link_to` call can contain a `:controller` entry. Using the `:controller` entry, you can jump from a page generated by `photos_controller.rb` to a page generated by a different controller. For example, when you add `:controller => 'videos'` to the `link_to` call, Rails links to a method in your `videos_controller.rb` file. You can bend a URL even further by tinkering with your project's `config\routes.rb` file. But I try to avoid messing with `routes.rb`. If you can't resist experimenting with the `routes.rb` file, look for my next book — *Ruby on Rails For Fanatics and Risk Takers.*

Rails finds a particular photo

Look at the `Show` link in Figure 10-3. Behind that link stands the `/photos/show/9` URL. When you click the `Show` link, the Rails Web server receives this `/photos/show/9` URL. Then, as if by magic, the Rails Web server processes the URL. The processing is shown in Figure 10-8.

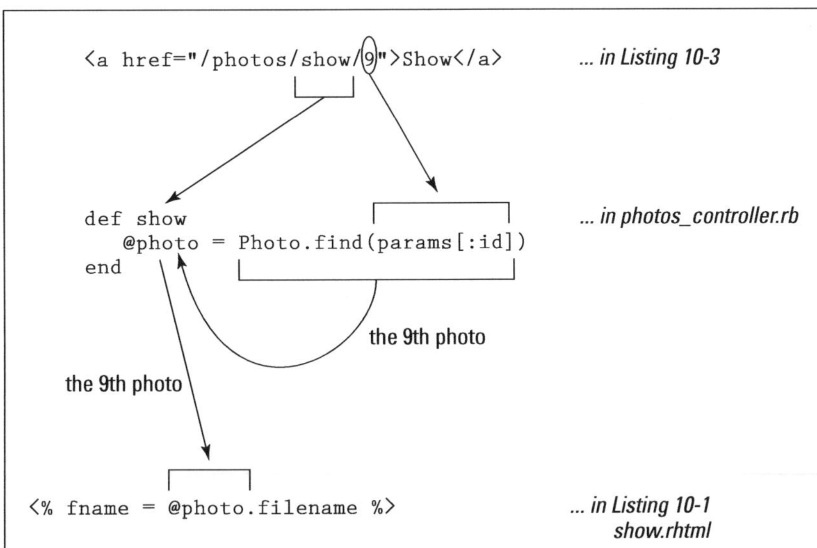

Figure 10-8: Rails passes a particular photo's id number from place to place.

When Lucy brings home Figure 10-8, Ricky says "Lucy, you've got some *'splainin'* to do!" So here's an explanation of some of the stuff in Figure 10-8.

- **Responding to the `/photos` part of the URL, the server looks inside the `photos_controller.rb` file.**
- **Responding to the `/show` part of the URL, the server looks inside the controller's `show` method.**

  The `show` method's code is as follows:

  ```
  def show
    @photo = Photo.find(params[:id])
  end
  ```

  There's that darn `:id` again! But by the time you reach the `show` method's code, `params[:id]` refers to a photo's number. (That is, the code refers to a single `id` value in a row of the database table, not an entire row of the database table.)

  You can display the value of the `show` method's variables. (For that matter, you can display the values of any controller method's variables.) Add statements such as `puts params[:id]` to the controller method's code. When Rails calls the method, the value of `params[:id]` appears in the Rails Console. (To see the value, you may have to find the Display Selected Console button. In the button's drop-down list, choose the Server option.)

- **The server executes the code inside the `show` method.**

  The code tells the server to find a row inside the database table — a row with a particular `id` number. After finding the row, Rails makes the `@photo` variable refer to this row.

- **Next, the server does what it always does after executing one of the controller methods. The server passes the baton to a view of the same name — in this example, the view named `show.rhtml`.**

  At last! The server reaches the code in Listing 10-1. This code uses the controller method's variables. More specifically, the code in Listing 10-1 is part of the `show.rhtml` file, so this code uses the `show` method's variables.

  The code in Listing 10-1 uses the `show` method's `@photo` variable. So in Listing 10-1, the name `@photo` refers to a row in the database table (one of possibly many photos).

That's how, in Listing 10-1, the variable `@photo` is able to refer to a photo in the project's database. I summarize the process in Figure 10-9.

The passing of an id number (from the database to a link's URL) takes place behind the scenes. As a programmer, you don't care whether the id number is `9`, `19`, or `9000000`. All you care about is that `link_to` retrieves the number and then uses that number to form a link's URL. As long as that happens, the link contains a reference to the correct photo in the database table.

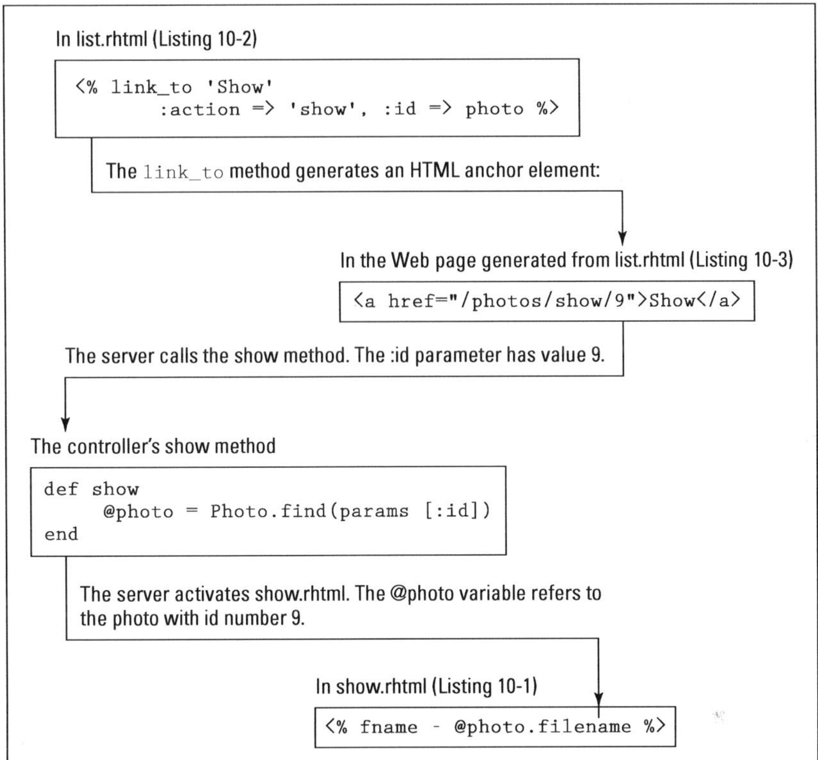

In list.rhtml (Listing 10-2)
<% link_to 'Show'
:action => 'show', :id => photo %>
The link_to method generates an HTML anchor element:
In the Web page generated from list.rhtml (Listing 10-3)
<a href="/photos/show/9">Show</a>
The server calls the show method. The :id parameter has value 9.
The controller's show method
def show
@photo = Photo.find(params [:id])
end
The server activates show.rhtml. The @photo variable refers to the photo with id number 9.
In show.rhtml (Listing 10-1)
<% fname - @photo.filename %>

Figure 10-9: How Rails creates part of the Show page.

Using JavaScript

Near the end of Listing 10-2, you see an innocent-looking pair of hash entries:

```
:confirm => 'Are you sure?', :post => true
```

These hash entries tell Rails to create a chunk of JavaScript code. (See Listing 10-3.)

```
onclick="if (confirm('Are you sure?'))
{ var f = document.createElement('form');
this.parentNode.appendChild(f);
f.method = 'POST'; f.action = this.href;
f.submit(); };return false;">
```

The JavaScript code makes the server display a confirmation dialog box — the dialog box in Figure 10-10. In Listings 10-2 and 10-3, this confirmation is associated with the Destroy link. So if you try to Destroy a photo, the server asks you to think twice about it.

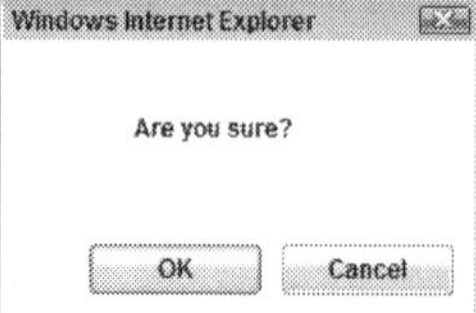

Figure 10-10: Do you really, really, really want to delete that photo?

This JavaScript in Listing 10-3 is an example of the cooperation between Rails and other Web technologies. I've met Web designers who have never heard of Ruby on Rails. (They think *Ruby on Rails* is an Agatha Christie murder mystery.) But these Web designers use JavaScript all the time.

In Listing 10-3, Rails uses JavaScript because it is the most efficient way to create a confirmation dialog box. In a similar way, Rails uses databases, HTML, and other tools to help you make the most of the World Wide Web.

To learn more about JavaScript, buy *JavaScript For Dummies,* 4th Edition, by Emily A. Vander Veer.

Importing Files

In the first section of this chapter, you add the Rails logo to the list of photos on your Web site. Of course, you may want to add something other than the Rails logo to your site. This section tells you how to do it.

Importing files the easy way

RadRails provides two ways to import photos and other files. One way is easy, but limited. The other way can be tricky, but it's more versatile. This section describes the easy way.

The instructions in this section apply only to Microsoft Windows users. If Windows isn't your thing, this section's drag-and-drop steps probably don't work for you. Skip directly to the next section.

1. **If you haven't already done so, create a simple photo album Web site.**

   Follow Steps 1 through 5 in the first section of Chapter 9.

2. **In the Rails Navigator view, find the project's `public\images` branch.**

   Refer to Figure 10-1.

3. **In Windows XP, choose Start➪My Computer. (In Windows Vista, choose the Start button and then select Computer.)**

   The My Computer (or Computer) window opens.

4. **In My Computer (or Computer), navigate to the directory containing the file you want to add to your Web site.**

5. **Select the file to add to your site.**

   I like photos of myself, so I select a file with my picture in it. The file's name is `mypic.jpg`. Of course, you may want to select a file with your picture or a picture of someone you love.

6. **Use your mouse to drag the file from the My Computer window to the `public\images` branch in the Rails Navigator view.**

   After dragging the file, you see the file's name in the Rails Navigator view. (See Figure 10-11.)

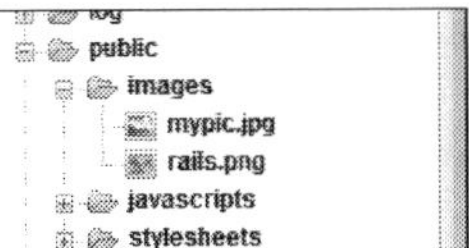

Figure 10-11: The public\images folder contains more than one image.

After finishing this section's steps, you can check to make sure that you successfully added an image file to your Rails project. To do so, double-click the file's branch in the Rails Navigator view. If all goes well, Windows displays the file with an image-viewing program (such as Windows Picture and Fax Viewer or Windows Photo Gallery).

When you follow this section's steps, RadRails makes a copy of the image file and places that copy in your Rails project directory. If you change your mind (and you no longer want the image to be part of your Rails project), you can delete the copy. To do so, select the file's branch in the Rails Navigator view and then press Delete. This action removes the copy from the Rails project. But the action doesn't delete the original file (the file that you find in Steps 3, 4, and 5).

Importing files the geeky way

With the RadRails Import Wizard, Windows, Linux, and Mac OS X users can add images to their projects. The Import Wizard is more difficult to use than the previous section's drag-and-drop technique. But the Import Wizard gives you more options than you have with dragging and dropping.

1. **If you haven't already done so, create a simple photo album Web site.**

   Follow Steps 1 through 5 in the first section of Chapter 9.

2. **In the Rails Navigator view, find the project's `public\images` branch.**

   Refer to Figure 10-1.

3. **Right-click the `public\images` branch. Then, in the resulting contextual menu, select Import.**

   The Import Wizard appears.

4. **In the Import Wizard's tree, choose General➪File System, as shown in Figure 10-12, then click Next.**

   Another Import Wizard page appears. Among other things, the page displays a From Directory field and two big panes. These panes are initially empty. (See Figure 10-13.)

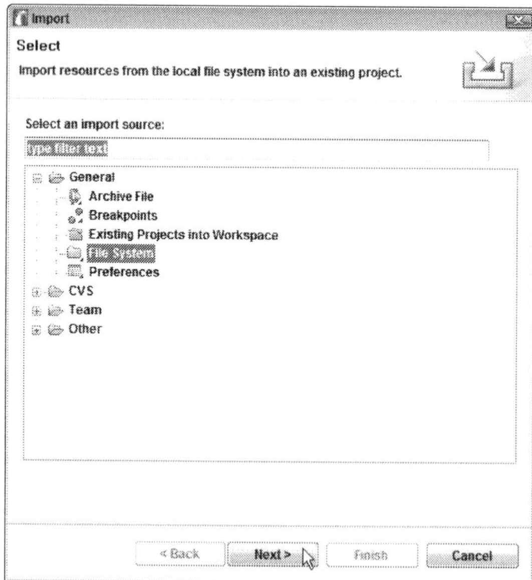

Figure 10-12: The Import Wizard.

Figure 10-13: The File System Import Wizard.

5. **In the From Directory field, type the name of a directory that contains an image file. (Optionally, you can click the Browse button and then navigate to the directory you need.)**

   In response, RadRails displays a folder tree in the pane on the left. Each branch of the tree has its own check box. (See Figure 10-14.)

   Sometimes, nothing happens when you put a name in the From Directory field. In particular, the two panes below the From Directory field remain empty until you click somewhere inside one of these panes.

6. **In the pane on the left, select the directory containing the image file.**

   Again, see Figure 10-14.

   In the pane on the left, leave all the check boxes unchecked. If you don't heed this advice, you end up with some unwanted folders in your Rails project tree.

7. **In the pane on the right, find the image file that you want to add to the Web site. Put a check mark in the box next to this image file.**

   Hey! Look at Figure 10-14!

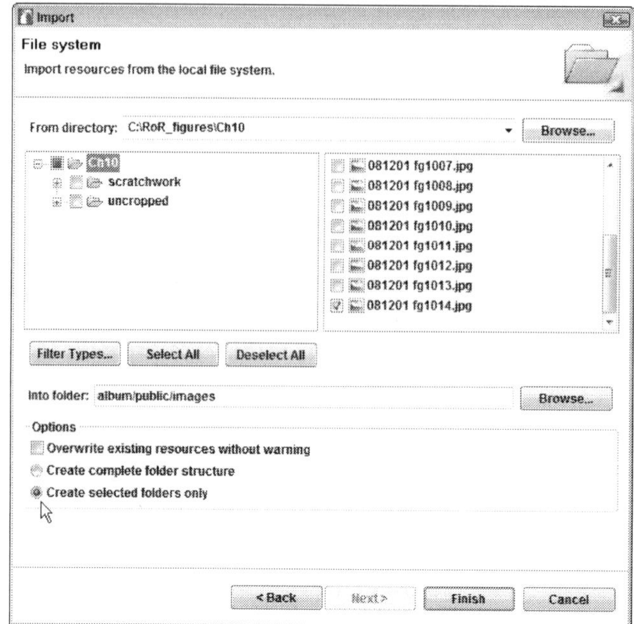

Figure 10-14: Selecting one or more image files.

When you check a branch in the right pane, RadRails automatically puts marks in some of the check boxes in the left pane's tree. You can safely ignore these marks. Because you don't add these marks yourself, these marks can't hurt you.

8. **In the Options group near the bottom of the Import Wizard, put a mark in the Create Selected Folders Only box.**

   RadRails gives you two ways to accidentally clutter up your project tree with unnecessary folders. One way is to ignore my advice in Step 6 about leaving boxes deselected. Another is to check Create Complete Folder Structure instead of Create Selected Folders Only.

9. **Click Finish.**

   After clicking Finish, you see the file's name in the Rails Navigator view.

To import images into your project, you can use the Import Wizard or you can drag and drop files. After importing the images, you can type the filenames in your application's New Photo page. (Refer to Figure 10-2.) If you repeat the process for several photos, you get a Web site full of photos.

But wait! In this chapter's examples, you can't import photos without sitting at your own computer. Your friends and relatives can't visit your Web site and upload photos to the site. Your friends aren't upset, but your relatives feel slighted. So to keep Uncle Joe happy, read Chapter 11.

Chapter 11

Image Is Everything

In This Chapter

- Storing photos (and other binary data) in a database
- Uploading images (and other data) to a Web site
- Working with a request and its response

Everyone has phobias. My uncle is afraid of heights. My best friend from high school is afraid of aging. (Too bad! Heights are easier to avoid than aging.) A student of mine is afraid of fish. A colleague in my department is afraid of mirrors (as well he should be). My cat is afraid of wolves. And me? I'm afraid of things that loosely dangle, such as hanging threads, orphan sentences, and other such things.

There must be a name for this kind of phobia. Maybe it's loosia-danglo-phobia. (Don't confuse this ailment with Lucy-phobia, which pertains only to old television sitcoms.) I don't know what bothers me about loosely dangling things. You can't account for taste or for phobias. Maybe I was frightened by a loosely dangling thing when I was a young child. (Or maybe I'm just crazy!)

Anyway, this book has a stunning example of a loosely dangling thing. It's a file stored in a Rails project's `public\images` directory.

The skeptics among you might ask "What's dangling about the `public\images` directory?" The answer is in Chapter 10. In that chapter, you create a database that supposedly stores all information about photos. But this big, hulking database doesn't store images. Instead, the database stores filenames. These filenames are frail tentacles that extend outside the database and into the rest of the file system. Each photo file dangles from the database, as if the database doesn't really own the file. Files can easily be misplaced. You can move or delete a file without even logging onto the database. That's dangerous. (And, yes, I also have losing-things-aphobia.)

So this chapter shows you how to store your photos in a database.

Enhancing Your Project's Code

This section wins a prize. It's a prize for the longest sequence of steps that I've ever written in a *For Dummies* book. If Paul weren't such a great project editor, he'd probably try to bully me into shortening the section.

Anyway, most of this section's steps involve plain, old typing. The only difficult part is typing exactly what's in the listings with all the commas, all the braces, all the bells, and all the whistles. Sometimes, you can mess things up by breaking a line where the line's not supposed to be broken. In other cases, line breaking doesn't matter. (The Ruby language is strange that way.)

Follow the book's longest step list

As you follow this section's instructions, remember to type carefully and to check everything that you type. If you do, your code will run correctly. And remember, if your fingers get tired or if you can't locate a typing error, you can download a customized version of RadRails from this book's Web site. The customized version contains a project that incorporates this section's code modifications.

1. **Create a new Rails project.**

   In this example, I name the project `album2`.

2. **Create a new database.**

   Use MySQL Administrator as you do in Chapter 3. If you name your project `album2`, the name of the database is `album2_development`.

3. **Using the RadRails Generators view, generate a model.**

   See Chapter 3 for advice on generating a model. In this example, I name the model `Photo`. Rails generates a `photo.rb` file in the project's `app\models` directory. Rails also generates a migration file (a file named `001_create_photos.rb`) in the project's `db\migrate` directory.

4. **Double-click the `db\migrate\001_create_photos.rb` file's branch in the Rails Navigator view.**

   As a result of your double-click, the `001_create_photos.rb` file opens in a RadRails editor.

5. **Using the editor, modify the `db\migrate\001_create_photos.rb` file.**

   The code that you type appears in bold in Listing 11-1. (The code that Rails creates for you doesn't appear in bold.)

Listing 11-1: Creating a Table Containing Binary Data

```
class CreatePhotos < ActiveRecord::Migration
  def self.up
    create_table :photos do |t|
      t.column :picture, :blob
      t.column :description, :text
    end
  end

  def self.down
    drop_table :photos
  end
end
```

6. **In the Rake Tasks view, run `db:migrate`.**

   For the basics of running `db:migrate`, see Chapter 3. And for more than you ever wanted to know about running `db:migrate`, see Chapter 9.

   After you run `db:migrate`, the `photos` table has three columns — `picture`, `description`, and `id`. The `picture` happens to be of type `blob`, which I describe in this chapter's "Creating a database table" section.

   What comes next in these steps is a bunch of typing. This might look like a lot of work, but it's really not. Just type each change in the appropriate file.

   To find each file, look for the file's branch in the Rails Navigator tree. For example, to modify the `app\controllers\photos_controller.rb` file, expand the tree's `app` branch and then expand the `controllers` branch within the `app` branch. Finally, double-click the `photos_controller.rb` branch inside the `controllers` branch. When you double-click the `photos_controller.rb` branch, the `photos_controller.rb` file opens in a RadRails editor.

7. **Modify the controller. Add a `get_picture` method inside the `app\controllers\photos_controller.rb` file.**

   Add the method in Listing 11-2.

Listing 11-2: A Method in the Controller

```
def get_picture
  @photo=Photo.find(params[:id])
  send_data(@photo.picture, :type=> 'image/jpeg')
end
```

Almost everything in this chapter applies to all kinds of image files (`.jpg`, `.gif`, `.png`, and others). But the code in Listing 11-2 works only with `.jpg` files. If you don't find any `.jpg` files on your hard drive, don't worry. Just choose whatever image files you have. When you choose a particular image file type (`.gif`, for example), stick with that type throughout the chapter. For `.gif` files, change `image/jpeg` to `image/gif` at the end of Listing 11-2. (Replacing `jpeg` with the file's three-letter extension works in many cases. For `.png` files, use `image/png`; for `.bmp` files, use `image/bmp`; and so on.)

8. **Modify the model — `app\models\photo.rb`.**

   The code that you type appears in bold in Listing 11-3.

Listing 11-3: A Method in the Model

```
class Photo < ActiveRecord::Base

  def photo=(photo_in)
    self.picture = photo_in.read
  end

end
```

In the previous two steps, you modify the controller and the model. In Steps 9 through 13, you modify the view.

9. **Modify `app\views\photos\_form.rhtml`.**

   The code that you type appears in bold in Listing 11-4.

Listing 11-4: Modifying the _form.rhtml File

```
<%= error_messages_for 'photo' %>

<!--[form:photo]-->
<p><label for="photo_picture">Picture</label><br/>
<%= file_field 'photo', 'photo' %></p>

<p><label for="photo_description">Description</label><br/>
<%= text_area 'photo', 'description'  %></p>
<!--[eoform:photo]-->
```

10. **Modify `app\views\photos\edit.rhtml`.**

    The code that you type appears in bold in Listing 11-5.

Listing 11-5: Modifying the edit.rhtml File

```
<h1>Editing photo</h1>

<%= start_form_tag( { :action => 'update',
                      :id => @photo },
```

```
                                   :multipart => true) %>
  <%= render :partial => 'form' %>
  <%= submit_tag 'Edit' %>
<%= end_form_tag %>

<%= link_to 'Show', :action => 'show', :id => @photo %> |
<%= link_to 'Back', :action => 'list' %>
```

In this example, someone uses a form to send an image (a bunch of bits) from his or her computer to your Web server. You must not forget to add **:multipart => true** to the `start_form` tag. In addition, you must add parentheses and curly braces for grouping the arguments in the `start_form_tag` call. If you forget any of this, the Web form fails to send the image to your server!

11. **Modify app\views\photos\list.rhtml.**

    The code that you type appears in bold in Listing 11-6.

Listing 11-6: Tweaking the Listing Photos Page (list.rhtml)

```
<h1>Listing photos</h1>

<table>
  <tr>
  <% for column in Photo.content_columns %>
    <th><%= column.human_name %></th>
  <% end %>
  </tr>

<% for photo in @photos %>
  <tr>

    <td>
      <img src="<%=url_for( :action => "get_picture",
                            :id => photo.id ) %>"
                            height="100" />
    </td>
    <td>
      <%= photo.send("description") %>
    </td>

    <td><%= link_to 'Show', :action => 'show',
                            :id => photo %></td>
    <td><%= link_to 'Edit', :action => 'edit',
                            :id => photo %></td>
    <td><%= link_to 'Destroy',
              { :action => 'destroy', :id => photo },
                :confirm => 'Are you sure?',
                :post => true %></td>
  </tr>
<% end %>
```

(continued)

Listing 11-6 *(continued)*

```
</table>

<%= link_to 'Previous page',
  { :page => @photo_pages.current.previous } if
  @photo_pages.current.previous %>
<%= link_to 'Next page',
  { :page => @photo_pages.current.next } if
  @photo_pages.current.next %>

<br />

<%= link_to 'New photo', :action => 'new' %>
```

12. **Modify `app\views\photos\new.rhtml`.**

    The code that you type appears in bold in Listing 11-7.

Listing 11-7: Adding Code to the New Photo Page (new.rhtml)

```
<h1>New photo</h1>

<%= start_form_tag( { :action => 'create' },
                    :multipart => true ) %>
  <%= render :partial => 'form' %>
  <%= submit_tag "Create" %>
<%= end_form_tag %>

<%= link_to 'Back', :action => 'list' %>
```

This is a reprise of an earlier warning. The more often you read this warning, the better. In a form in which you upload an image, a video, or some other binary data, you must not forget to include **`:multipart => true`** in the `start_form_tag` argument list. In addition, you must add parentheses and curly braces for grouping the arguments in the `start_form_tag` call.

13. **Modify `app\views\photos\show.rhtml`.**

    The code that you type appears in bold in Listing 11-8.

Listing 11-8: Modifying the Show Page (show.rhtml)

```
<img src="<%=url_for( :action => "get_picture",
                      :id => @photo.id ) %>" /><p>

<b><%=@photo.description %></b><p>

<%= link_to 'Edit', :action => 'edit', :id => @photo %> |
<%= link_to 'Back', :action => 'list' %>
```

14. **Run the application!**

    For instructions on running an application of this kind, see the last section of Chapter 3.

    Figures 11-1 through 11-3 show what happens when you run the new Rails application.

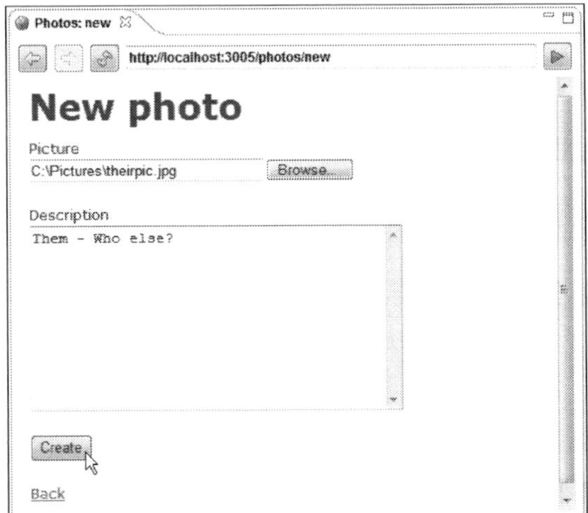

Figure 11-1: The New Photo page.

Figure 11-2: The Listing Photos page.

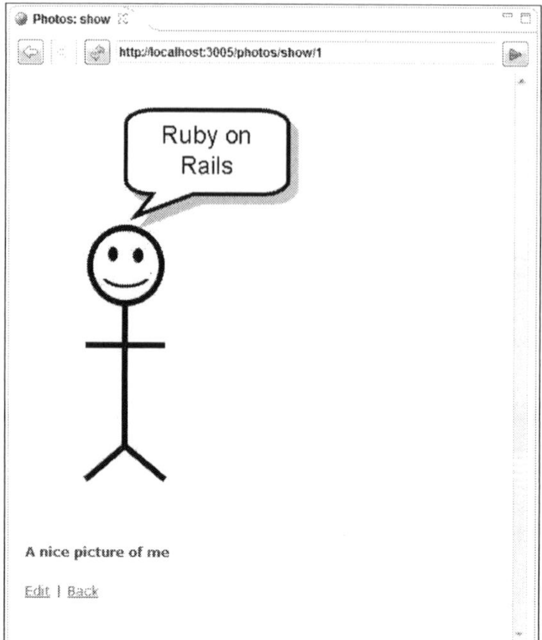

Figure 11-3: The Show page.

Know the flow

Figure 11-4 illustrates the flow in the photo album application.

In Figure 11-4, the circled numbers represent parts of the photo album application cycle. The following paragraphs describe the cycle.

1. A *visitor* (Uncle Joe, or someone else who visits your photo album Web site) fills in the fields on the New Photo page. The visitor clicks the page's Create button. (See Figure 11-1 and, of course, Figure 11-4.)
2. The button click creates an HTTP request. (For more info about HTTP requests and responses, see Chapter 7.) The visitor's Web browser sends the request along the Internet to your server. The request contains the bits from an image file on the visitor's hard drive.
3. Your server (running a Rails application) reads the image into a variable named `@photo.picture`.
4. Rails automatically stores the image in the picture column of the `photos` database table.

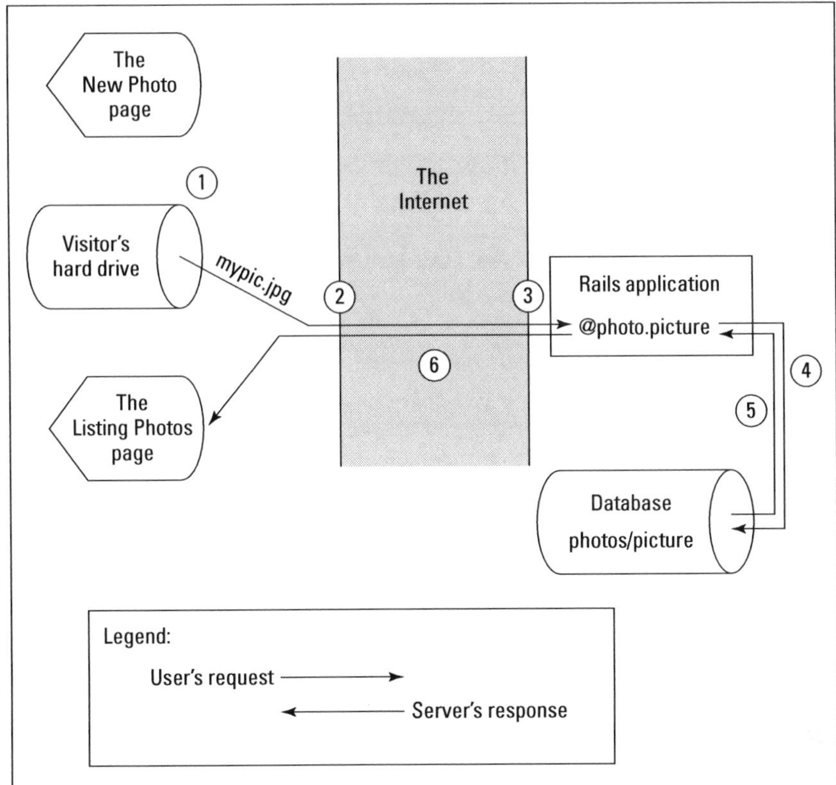

Figure 11-4: A visitor's request and your server's response.

After accepting the visitor's request, your server responds to this request. As part of the HTTP response, Rails composes a Listing Photos page.

5. Rails retrieves the image from the database, and stores the image in an `@photo.picture` variable.

   Rails adds the bits in the `@photo.picture` variable to the Listing Photos page. (Actually, the code in Listing 11-6 that creates an HTML image tag is inside a loop. So Rails adds the bits from several photos to the Listing Photos page.)

6. Rails sends the response (the Listing Photos page in Figure 11-2) back to the visitor.

The server sends a similar response (the Show page in Figure 11-3) whenever the visitor clicks a Show link.

The next section walks you through the relevant Rails code.

Understanding the Enhanced Code

In the previous section, you perform 14 steps. You probably want to know why you perform all these steps. To explain why, this section describes the new photo album application and the reasons why all the code works.

Creating a database table

Listing 11-1 defines a database table. In the table, the `description` column has type `text`. The type `text` is old news.

In the same table, the `picture` column has type `blob` (*b*inary *l*arge *ob*ject). Most databases (MySQL included) can store data of type `blob`. A *blob* is a bunch of bits, containing no particular letters, numeric values, or any other human readable data. The `blob` data type is good for storing images (`.png` images, `.jpg` images, `.gif` images, and others).

Moving on to more code . . .

The next several sections jump from one piece of code to another, like the shiny, silvery orb in a pinball machine. To keep you from becoming dizzy, I offer Figure 11-5. The figure shows you which Rails file participates in each step of the application's cycle.

As you read the next several sections, remember that the sections describe everything from the server's point of view. (After all, the server runs all your Rails code.) Imagine yourself sitting on top of the circled number 3 in Figure 11-4. Before the visitor can fill in the New Photo page's fields, you must write the Rails code to create the New Photo page (the code in Listings 11-4 and 11-7).

Creating a file input field

Working together, Listings 11-4 and 11-7 present the New Photo page to the visitor. Listing 11-4 contains a *partial* — a partial Web page, that is. Listing 11-7 incorporates the partial by calling `render :partial => 'form'`.

For Rails enthusiasts, the word *partial* is a noun. For information on partials, see Chapter 8.

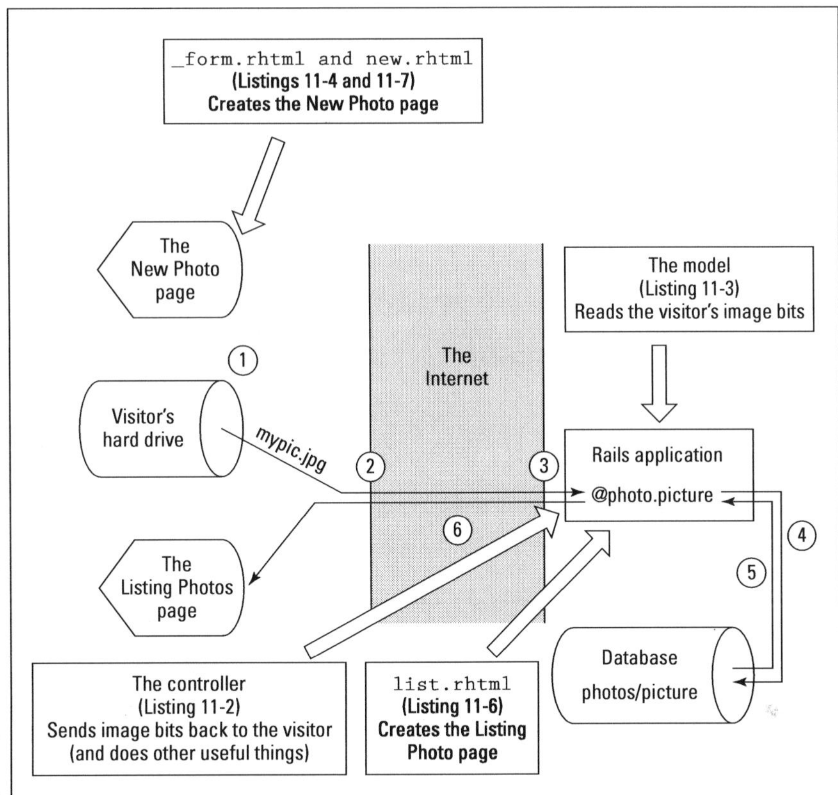

Figure 11-5: How code cooperates to create the photo album application.

In Listing 11-4, a call to the Rails `file_field` method tells the server to generate the following HTML tag:

```
<input id="photo_photo" name="photo[photo]"
  size="30" type="file" />
```

See Figure 11-6. This HTML tag becomes part of the New Photo Web page. Because of the words `type="file"` in the tag, the visitor's browser displays a text box with a Browse button. (Refer to Figure 11-1.) Clicking this Browse button opens a standard Choose File dialog box.

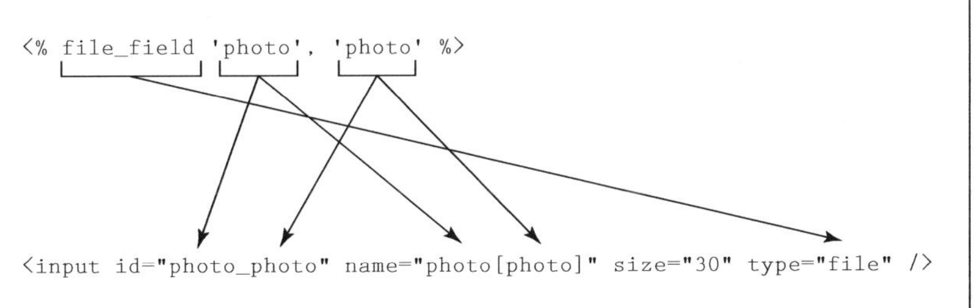

Figure 11-6: The Rails file_field method creates an HTML input tag.

In Listing 11-7, the words `:multipart => true` help to generate another HTML tag:

```
<form action="/photos/create"
  enctype="multipart/form-data" method="post">
```

In this tag, the words `enctype="multipart/form-data"` cause the visitor's browser to send an image file's bits (instead of the image file's name) to your Web server.

Creating a Photo instance

The controller has a `create` method containing the following line:

```
@photo = Photo.new(params[:photo])
```

The line creates a new `Photo` instance and makes `@photo` refer to that instance.

(In case you're wondering, the `create` method doesn't appear in any of this chapter's code listings, and this part of the controller's contribution doesn't appear in Figure 11-5.)

Reading the image bits

Quoting quickly from the previous section, a line of code "creates a new `Photo` instance and makes `@photo` refer to that instance." What do I mean when I write that the code "makes `@photo` refer to that instance"?

Listing 11-3 defines what "making something refer to a `Photo` instance" means. Listing 11-3 is the `Photo` model. The model describes the characteristics of each `Photo` instance.

For starters, a `Photo` instance has all the characteristics of an `ActiveRecord::Base` instance. (See the discussion of subclasses in Chapter 6.) A `Photo` instance has methods named `find`, `create`, `establish_connection`, `delete`, and so on.

Listing 11-3 adds an additional method. A `Photo` instance has an assignment method (a method denoted as `photo=` in Listing 11-3). The assignment method tells Rails to call `read` when making something refer to a `Photo` instance. That's good because the `read` method gets the image bits from the visitor's request.

Listing 11-3 reads image bits and assigns these bits to the `picture` variable in a `Photo` instance. Then, using object-relational mapping, Rails stores the image's bits in the `picture` column of the database table. (For a discussion of object-relational mapping, see Chapter 9.)

Composing an image tag

Listings 11-6 and 11-8 have a lot in common. Both contain code to construct an HTML image tag.

```
<img src="<%=url_for( :action => "get_picture",
                      :id => @photo.id ) %>" />
```

The code in Listing 11-6 has an additional `height="100"` part because the tag in Listing 11-6 is on the Listing Photos page. On that page, you don't want to display very large versions of the images. (See Chapter 10.)

In Chapter 10, I create an HTML image tag using the Rails `image_tag` method. But in Listings 11-6 and 11-8, I forgo the `image_tag` method. Instead, I plop some HTML code (`<img src= . . . >`) right into my Rails `rhtml` file. Why do I do it differently in Listings 11-6 and 11-8? I do it because, by the time I get around to writing Listings 11-6 and 11-8, my mood changes. That's the only difference.

In Listings 11-6 and 11-8, the call to the Rails `url_for` method creates a URL. This URL is something like `/photos/get_picture/3` or `/photos/get_picture/2158`.

So, after Rails calls the `url_for` method, the HTML image tag looks something like this:

```
<img src="/photos/get_picture/3" />
```

See Figure 11-7.

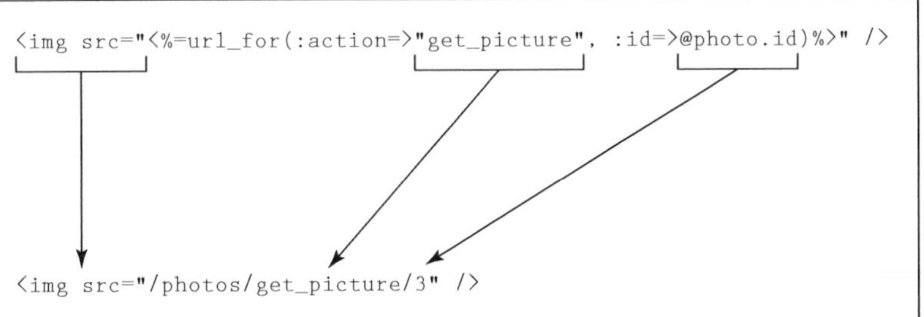

Figure 11-7: The Rails url_for method creates a URL.

At this point in the process, things bounce back and forth between the visitor's browser and your Web server. Your server sends the image tag to the visitor's Web browser as part of a Listing Photos or Show Photo page. When the browser encounters the image tag, the browser sends a follow-up request to your server. "Please send me `/photos/get_picture/3` so I can display it in my window," says the visitor's browser.

When your server receives the "Please send me . . . `get_picture`" message, your server calls the `get_picture` method in Listing 11-2. Fortunately, the `get_picture` method is ready to send an image's bits to the visitor's browser.

Sending image bits to the visitor's browser

Listing 11-2 is part of the controller. In Listing 11-2, the `get_picture` method calls the Rails `send_data` method. The Rails `send_data` method fulfills its cosmic purpose by sending an image's bits to the visitor's Web browser.

Whew!

The whole cycle (the visitor's request followed by your server's response) takes place in a few seconds. On a good day it can take less than a second. That's amazing when you think about the amount of work that Rails does.

Every Intel processor contains a *time-of-day clock.* One hundred times each second, the time-of-day clock sends out a signal. This signal tells the processor to stop whatever it's doing, and perform some housekeeping tasks. In other words, 100 times per second, the computer dawdles for a while and ignores the user's immediate needs. In spite of this, the computer gets more work done in a second than a thousand monkeys can do between now and eternity. What a marvelous beast the computer is!

Chapter 12

More Model Magic

In This Chapter

- Validating input
- Creating relationships between database tables
- Creating forms with check boxes, drop-down lists, and more

My next book is entitled *Lucid Dreaming For Dummies.* The book is about dreams in which I know that I'm dreaming.

In one chapter, I can't pay the check at a fancy restaurant. Instead of becoming upset, I remind myself that the restaurant isn't real, and that if I wake up, I'll avoid any possible embarrassment.

In another chapter, I walk into a crowded room. I tell everyone to leave immediately because they're in my dream and they don't belong there.

In yet another, I ask someone what it's like to be a character in my dream. He replies that he doesn't know because he's not a real person. I remind him that he's part of my mind, so I can answer the question on his behalf. He challenges me to do so. I become angry. I decide that in future dreams, I'll be giving my characters much less independence.

The list of good chapters goes on and on. Strangely enough, Wiley Publishing hasn't yet approved the project.

Blogging Your Dreams

Every good book comes with a good Web site. So to accompany my *Lucid Dreaming For Dummies* book, I have a site on which people can post descriptions of their dreams. In an unusual moment of cleverness, I named the site `TextfieldOfDreams.com`.

Using Ruby on Rails, you can re-create the `TextfieldOfDreams` site. Follow the usual steps in creating a Rails application. (For details, see Chapter 3.) In this chapter's application, do the following:

- **Name your new project `dreaming`.**

  The corresponding database name is `dreaming_development`.

- **Name your new model `Dream`.**

  When you generate a `Dream` model, you get files named `dream.rb` and `001_create_dreams.rb`.

- **Add columns named `title` and `description` to the database. (See Listing 12-1.)**

  REMEMBER: For detailed instructions on creating a project, a model, or the columns in a database, see Chapter 3.

Listing 12-1: Defining a Database Table

```
class CreateDreams < ActiveRecord::Migration
  def self.up
    create_table :dreams do |t|
      t.column :title, :string
      t.column :description, :text
    end
  end

  def self.down
    drop_table :dreams
  end
end
```

- **Perform the usual steps in building a Rails application.**

  Run the migration, create a **`Dream`** scaffold, and so on.

The finished product's Show page looks like the page in Figure 12-1.

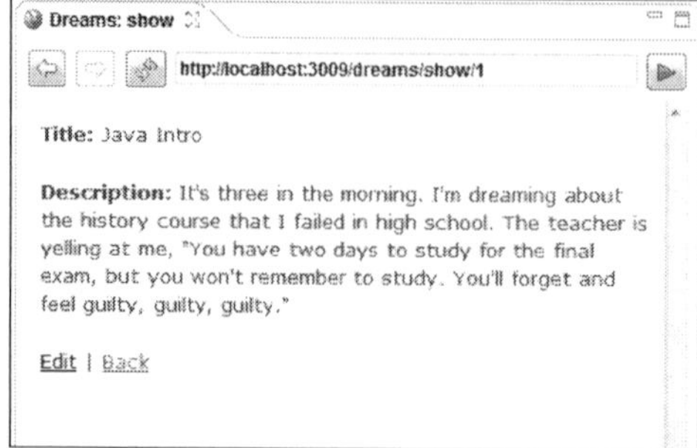

Figure 12-1: A dreamy Web page.

Validating the Visitor's Input

One day, I visited my dreams Web site and saw the stuff in Figure 12-2. I admired the cool logo that I'd added to the Listing Photos page. But I also noticed that someone had added three blank entries — three dreams with neither titles nor descriptions.

Figure 12-2: The database has three blank entries.

To keep people from adding unwanted entries, I used the RadRails editor to modify the Dream model (the `dream.rb` file). I added the bold lines in Listing 12-2.

Listing 12-2: Validating Input

```
class Dream < ActiveRecord::Base
  validates_presence_of :title, :description
  validates_length_of :description, :minimum => 10
  validates_length_of :description, :maximum => 500
  validates_uniqueness_of :title
end
```

Listing 12-2 makes four calls to Rails validation methods. Of all the Rails features, validation methods may give you the most bang for your buck. With the addition of one `validates_`*`something`* call, Rails checks the correctness of the incoming data. After you add the code in Listing 12-2, people can't create blank entries. If they try, they see a page like the one in Figure 12-3.

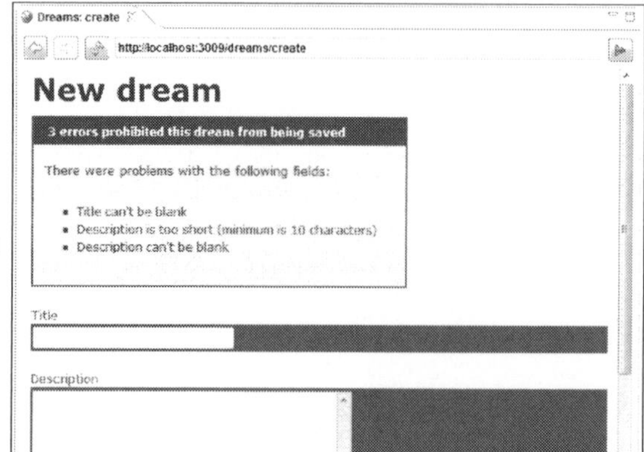

Figure 12-3: Sorry, pal. Your entry isn't good enough.

In Listing 12-2, the `validates_presence_of` call insures that the visitor types both a title and a description. Actually, the requirement that a description be present is redundant. Later in Listing 12-2, a `validates_length_of` call insists that the description have at least 10 characters. So a blank description or a very brief description (`My dream`) doesn't pass muster.

The `validates_uniqueness_of` call is very handy. With this call, Rails prevents the `dreams` database table from containing duplicate title entries. For example, if you start with the page in Figure 12-2 and try to add another dream with the title `Java Intro`, Rails barks at you with the message in Figure 12-4.

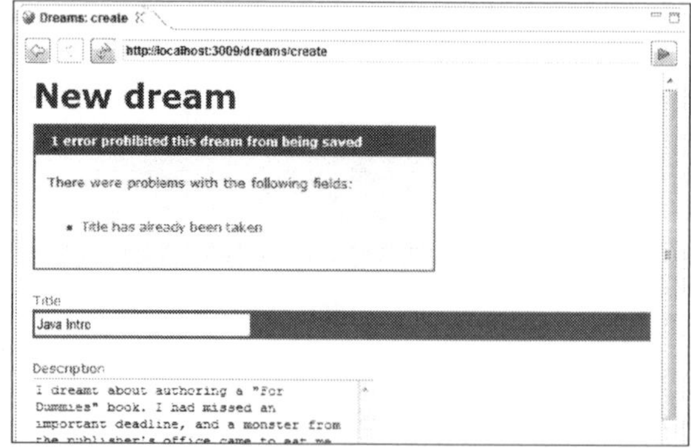

Figure 12-4: Too many people are posting "Java Intro" dreams.

By default, Rails checks a value when your code saves the value to a database. Using arguments to the `validates` methods, you can fine-tune this behavior. But you can't force Rails to check a value whenever you show that value. (You can write detailed code to check values whenever you want. But writing detailed code is more difficult than using the Rails `validates` methods.)

This section covers three validation methods — `validates_presence_of`, `validates_length_of`, and `validates_uniqueness_of`. In addition, Rails has methods for validating the format of a visitor's input, the numericality of input, acceptance of an agreement, and lots of other stuff. For an example of format checking, see this chapter's "Connecting dreams with keywords" section. For information about the other Rails validation methods, visit `http://api.rubyonrails.org/classes/ActiveRecord/Validations/ClassMethods.html`.

Adding Comments

Usually, when people tell me about their dreams, I respond with a polite comment. "That's interesting," I say, and then I quickly change the subject. In most cases, a dream is interesting only to the person who has the dream. But at `TextfieldOfDreams.com`, everyone takes an interest in everyone else's dreams. After someone posts a dream, others read the dream's description and add comments of their own.

The Joy of Ruby

Listing 12-4 dynamically adds methods to instances of the `Comment` class. In other words, calling one method (the `belongs_to` method) effortlessly changes the number of methods associated with certain objects. This spontaneous creation of methods doesn't take place during some sluggish code compilation stage or class loading stage. Instead, this sleight-of-hand takes place while Listing 12-4 runs.

In most other languages, you'd have to jump through hoops to add methods while a program runs. But in Ruby, you can create methods by typing one line of code. The Ruby language makes a system more pliable, more flexible, more responsive to change than systems written in other languages. And Rails takes full advantage of Ruby's dynamic qualities.

It was either Charles Nutter or Thomas Enebo who told me that Rails stretches Ruby to its limits. Rails uses more of Ruby's features than other Ruby-based frameworks tend to use. Listing 12-4 is only one, tiny example of the Ruby language's power. But Listing 12-4, with its astounding simplicity, provides a hint of Ruby's richness.

Where do I store these comments? The previous section's `dreams` table has only three columns — title, description, and id. I could add an additional column to store one comment, but that strategy wears thin when a dream acquires its second, third, and fourth comments.

The best way to deal with comments is to store them in a separate database table. So I create a second table (named `comments`). Then I do something "Railsian" to connect the old `dreams` table with the new `comments` table. You can do it too. Here's how:

1. **Create the `dreaming` project described in the first section of this chapter.**
2. **Make sure that your `dreaming` project has a `Dream` model, `Dream` scaffolding, and the works.**

   Chapter 3 has all you'd ever need to know about such matters.
3. **Add a second model to your project. Give this second model the name `Comment`.**

   In other words, use the Rails Generators view to create an `app\models\comment.rb` file.
4. **Perform the migration shown in Listing 12-3.**

   Again, a migration is a Ruby program that adds tables and columns to a database. For nuts and bolts details, see Chapter 3.

Listing 12-3: The File 002_create_comments.rb

```
class CreateComments < ActiveRecord::Migration
  def self.up
    create_table :comments do |t|
      t.column :body, :text
      t.column :dream_id, :int
    end
  end

  def self.down
    drop_table :comments
  end
end
```

With Listing 12-3, you depart from the previous chapters' hum-drum migrations. Sure, each comment has a body — a bunch of text that someone writes about someone else's dream. But Listing 12-3 says more. Listing 12-3 says that each comment has a `dream_id`. That is, each comment is associated with a particular dream.

Remember the Rails mantra, "Convention over configuration." (If you don't remember the mantra, see Chapter 8.) In Listing 12-3, you create a column named `dream_id`. The Rails convention dictates that a column named `othertable_id` is a reference to the other table's rows.

So, imagine that you create a comment. The comment's `body` is `"I agree"` and the comment's `dream_id` is `7`. Then your `dreams` table must have a row with id `7`. Rails associates the `"I agree"` comment with the `dream` that has id `7`. (For details about a table's id numbers, see Chapter 10.)

In your Rails code, a row's id number is almost always a variable. You never assume that a particular table row has a particular id number.

5. **Tell Rails that each comment belongs to a particular dream.**

   That means you add code to the Comment model (the `comment.rb` file) as shown in Listing 12-4.

Listing 12-4: The Comment Model

```
class Comment < ActiveRecord::Base
  belongs_to :dream
end
```

In Listing 12-4, the `belongs_to` method says "A comment without a dream is like a day without sunshine." Of course, I can make the same point without all the silliness. Listing 12-4 adds additional methods to each `Comment` instance. In particular, each `Comment` instance has its own `dream` method. In your code, you can type

```
@comment = Comment.new
puts @comment.dream
```

Because of the `belongs_to` call in Listing 12-4, Ruby doesn't complain when you run these two lines of code. (You don't put these particular lines of code in any of your dreaming project's files, but it's nice to know that you could add them if you wanted to do so.)

6. **Tell Rails that each dream has many comments.**

   That is, add code to the Dream model (the `dream.rb` file) as shown in Listing 12-5.

Listing 12-5: The Enhanced Dream Model

```
class Dream < ActiveRecord::Base
  has_many :comments
end
```

Listing 12-5 does for dreams what Listing 12-4 does for comments. The big difference is that Listing 12-5 tells Rails that a dream can have not just one, but several comments. In particular, the call to `has_many` in Listing 12-5 adds a `comments` method to each `Dream` instance. A listing later in this chapter contains the code `for comment in @dream.comments`. That code, with its reference to `@dream.comments`, would crash the program if the `Dream` model didn't contain a `has_many :comments` call.

A comment belongs to a dream. (See Listing 12-4.) Because of this, the `comments` database table has a `dream_id` column. (See Listing 12-3.) But a dream has many comments and, as a result, the `dreams` database table doesn't have a `comment_id` column. (See Listing 12-1.)

The method call in Listing 12-4 is `belongs_to :dream`. The argument in a `belongs_to` call is singular. But the method call in Listing 12-5 is `has_many :comments`. The argument in a `has_many` call is plural.

7. **Add code to the `app\views\dreams\show.rhtml` file.**

   The code that you type appears in bold in Listing 12-6. (The code that Rails creates for you doesn't appear in bold.)

Listing 12-6: Adding Code to the show.rhtml File

```
<% for column in Dream.content_columns %>
<p>
  <b><%= column.human_name %>:</b>
  <%=h @dream.send(column.name) %>
</p>
<% end %>


<b>Comments:</b><br>

<% if @dream.comments.empty? %>
    (None)<p>
<% else %>
  <% for comment in @dream.comments %>
    <%= comment.body %><br>
  <% end %>
<% end %><p>

<%= start_form_tag :action => "add_comment",
                   :id => @dream %>
  <b>Add a comment:</b><br>
  <%= text_area "comment", "body", "rows" => 5 %><br>
  <%= submit_tag %>
<%= end_form_tag %><p>


<%= link_to 'Edit', :action => 'edit', :id => @dream %> |
<%= link_to 'Back', :action => 'list' %>
```

The new code adds two sections to each dream's Show page. The first section lists all the comments belonging to a particular dream. The second section contains a form for adding new comments.

Notice the use of the expression `@dream.comments` in Listing 12-6. This expression is illegal if you don't add `has_many :comments` to the model in Listing 12-5.

Notice also the use of Ruby's `empty?` method in Listing 12-6. In Ruby, the name of a method may end with a question mark. A method of this kind returns `true` or `false` in response to a question. ("Is the `@dream.comments` array devoid of any comments?")

Listing 12-6 contains several `<%= %>` tags. Forgetting the equal sign in one these tags is a bad mistake. Errors involving these equal signs can be difficult to debug. Always double-check your work to make sure that you haven't used `<% %>` when you should be using `<%= %>`. When you're not sure whether you should be adding the equal sign, take a few minutes to do some research. Check the Rails documentation, or compare your code with some code that's known to be correct.

8. **Add a method to the `app\controllers\dreams_controller.rb` file.**

   To do this, double-click the `dreams_controller.rb` file's branch in the `app\controllers` branch of the Rails Navigator's tree. When you do, the `dreams_controller.rb file` opens in a RadRails editor.

   Add the method in Listing 12-7.

Listing 12-7: How to Add a Comment

```
def add_comment
  Dream.find(params[:id]).
    comments.create(params[:comment])
  flash[:notice] = 'Comment was successfully added'
  redirect_to :action => 'show', :id => params[:id]
end
```

The form in Listing 12-6 calls the `add_comment` method in Listing 12-7. The `add_comment` method does what its name suggests; namely, the method adds a new comment to an existing dream. Most of the work takes place in the method's first statement.

```
Dream.find(params[:id]).
  comments.create(params[:comment])
```

This statement finds a dream whose id matches that of the dream in the Show page. The statement calls that dream's `comments` method, which returns an array containing all comments associated with that particular dream. (Once again, this call to a `comments` method owes its existence to the `has_many :comments` line in Listing 12-5.)

After fetching an array of comments, the first statement in Listing 12-7 calls the `create` method. In one fell swoop, this `create` call adds a comment to the existing array and deposits the updated array information into the `comments` database table. (For an introduction to the `create` method, see Chapter 9.)

9. Go!

Put your Web site through the paces. Add comments. See the results. (Better yet, see Figures 12-5 and 12-6.)

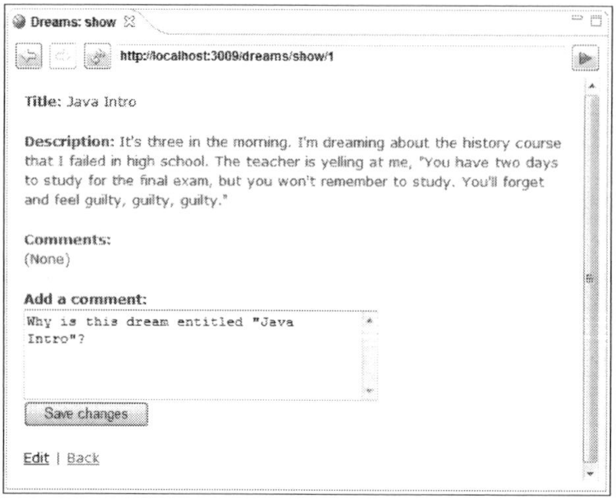

Figure 12-5: Adding a comment.

Figure 12-6: A dream with several comments.

Adding Keywords

Often, when I dream, I'm aware that I'm dreaming. I dream about dreaming, and occasionally, I dream about dreaming about dreaming. This kind of dreaming is called "lucid dreaming." And, as I indicate at the start of this chapter, I'm a frequent lucid dreamer.

To my `TextFieldOfDreams.com` Web site, I want to add keywords. Each dream has keywords. For example, I dream that I'm flying. While I'm flying I say "Dreams are wonderful! I wouldn't be able to fly if I weren't dreaming." When I post this dream, I give the dream at least two keywords — Lucid and Flying. A visitor to the Web site can scan keywords and quickly discover which dreams match his or her interests.

Some Web sites have thingies that they call *tags.* Their tags are the same as my keywords. But in this book, I use the word *tag* to mean *HTML tag* and *ERb tag.* So to avoid confusion, I call my things *keywords.*

Regular expressions

In Ruby, anything enclosed inside `%r{ }` is a *regular expression.* A regular expression separates strings of characters into two groups — strings that match the expression and strings that don't match. For example, in a regular expression, `[A-F]` stands for a letter in the range `A` to `F`. If you change the `:with` entry in Listing 12-10 to `:with => %r{^[A-F]+$}`, the application doesn't accept `BARRY` as a new keyword. (The word `BARRY` contains `R`s and a `Y`, which aren't in the range `A` to `F`.)

In Listing 12-10, `[A-Za-z]` stands for any letter of the Roman alphabet, from uppercase `A` to uppercase `Z`, and from lowercase `a` to lowercase `z`. Hey! It's beginning to look as if blank spaces, digits, and punctuation characters aren't permitted in a keyword's name (at least not as far as the code in Listing 12-10 is concerned).

In a regular expression, a plus sign (+) stands for "one or more occurrences of. . . ." So in Listing 12-10, `[A-Za-z]+` means "one or more letters of the Roman alphabet."

Finally in Listing 12-10, the hook (^) stands for the start of a string, and the dollar sign ($) stands for the end of a string. So the entire expression `%r{^[A-Za-z]+$}` matches any string that contains nothing but letters of the Roman alphabet from beginning to end.

Regular expressions are very powerful (and they can also be very complicated). For more information on regular expressions, visit `http://www.regular-expressions.info`.

Connecting dreams with keywords

I don't want to let people make up their own keywords. If I do, then I'll quickly see posts with keywords like Viagra, Confidential, and Refinance. Instead, I create a database table containing keywords. I let visitors attach words from the table to each dream.

My database contains many dreams and many keywords, and the relationship between dreams and keywords is *many-to-many.* That is, each dream can have many keywords, and each keyword can be associated with many different dreams.

I need a quick Rails-ish way to define this many-to-many relationship. And indeed I have a way: *`has_and_belongs_to_many`* (abbreviated *habtm* by most authors). Putting a habtm relationship in your code is quick and easy. But tailoring your controller and views to accommodate the new habtm relationship can be tricky. This section shows you what to do.

1. **If you haven't already done so, create the `dreaming` project (complete with `Dream` model and scaffolding) described in the first section of this chapter.**

   Optionally, you can follow all the steps in this chapter's "Adding Comments" section.

2. **Add an additional model to your project. Give this new model the name `Keyword`.**

   In other words, use the Rails Generators view to create an `app\models\keyword.rb` file.

3. **Perform the migration shown in Listing 12-8.**

Listing 12-8: Defining the keywords Table

```
class CreateKeywords < ActiveRecord::Migration
  def self.up
    create_table :keywords do |t|
      t.column :name, :string
    end
  end

  def self.down
    drop_table :keywords
  end
end
```

   Big deal! With the default migration written by RadRails, you can create Listing 12-8 by deleting one pound sign!

   Anyway, when you perform this migration, you create a new `keywords` database table. Unlike the `comments` table in this chapter's "Adding

Comments" section, the new keywords table has no dream_id column. That's the way the habtm relationship works.

Like so many other Rails tables, the new keywords table has an id column. But the keywords table has no dream_id column.

4. **Tell Rails that dreams and keywords participate in a habtm relationship.**

   More specifically, add has_and_belongs_to_many method calls in both the dream and keyword models. (See Listings 12-9 and 12-10.)

Listing 12-9: The Dream Model

```
class Dream < ActiveRecord::Base
  has_many :comments
  has_and_belongs_to_many :keywords
end
```

Listing 12-10: The Keyword Model

```
class Keyword < ActiveRecord::Base
  validates_format_of :name, :with => %r{^[A-Za-z]+$}
  has_and_belongs_to_many :dreams
end
```

The habtm relationship is symmetrical. Both Listings 12-9 and 12-10 contain has_and_belongs_to_many calls. This differs from the situation in the "Adding Comments" section. In that section, one model calls has_many, and the other model calls belongs_to. The has_many/belongs_to relationship is not symmetrical.

In Listing 12-9, the line has_many :comments is optional. If you followed the steps in this chapter's "Adding Comments" section, then keep the has_many call in Listing 12-9. But if you haven't already added comments to your Web site, then don't bother. This section's *keywords* don't depend on the previous section's *comments.*

Listing 12-10 also contains an optional statement — a statement that has nothing to do with the habtm relationship. Listing 12-10 calls the validates_format_of method. This method tells the model to check a keyword's name against a *regular expression.* If I try to create a keyword that doesn't match the regular expression, Rails displays an error message. In Listing 12-10, the regular expression %r{^[A-Za-z]+$} stands for any sequence of characters containing only letters. No blank spaces, digits, or punctuation characters are allowed in a new keyword's name. (See the sidebar "Regular expressions.")

At this point in the process, you have two related tables — a dreams table and a keywords table. Neither of these tables has an _id column pointing to the other table. So how does Rails keep track of the keywords associated with each dream? The answer is in Step 5.

5. **Create an additional database table named dreams_keywords.**

The name of this table is not negotiable. Rails keeps track of a habtm relationship by depositing values into an additional database table. By default, the additional table's name comes from the names of the two original tables. (The additional table's name is *alphabeticallyFirst_alphabeticallySecond*.) In this example, Rails wants the additional database table to be named `dreams_keywords`.

Listing 12-11 contains the `004_create_dreams_keywords.rb` file. The code that you type appears in bold in Listing 12-11.

Listing 12-11: A Table Describes the Relationship between Two Other Tables

```
class CreateDreamsKeywords < ActiveRecord::Migration
  def self.up
    create_table :dreams_keywords, :id => false  do |t|
      t.column :dream_id, :int
      t.column :keyword_id, :int
    end
  end

  def self.down
    drop_table :dreams_keywords
  end
end
```

In performing this step, you generate a new migration. But you don't generate a new model. To learn how to generate a migration out of the blue, see Chapter 9.

Each row of the new `dreams_keywords` table contains two values — the id number of a dream, and the id number of a keyword. If keyword 42 is associated with dream 9, Rails puts `9 42` into one of the rows in the `dreams_keywords` table.

In the previous paragraph, *two values* means two values. It doesn't mean three values (two ordinary content values plus an additional id value). A table that stores habtm information must not contain its own id column. That's why Listing 12-11 contains the code `:id => false`.

A table that stores habtm information must not contain its own id column. If you omit the `:id => false` code in Listing 12-11, Rails may complain when you try to add entries. (Rails complains that the table contains duplicate entries, even though the table doesn't contain duplicate entries.)

6. **Create a `Keyword` scaffold.**

   Use the Rails Generators view to create files named `app\controllers\keywords_controller.rb`, `app\views\keywords\list.rhtml`, and so on.

   Some of your applications' models don't need their own scaffolds. (For example, in the previous section, the `Comment` model has no scaffold.) But using the `Keyword` model's scaffold, you can create new keywords as needed. When you create a new keyword, you don't have to associate that keyword with a particular dream. In the habtm relationship, both dreams and keywords have lives of their own.

7. **Add methods to the `app\controllers\dreams_controller.rb` file.**

   To do this, double-click the `dreams_controller.rb` file's branch in the `app\controllers` branch of the Rails Navigator's tree. When you do, the `dreams_controller.rb file` opens in a RadRails editor.

   Add the methods in Listing 12-12.

Listing 12-12: Methods in the Dream Controller

```
def remove_keyword
  @dream = Dream.find(params[:id])
  @dream.keywords.delete(
    Keyword.find(params[:which_keyword]))

  if @dream.save
    flash[:notice] = 'Keyword has been removed.'
  end
  redirect_to :action => 'show', :id => @dream
end

def add_keyword
  @dream = Dream.find(params[:id])
  @dream.keywords.push_with_attributes(
    Keyword.find(params[:keyword][:id]))

  if @dream.save
    flash[:notice] = 'Keyword has been added!'
  end
  redirect_to :action => 'show', :id => params[:id]
end

def add_some_keywords
  @dream = Dream.find(params[:id])
  @unused_keywords =
    Keyword.find(:all) - @dream.keywords

  if @unused_keywords.any?
    @keywords_to_add = @unused_keywords.select { |key|
      (@params['key'+key.id.to_s]['checked'] == '1')}
    @keywords_to_add.each { |key|
      @dream.keywords.push_with_attributes(key)}
  end

  if @keywords_to_add.any? and @dream.save
    flash[:notice] = 'Keywords have been added!'
  end
  redirect_to :action => 'show', :id => @dream
end
```

I admit it. If you don't download the code from this book's Web site, Listing 12-12 involves lots and lots of typing. But typing and understanding are two completely different things. Typing or no typing, you can understand the code in Listing 12-12. To so do, read the next section.

8. **Optionally, modify the `app\views\dreams\list.rhtml` file.**

   Listing 12-13 shows the top half of the modified `list.rhtml` file. In this listing, the code that you type appears in bold. (The code that Rails creates for you doesn't appear in bold.) You make no changes in the bottom half of the `list.rhtml` file (the half that doesn't appear in Listing 12-13).

Listing 12-13: Changing a Few Lines in the dreams\list.rhtml File

```
<h1>Listing dreams</h1>

<table>
  <tr>
    <th>Title</th>
  </tr>

<% for dream in @dreams %>
  <tr>
    <td><%= dream.title %></td>

    <td><%= link_to 'Show', :action => 'show', :id =>
            dream %></td>
    <td><%= link_to 'Edit', :action => 'edit', :id =>
            dream %></td>
    <td><%= link_to 'Destroy',
             { :action => 'destroy', :id => dream },
               :confirm => 'Are you sure?',
               :post => true %></td>
  </tr>
<% end %>
</table>

# ... And so on.
```

If you don't make the changes in Listing 12-13, nothing terrible happens. Your site's Listing Dreams page displays the description of each dream (like the page in Figure 12-2). Displaying a description isn't awful, but having descriptions on the Listing Dreams page defeats the purpose of having titles and Show pages. So at this point in the process, I make an executive decision to modify the `list.rhtml` file. The revised `list.rhtml` file displays titles, but no keywords and no descriptions.

9. **Modify the `app\views\dreams\show.rhtml` file.**

   The code that you type appears in bold in Listing 12-14. The code that Rails creates for you (and the code that may be left over in your `show.rhtml` file from Listing 12-6) doesn't appear in bold.

Listing 12-14: The Show Page for a Dream

```
<% for column in Dream.content_columns %>
<p>
  <b><%= column.human_name %>:</b>
  <%=h @dream.send(column.name) %>
</p>
<% end %>

<b>Keywords:</b><br>

<% if @dream.keywords.empty? %>
    (None)<p>
<% else %>
  <% for keyword in @dream.keywords %>
    <%= keyword.name %> 
    <%= link_to 'Remove', { :action => 'remove_keyword',
    :id => @dream, :which_keyword => keyword.id },
    :confirm => 'Are you sure?', :post => true %>
    <br />
  <% end %>
<% end %>

<% @unused_keywords =
     Keyword.find(:all) - @dream.keywords %>

<% if @unused_keywords.any?  %>
  <%= start_form_tag :action => "add_keyword",
                     :id => @dream %>
    <b>Add a keyword:</b><br>
    <%= collection_select(:keyword, :id,
         @unused_keywords, :id, :name) %><br/>
    <%= submit_tag %>
  <%= end_form_tag %><p>

  <%= form_tag :action => "add_some_keywords",
                :id => @dream %>
    <% @unused_keywords.each {|key| %>
      <%= check_box('key'+key.id.to_s, 'checked') +
         key.name %><br/>
    <% } %>
    <%= submit_tag %>
  <%= end_form_tag %>
<% end %><p>

<b>Comments:</b><br>

<% if @dream.comments.empty? %>
    (None)<p>
<% else %>
```

(continued)

Listing 12-14 *(continued)*

```
  <% for comment in @dream.comments %>
    <%= comment.body %><br>
  <% end %>
<% end %><p>

<%= start_form_tag :action => "add_comment",
                   :id => @dream %>
  <b>Add a comment:</b><br>
  <%= text_area "comment", "body", "rows" => 5 %><br>
  <%= submit_tag %>
<%= end_form_tag %><p>


<%= link_to 'Edit', :action => 'edit', :id => @dream %> |
<%= link_to 'Back', :action => 'list' %>
```

Listing 12-14 contains a heck of a lot of code. Typing this code is even more challenging than typing the code in Listing 12-12, because the code in this listing contains more punctuation (more things that are easy to type incorrectly). Anyway, whether you type this code or you download it from the Web, your best bet is to understand how the code works. For a look inside the workings of the code in Listing 12-12, see the next section.

Hey! Don't you think it's time you tested your new Web application?

10. **Visit `http://localhost:300x/keywords/new`.**

    Create a few keywords. (See Figure 12-7.)

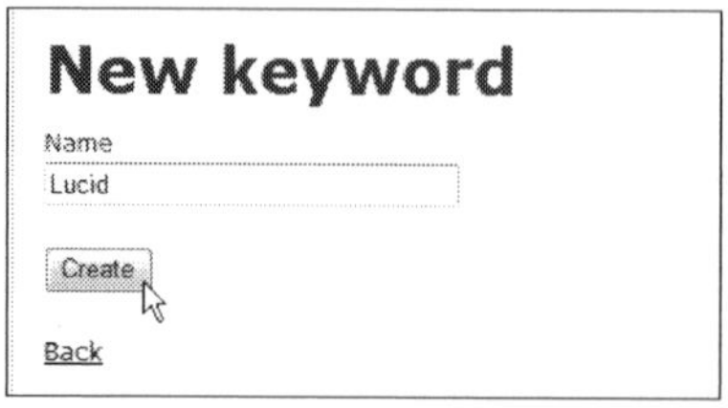

New keyword

Name

Lucid

Create

Back

Figure 12-7: Adding a keyword.

11. **Visit `http://localhost:300x/dreams`.**

    As usual, I encourage you to goof around with the application's pages. Add dreams, add keywords to dreams, remove keywords from dreams, and so on. Figures 12-8 and 12-9 are screenshots.

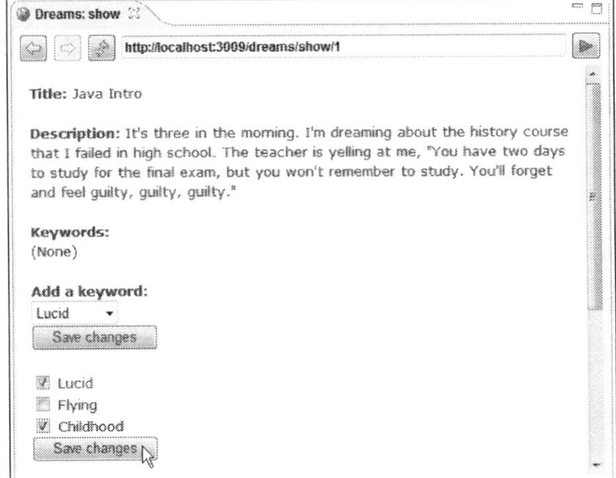

Figure 12-8: Using check boxes.

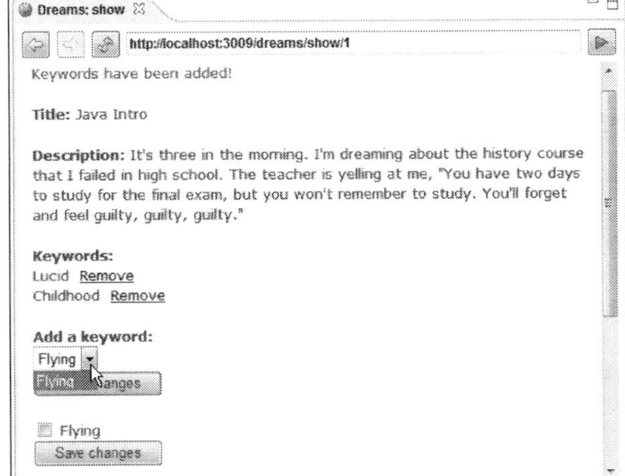

Figure 12-9: Using a drop-down list.

How the Rails code does what it does

By far, the most challenging part of adding keywords to the dreams Web site is digesting the code in Listings 12-12 and 12-14. This section covers the highlights in those listings.

Removing a keyword

In Listing 12-14, the first bold chunk of code lists the keywords associated with a particular dream. A link appears beside each keyword's name. The link (labeled *Remove*) points to a controller action named `remove_keyword`.

Rails doesn't insist that the controller's action be named `remove_keyword`. The only requirement is consistency. If you replace `:action => 'remove_keyword'` with `:action => 'razzle-dazzle'` in Listing 12-14, you must add a method named `razzle-dazzle` in the controller. Of course, the name `razzle-dazzle` would make your program difficult to read and understand. The name `remove_keyword` is much better.

When a visitor clicks the Remove link, the link sends two values to the controller. One value (the `:id` value) is a dream's id. The other value (the `:keyword` value) is a keyword's id.

In the controller (Listing 12-12), the `remove_keyword` method isn't very exciting. The method finds a dream with a particular id, finds a keyword with another id, and deletes the keyword from the dream. The call to `delete` (inside the `remove_keyword` method) behaves nicely. Behind the scenes, Rails responds to the `delete` call by eventually removing a row from the `dreams_keywords` table.

Using a drop-down list to add a keyword

In Listing 12-14, the Ruby statement

```
@unused_keywords =
  Keyword.find(:all) - @dream.keywords
```

finds the *difference* between two arrays. In this case, the difference is an array consisting of all keywords minus any keywords belonging to a particular dream. (So, the variable `@unused_keywords` contains all keywords that aren't associated with this Show page's dream. Pretty slick, heh?)

Listing 12-14 also contains an `add_keyword` form, and the form contains a `collection_select` call. The Rails `collection_select` method adds a drop-down list to a Web page. (Refer to Figures 12-8 and 12-9.) To be painfully precise, the `collection_select` method adds an HTML `select` element to a Web page. When a Web browser receives a `select` element, the browser displays a drop-down list.

A `select` element consists of two tags, a *select start tag* and a *select end tag*. But many people use the phrase *select tag* to refer to the whole kit and caboodle — the start tag, the end tag, and all the text between the start and end tags.

The collection_select call and the select element that the call creates are shown in Figure 12-10.

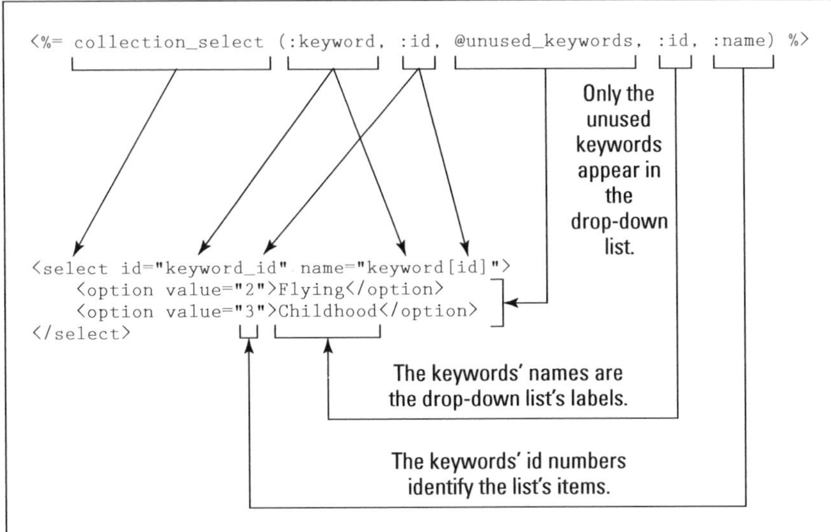

Figure 12-10: A Rails collection_select call generates an HTML select element.

In Listing 12-14, a call to the Rails submit_tag method accompanies the collection_select call. The submit_tag call puts a button on the Web page. (By default, the label on the button is Save Changes. See Figures 12-8 and 12-9.) A visitor selects an entry in the drop-down box and then clicks the button that's immediately below the box. As a result, Rails calls the Dream controller's add_keyword method.

In Listing 12-12, the add_keyword method contains the following Ruby statement:

```
@dream.keywords.push_with_attributes(
    Keyword.find(params[:keyword][:id]))
```

In this statement, the value of params[:keyword][:id] is the id number of the keyword that the visitor selected. In order for this to work correctly, some words in the Ruby statement must be identical to words in the HTML select element. In particular, the words [:keyword][:id] in the Ruby statement match up with keyword[id] in the select element. (See Figure 12-11.)

The add_keyword method in Listing 12-12 contains a push_with_attributes method call. This call does the real grunt work — adding a keyword to a dream. In the end, Rails adds a new row to the dreams_keywords table.

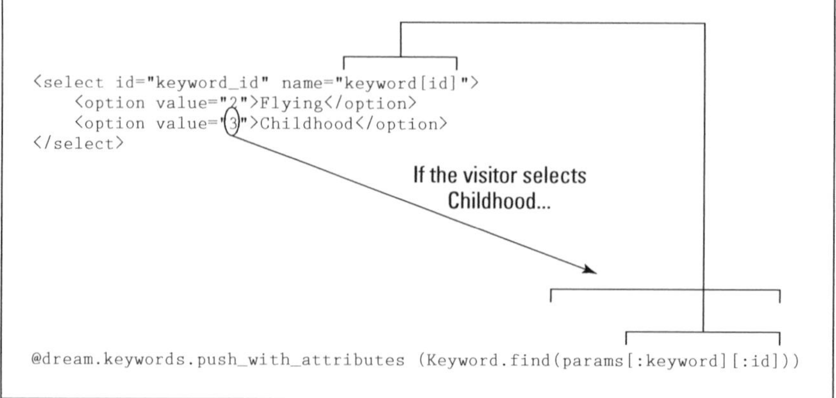

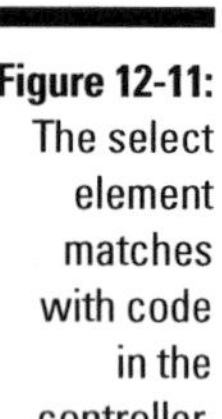

Figure 12-11: The select element matches with code in the controller.

Using check boxes to add keywords

The page in Figure 12-8 has a strange feature. The page offers two ways to add keywords. The first way involves a drop-down box, and the second way involves check boxes. Normally, you wouldn't offer both ways on the same page. (Well, maybe you would. But you probably wouldn't offer both ways so close to one another on the page.) In any case, the code in this chapter shows you both features of Rails — drop-down boxes and check boxes.

Listing 12-14 contains an `add_some_keywords` form. The form calls the Rails `check_box` method once for each unused keyword. (See Figures 12-8 and 12-9.) In particular, the call

```
check_box('key'+key.id.to_s, 'checked')
```

creates a check box whose name is something like `key2[checked]` or `key3[checked]`. The expression `'key'+key.id.to_s` performs several steps:

- **Finds `key.id` — a certain keyword's id number.**

  In this example, the id number may be `2`.

- **Turns the numeric value 2 into a string of digits.**

  The Ruby method `to_s` turns any number into a string of digits. In this example, the string contains only one digit. The string is `"2"`.

- **Adds `key` to the beginning of the string.**

  A name that starts with a digit (a name such as `2[checked]`) is considered bad form. So I slap the word `key` in front of the check box's name. The end result is a name such as `key2[checked]`.

A visitor checks some of the check boxes and then presses the corresponding Save Changes button. As a result, the browser calls the controller's add_some_keywords method. For each check box, the add_some_keywords method does the following:

- **Reconstructs the check box's name using the expression 'key'+key.id.to_s.**
- **Retrieves the check box's value using the expression @params['key'+key.id.to_s]['checked'].**

  For a box that's checked, the value of @params['key'+key.id.to_s]['checked'] is '1'. For a box that's not checked, the value of @params['key'+key.id.to_s]['checked'] is '0'.
- **Compares the check box's value with '1'.**

  If the value is '1', then the add_some_keywords method calls the push_with_attributes method. The parameter in the call to push_with_attributes is the keyword associated with the particular check box. The push_with_attributes call adds that keyword to a dream.

Using the Rails check_box method is like walking through a virtual mine field. The most dangerous part is distinguishing between integers and strings. By default, a box that's checked has value '1'. And in Ruby, the string '1' isn't equal to the integer 1. So if, in Listing 12-12, you write == 1 instead of == '1', the example doesn't work. Sorry about that!

This chapter describes the Rails has_many and has_and_belongs_to_many methods. Are you hungry for more? If so, visit http://api.rubyonrails.org/classes/ActiveRecord/Associations/ClassMethods.html#M000531 to learn about the Rails has_one method. The fun never ends!

Chapter 13

Cool Things on Rails

In This Chapter

- Making Web pages more user-friendly
- Sending e-mail from a Web page
- Entering the world of Web services

Rails eases the pain of constructing a Web-based database application. And how does Rails ease the pain? Rails makes liberal use of generators, convention over configuration, and other tricks. You open the RadRails Generators view, fill in a field or two, click a button, and then . . . Voila! You have a scaffold.

This generator stuff helps with other kinds of problems, too — problems that don't center around databases. After all, so many problems involve boilerplate code. These problems have related names that apply to several different things — a `MyMailer` class inside a `my_mailer.rb` file or an e-mail `setup` controller method with a `setup.rhtml` view.

Rails has components to help you solve these problems. And the best part is that you can have fun doing it.

Using Ajax

Several years ago, someone posed an interesting question. If Web pages are good for displaying information, are Web pages also good for editing information? Can you create a useful word processing program that runs in a Web browser? Can you comfortably read and compose e-mail through a Web-based interface? Can you collaborate with a coworker using an online spreadsheet?

The idea sounds promising. But despite the promise, Web-based applications haven't become very popular. When I want to read e-mail, I open Microsoft Outlook, Mozilla Thunderbird, or some other desktop application. I use a Web interface only when I'm traveling or when desktop applications are otherwise unavailable.

Why do I avoid Web-based e-mail? I avoid it because Web-based applications are clunky. Every action requires a page refresh. For example, I delete 1 message in a list of 20. With a slow Internet connection, I wait patiently for my Web browser to fetch a whole new page. But what's on that new page? The new page contains 19 of the original message subjects with an additional (less recent) message's subject added at the end. What a waste! The entire page reloads (images, and all) in order to change only 1 of 20 message subjects.

Another part of the same Web-based e-mail interface displays a tree of mail folders. I can click a plus sign to expand one of the tree's branches. But once again, I see more than one expanding branch. I watch as the entire Web page repaints itself.

Sure, I'm spoiled by desktop applications. But if browser-based applications can be just as slick, why aren't they?

Refresh part of a page, not the entire page

One alternative to the ugliness of a full-page refresh is to use Ajax. The term *Ajax* stands for *Asynchronous JavaScript and XML.* The term was coined in 2005 by Jesse James Garrett. As Ajax fans are quick to point out, Ajax isn't a new technology. Ajax is a new name for a combination of existing technologies — technologies which enable you to update only part of a Web page. These technologies include HTML, JavaScript, DOM (the *D*ynamic *O*bject *M*odel), XML (the e*X*tensible *M*arkup *L*anguage), XSLT (e*X*tensible *S*tylesheet *T*ransformations), and others.

At the heart of Ajax is something called the `XMLHttpRequest` *object.* When embedded in a Web page, this `XMLHttpRequest` thingie sends a request to a Web server. And the good news is that the request is *asynchronous.* Your browser doesn't stop what it's doing to wait for a response. Instead, the browser keeps doing whatever it was doing before issuing the request. At some future moment, when a response arrives back from the server, your browser processes the response and updates only a portion of the current page.

Incorporating Ajax into a Rails page

You can easily incorporate Ajax into your Rails applications. (Big surprise, heh? Imagine reading "Despite Ajax's enormous benefits, you can't use Ajax in your Rails applications." What a letdown that would be!) This section presents a basic Ajax example.

1. **Create a Rails project named `discussion`.**

   For details, see Chapter 3.

2. **Create a database named `discussion_development`.**

   For details, see Chapter 3 again. In fact, bookmark Chapter 3. You need sections in Chapter 3 for many of the steps that follow.

3. **Within the `discussion` project, generate a model named `Comment`.**

4. **Create a database table named `comments` using the migration file in Listing 13-1.**

Listing 13-1: Migrate that Database

```
class CreateComments < ActiveRecord::Migration
  def self.up
    create_table :comments do |t|
      t.column :title, :string
      t.column :body, :text
    end
  end

  def self.down
    drop_table :comments
  end
end
```

Don't make the mistake that I often make. Don't become so excited about the migration file that you forget to perform the `db:migrate` Rake task.

5. **Generate a `Comment` scaffold.**

6. **Add a method to the project's `app\controllers\comments_controller.rb` file.**

   To do this, double-click the `comments_controller.rb` file's branch in the `app\controllers` branch of the Rails Navigator's tree. When you do, the `comments_controller.rb file` opens in a RadRails editor.

   Add the method in Listing 13-2.

Listing 13-2: A Method for Your Controller

```
def show_body
  @comment = Comment.find(params[:id])
  render :text => @comment.body
end
```

The code fetches a particular comment from the database. Then the code displays the comment's body. But where does the comment's body appear? (Remember, this is Ajax!)

7. **Modify `app\views\comments\list.rhtml`.**

   The code that you type is bold in Listing 13-3.

Listing 13-3: Modifying the Listing Comments Page

```
<head>
  <%= javascript_include_tag "prototype" %>
</head>

<h1>Listing comments</h1>

<table>
  <tr>
  <% for column in Comment.content_columns %>
    <th><%= column.human_name %></th>
  <% end %>
  </tr>

<% for comment in @comments %>
  <tr>

    <td><%= comment.title %></td>
    <td>
      <div id="comment_<%= comment.id.to_s %>">
        <%= link_to_remote( "Show Body",
              :update => "comment_#{comment.id.to_s}",
              :url => { :action => :show_body,
                        :id => comment }) %>
      </div>
    </td>

    <td><%= link_to 'Show',
            :action => 'show', :id => comment %></td>
    <td><%= link_to 'Edit',
            :action => 'edit', :id => comment %></td>
    <td><%= link_to 'Destroy',
            { :action => 'destroy', :id => comment },
            :confirm => 'Are you sure?', :post => true %>
    </td>
  </tr>
<% end %>
</table>

<%= link_to 'Previous page',
  { :page => @comment_pages.current.previous } if
  @comment_pages.current.previous %>
<%= link_to 'Next page',
```

```
  { :page => @comment_pages.current.next } if
  @comment_pages.current.next %>

<br />

<%= link_to 'New comment', :action => 'new' %>
```

Listing 13-3 contains two new pieces of code. The first piece imports some JavaScript code into the Listing Comments Web page. This JavaScript code comes from the project's `public\javascripts\prototype.js` file. Among other things, the code creates an `XMLHttpRequest`:

```
var Ajax = {
  getTransport: function() {
    return Try.these(
      function() {return new XMLHttpRequest()},
```

If you're a fan of JavaScript, you can examine the `prototype.js` code. To do so, double-click the `public\javascripts\prototype.js` branch in the Rails Navigator view.

In Listing 13-3, the other new piece of code contains a `link_to_remote` call. The Rails `link_to_remote` method adds an HTML anchor element to the Listing Comments Web page. The anchor element and its enclosing `div` element look something like this:

```
<div id="comment_4">
  <a href="#" onclick="new Ajax.Updater('comment_4',
    '/comments/show_body/4', {asynchronous:true,
    evalScripts:true}); return false;">Show Body</a>
</div>
```

You can see the HTML anchor element that Rails generates. To do so, visit the Listing Comments page in the Rails browser. Then right-click in any neutral space on the Listing Comments page. In the resulting contextual menu, select View Source.

The HTML anchor element creates a link with the text *Show Body.* (See Figure 13-1.)

Figure 13-1: You see a link instead of the body of the comment.

When you click the link, the Web browser calls some JavaScript code, which creates an `XMLHttpRequest` and calls the `show_body` method in Listing 13-2.

Notice the `<div>...</div>` element in Listing 13-3. The tagname `div` stands for the word *division* — a section or portion of an HTML document. The `id` attribute of this `div` element has a value such as `comment_1` or `comment_2`. (The Listing Comments page contains several comments. The exact value of the `div` element's `id` attribute varies from one comment to another.)

The call to `link_to_remote` in Listing 13-3 also refers to `comment_someIdNumber`. So, when a visitor clicks one of the Show Body links, the stuff rendered by the `show_body` method replaces the text inside the appropriate `div` element. (See Listing 13-2.)

8. **Try it!**

   Fire up the discussion project's server. Add a few comments and then look at the Listing Comments page. At first, the page displays only titles and Show Body links. (Refer to Figure 13-1.) But when you click a Show Body link, the browser displays the body of the comment. (See Figure 13-2.)

Figure 13-2: Comment bodies in place of some links.

Alas! The coolest part of this example isn't visible in Figures 13-1 or 13-2. When you click a Show Body link, the Web browser doesn't refresh the whole page. Instead, the browser replaces the Show Body link with the appropriate comment's body. The rest of the page remains the same. (The other items on the page move over a bit to accommodate the body's size, but that's not nearly as jolting as seeing a refresh of the entire page.)

Sending E-Mail

"Why would anyone want to do that?" I asked. It was 1979. My question was a response to an engineer's remarks. He told me about his system at work for typing text instead of making a phone call. "Isn't typing more difficult than talking?" I said.

Since then, I've been tempted to open an anti-consulting business. Pay me to predict what the future holds for your company, but first sign an agreement to do the opposite of whatever I advise. I can make some good money doing anti-consulting.

These days, I send e-mail to my wife. I work in the living room and she works upstairs in the den. I know I won't remember to tell her that Mary called, so I send her a quick e-mail message. That way, the burden of remembering Mary's call is out of my hands.

Of course, some things in a marital relationship aren't suited to e-mail. For example, if I have an urgent need for my wife's attention, I use instant messaging.

Don't blame me if it doesn't work

This brief section contains some discouraging news. Sending e-mail can be a dicey business. You need access to a mail server, and the server's configuration must allow you to send mail through the server. In the past few years, mail servers have become more restrictive. (Any unrestrictive server becomes a launching pad for spam.) So many SMTP servers (outgoing e-mail servers) require authentication of one kind or another.

My family's Internet provider doesn't require authentication for outgoing e-mail, so the code in this section works on my home computer. But your provider may be different, and (unfortunately) I can't predict what special incantations you may need in order to make this section's example work with your provider.

My advice is this: If this section's example doesn't work for you, try tinkering a bit, but don't get hung up on the task. If you know an e-mail guru who's familiar with your provider's configuration, ask that person. But if at first you don't succeed, don't try, try again and again.

Rails mail

To create an e-mail-enabled Web site, follow these steps.

1. **Create a Rails project named `email`.**

   For details on creating a Rails project, see Chapter 3. In fact, for details on each of this section's steps (up to and including Step 5), see Chapter 3.

2. **Create a database named `email_development`.**
3. **Within the `email` project, generate a model named `Message`.**
4. **Create a database table named `messages` using the migration file in Listing 13-4.**

Listing 13-4: The Elements of an E-Mail Message

```
class CreateMessages < ActiveRecord::Migration
  def self.up
    create_table :messages do |t|
      t.column :subject, :string
      t.column :custname, :string
      t.column :amount, :float
      t.column :recipients, :string
      t.column :sender, :string
    end
  end

  def self.down
    drop_table :messages
  end
end
```

5. **Generate a `Message` scaffold.**
6. **Add the code in Listing 13-5 to the end of your project's `config\environment.rb` file.**

Listing 13-5: Configuring the Mailer

```
ActionMailer::Base.server_settings = {
  :address => "mail.cheapprovider.net",
  :domain => "burdbrain.com",
}
```

In Listing 13-5, the `address` is the name of your Internet service provider's e-mail server. I found the server's name by opening my Outlook configuration page and copying the text in the SMTP (outgoing) server name field. If you get this address wrong, you can't send any e-mails.

The `domain` in Listing 13-5 is the Rails Web site that originates the e-mail. The domain value helps assure your Internet provider that you're not sending malicious e-mail. Many outgoing e-mail servers don't check this field because it's easy to fake. So if you get this domain value wrong, you can probably send e-mail anyway.

If your outgoing server requires authentication, try adding `:user_name` and `:password` values to the `ActionMailer::Base.server_settings`. This helps with the kind of authentication that *some* outgoing servers use.

Ruby reads the `environment.rb` file only when your Rails project's server starts. So if you edit the `environment.rb` file while the project's server is running, save the `environment.rb` file changes and then restart the server.

7. **Generate a `MyMailer` mailer with a method named `setup`.**

   Use the RadRails Generators view (as shown in Figure 13-3).

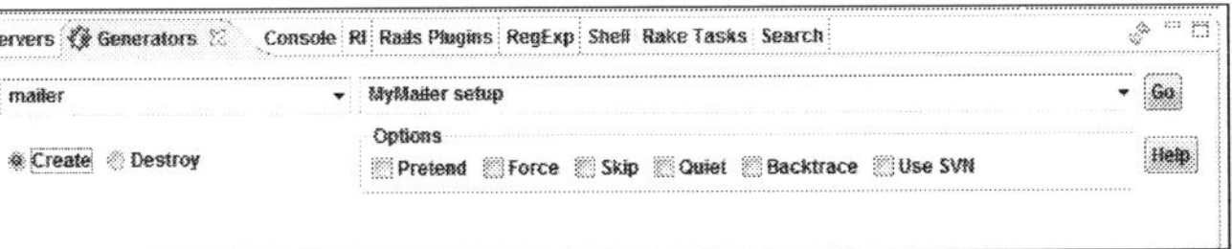

Figure 13-3: Generating a mailer.

   Rails creates an `app\models\my_mailer.rb` file and an `app\views\my_mailer\setup.rhtml` file.

8. **Add a few lines of code to the `create` method in the project's `app\controllers\messages_controller.rb` file.**

   Add the bold lines shown in Listing 13-6.

Listing 13-6: How to Mail a Message

```
def create
  @message = Message.new(params[:message])

  my_message = MyMailer::create_setup(@message)
  my_message.set_content_type 'text/html'
  MyMailer::deliver my_message

  if @message.save
    flash[:notice] = 'Message was successfully created.'
    redirect_to :action => 'list'
  else
    render :action => 'new'
  end
end
```

When you create a new message, the server does its usual Rails stuff (creates the @message object, saves the object in a database, and so on). But the server also calls create_setup. (See Listing 13-6.) This create_setup call builds a "mailable" object from the stuff in the @message variable. Then the code in Listing 13-6 sets the mailable object's content type (so that programs such as Outlook recognize any HTML tags in the message's body).

Finally in Listing 13-6, the server executes the deliver method to send an e-mail message.

The trickiest thing in Listing 13-6 is the method name create_setup. This name is a combination of create_, which is hard-wired into the Rails e-mail code, and the name setup, which a programmer invents on his or her own. In the next step, you see the definition of a method named setup. But remember, some other name (such as johnsmith or malarkeyonfire) would work just as well. Whatever you name the next step's method, you append the prefix create_ to that name in Listing 13-6. You do this even if the call to create_*whatever* isn't inside a controller's create method. (The similarity between def create and create_setup in Listing 13-6 is purely coincidental.)

9. **Edit the app\models\my_mailer.rb file. When you're done, it should look like what you see in Listing 13-7.**

Listing 13-7: The My Mailer Class

```
class MyMailer < ActionMailer::Base

  def setup(message, sent_at = Time.now)
    @subject      = message.subject
    @body['custname'] = message.custname
    @body['amount']   = message.amount
    @recipients = message.recipients
    @from         = message.sender
    @sent_on      = sent_at
    @headers      = {}
  end
end
```

The method in Listing 13-7 sets some important values. The method gets most of these values from the message parameter. Rails surreptitiously turns the create_setup call in Listing 13-6 into a call to the setup method in Listing 13-7. In the process, Rails hands this message parameter to the setup method.

The most interesting lines in Listing 13-7 are the `@body` assignments. The `@body` variable refers to a hash, and the `setup` method creates two hash entries. How do these hash entries affect the content of the outgoing e-mail message? For an answer, proceed to the next step.

Your code doesn't explicitly call the `setup` method in Listing 13-7. Instead, your code calls the `create_setup` method. (See Listing 13-6.)

In Listing 13-7, names such as `setup` and `message` aren't cast in stone. You can use other names as long as you name things consistently throughout this example's `email` project. But avoid the temptation to change the word `sender` to the word `from` in Listing 13-7. The word `from` is an SQL keyword. If you use the word `from`, you may confuse the database software.

10. **Edit `app\views\my_mailer\setup.rhtml` so that the file contains the code in Listing 13-8.**

Listing 13-8: The Outline of a Cordial but Forceful Message

```
<head>
  <style type="text/css">
    p.indent { margin-left: 60px }
  </style>
</head>

<h1>Third Notice!</h1>

Dear <%= @custname %>,<p>

Your bill is overdue. Please pay
<%= number_to_currency(@amount) %> immediately.<p>

<p class="indent">Signed,<br>Your <i><b>friends</b></i>
at Burd Brain Consulting</p>
```

When you create a mailer in Step 7, you add a method named `setup`. Rails automatically adds a view named `setup.rhtml`. When you send a message, Rails consults this `setup.rhtml` file to form the content of the e-mail message.

In Listing 13-8, the `setup.rhtml` file contains two ERb tags. Each tag displays the value of a variable — a variable whose name is a hash key in Listing 13-7. Ruby does some juggling to feed the correct values to the `@custname` and `@amount` variables in Listing 13-8, and the message goes to the recipient with the desired wording.

11. **Visit `http://localhost:300x/messages/new`.**

12. **Create a new message as shown in Figure 13-4. (But please don't use my e-mail addresses. Put your own e-mail address in both the Recipients and Sender fields!)**

Figure 13-4: Filling in the fields.

After creating a new message, you see the usual Listing Messages page (Figure 13-5). And your recipient gets an e-mail message like the one shown in Figure 13-6.

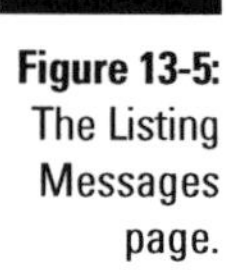

Figure 13-5: The Listing Messages page.

Be patient. Your Internet provider may not send the message immediately. If you don't receive the message, wait at least ten minutes before concluding that something's amiss.

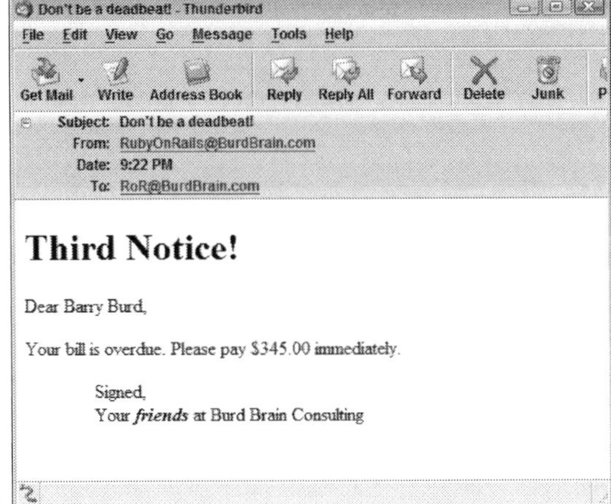

Figure 13-6: Wow! I actually sent myself an e-mail message!

With all the ranting and raving I do about e-mail clients in the section on Ajax in this chapter, you'd think I'd devote some space to the creation of an Ajax-based e-mail client. But mixing Ajax and e-mail in one introductory example would be burdensome. Besides, this section isn't about reading e-mail. It's about sending e-mail.

Anyway, you can mix and match Rails technologies. Using this section's tools combined with Ajax, you can create a Web page that sends e-mail and avoids refreshing entire pages. The possibilities are endless.

Creating and Consuming Web Services

Web services have been hot stuff in the computing industry for several years. A Web service is a program that produces a special kind of Web page. This special Web page contains only data, with no attention to the data's layout or visual formatting.

For example, an ordinary Web page with weather information may contain the following HTML code:

```
<h1>Welcome to Burd Brain Consulting</h1>
Today's temperature is a pleasant 71&deg; F.<p>
Expect light showers in the afternoon, with a chance of
snow later this evening.<p>
<font size=-1>&copy; 2007, Burd Brain Consulting</font>
```

The HTML code tells a Web browser to display a Welcome heading with big bold characters, to display the copyright line with small letters, and so on.

This HTML code is fine for a person browsing the Web. You can't easily write a computer program to fetch weather information from this HTML code, however. A program would have to remove the extraneous display information. After all, the program doesn't feel warmed by being welcomed to the Burd Brain Web site. The program probably doesn't know what the word *pleasant* means, and the program doesn't care about the font size in a copyright line. All the computer program wants is the current temperature along with the time and status of each weather prediction.

A program that reads the HTML code, with all the code's extraneous information, does something called *screen scraping*. The program scrapes the relevant information from a page full of relevant and irrelevant information. This screen scraping process is both inefficient and error-prone. If the Webmaster at Burd Brain consulting changes anything about the HTML page's layout, then the screen scraper is likely to filter out the wrong information.

How to avoid screen scraping

With the Web services approach, a page contains only the information that a computer program actually requires. No formatting and no layout. Just the facts.

The page's coding is XML rather than HTML, so the page's tags obey very rigid rules. A bunch of weather information coded in XML may look something like this:

```
<?xml version="1.0" encoding="UTF-8"?>
<weather>
  <current>
    <what><temp number="71" scale="F" /></what>
  </current>
  <prediction>
    <what>light showers</what>
    <when>1500h</when>
  </prediction>
  <prediction>
    <what>snow</what>
    <when>2100h</when>
  </prediction>
</weather>
```

When called into action, the Web service returns an XML document containing concise, self-describing information. A program uses this information efficiently and reliably.

Building a Web service using Ruby on Rails

With Ruby on Rails, you can quickly generate code to create and consume a Web service. This section presents an example.

Unfortunately, the output of this section's example isn't startling. In fact, when you run the code, you may wonder what all the fuss over Web services is about. All the Web services business (the protocol for invoking the service, the XML-coded result, and so on) lurks quietly underneath the mechanics of this example. Rails hides most Web service complexities from your view.

The main thing to take away from this example is not what the example does. (The example tells you the time. Big deal!). Rather, the thing to take away is how easily this example does what it does. With only a few steps, this example creates a portable, network-ready Web service. Any enterprise using the Web services standards can provide and retrieve information using this example's techniques.

1. **Create a Rails project named `timeProject`.**
2. **Generate a Web service named `TimeService` with a method named `get_time`. (See Figure 13-7.)**

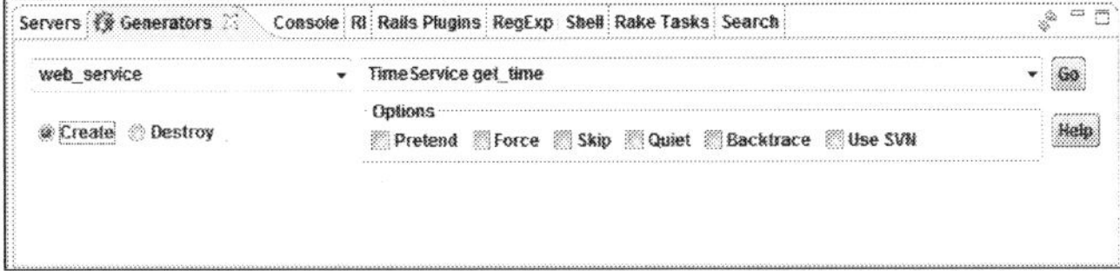

Figure 13-7: Generating a Web service.

To reward you for your efforts, Rails creates files named `app\apis\time_service_api.rb` and `app\controllers\time_service_controller.rb`.

3. **Add code to the `app\apis\time_service_api.rb` file, as shown in Listing 13-9.**

Listing 13-9: Describing the Web Service Interface

```
class TimeServiceApi < ActionWebService::API::Base
  api_method :get_time, :expects => [:bool],
                        :returns => [:time]
end
```

Listing 13-9 tells Rails that the Web service's `get_time` method takes a parameter of type `bool` and returns a value of type `time`. A `bool` (short for *boolean*) value is either `true` or `false`. (For more information on Ruby's `true` and `false` values, see Chapter 3.) A `time` value is a point in time, which includes year, month, and day values as well as hours, minutes, seconds, and even microseconds values.

Rails doesn't know it yet, but the `get_time` method's boolean parameter stands for "true, I want Greenwich Mean Time," or "false, I don't want Greenwich Mean Time. I want a computer's local time instead." (Rails learns all this in the next step.)

4. **Add code to the `app\controllers\time_service_controller.rb` file as shown in Listing 13-10.**

Listing 13-10: The Service Gets the Time of Day

```
require 'time'

class TimeServiceController < ApplicationController
  wsdl_service_name 'TimeService'
  web_service_scaffold :use_service

  def get_time(gmt)
    (gmt)?(Time.now.getgm):(Time.now)
  end
end
```

Listing 13-10 has lots to say:

- **The `TimeServiceController` class uses definitions from Ruby's built-in `time.rb` file.**

  You `require 'time'` at the top of Listing 13-10.

- **The `TimeServiceController` class grants a WSDL name to your Web service.**

  The acronym *WSDL* stands for *Web Service Description Language.* A WSDL document is an XML document describing your Web service for the benefit of potential clients. (After all, someone who gets the time from your Web service may not be running Ruby and may not be able to look inside the code in Listing 13-9.)

• **The `TimeServiceController` class creates a scaffold.**

This scaffold is similar to a scaffold that you generate for an ordinary Rails model. But the special `web_service_scaffold` is a bit simpler than a model's scaffold.

For one thing, Rails doesn't have a handy generator script for creating a `web_service_scaffold`. You can't use the RadRails Generators view to create the `web_service_scaffold`. Instead, you add a line to the `TimeServiceController` class's code. (See Listing 13-10.)

In the `web_service_scaffold` method call, the parameter name `:use_service` becomes part of the URL that you use to visit the scaffold's Web pages. (If you can't wait to find out about this, see Step 5.)

You can create an old-fashioned model scaffold the way you create a `web_service_scaffold` in Listing 13-10. For example, if your model is named `Photo`, add the line `scaffold :photo` inside the code of the `PhotoController` class. But remember, to use this application's Web interface, visit `http://localhost:300x/photo`, where the word `photo` is singular, not plural.

• **The `get_time` method takes a parameter.**

In Listing 13-10, I give this parameter the name **`gmt`**.

• **The `get_time` method returns either the Greenwich Mean Time or the local time, depending on the value (`true` or `false`) of the `gmt` parameter.**

Ruby's built-in `getgm` method turns a local time into a Greenwich Mean Time.

5. **Visit `http://localhost:300x/time_service/use_service`.**

You see a Web page like the one shown in Figure 13-8.

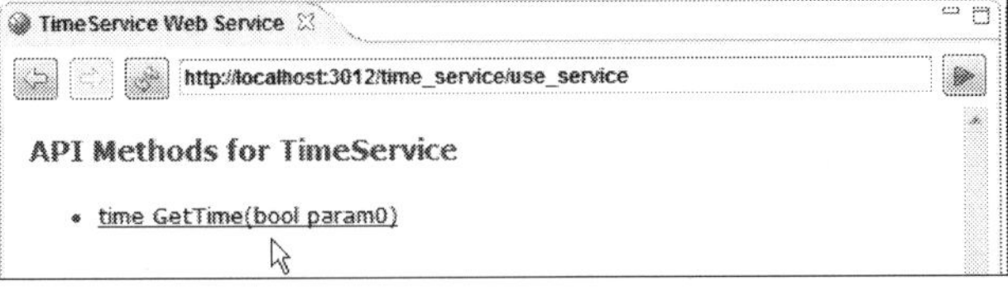

Figure 13-8: An interface to a service.

On this Web page, a link points to your `GetTime` method (also known as your `get_time` method).

6. **Click the Web page's `GetTime` link.**

   The link takes you to another Web page. (See Figure 13-9.) This page contains a form that's specific to the `GetTime` method. In particular, the form has radio buttons for specifying the value (`true` or `false`) of the method's `gmt` parameter.

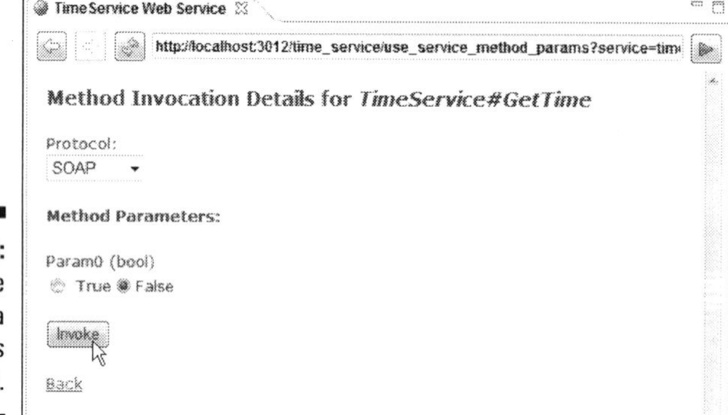

Figure 13-9: An interface to a service's method.

7. **Select one of the two radio buttons (True or False).**
8. **Click the Invoke button.**

   As a result of this click, Ruby sends a message to your Web service. The Web service answers back, and your browser receives a page displaying the current time. After a brief pause, you see a page like the one shown in Figure 13-10.

This section's example is a Web service that tells you the current time. I admit, instead of creating a Rails Web service, you can glance at your watch. And if you don't have a watch, you can write a one-line Ruby program to achieve the same result. (The entire Ruby program is `puts Time.now`.)

But what if you want the world to retrieve the time from your Web server? What if you want programs running half-way around the world to retrieve stock quotes, weather reports, news analysis, product lists, or other valuable pieces of information from your Web server? Then the standard way to make this happen is to create a Web service. And using Rails, you can create a Web service without muss or fuss.

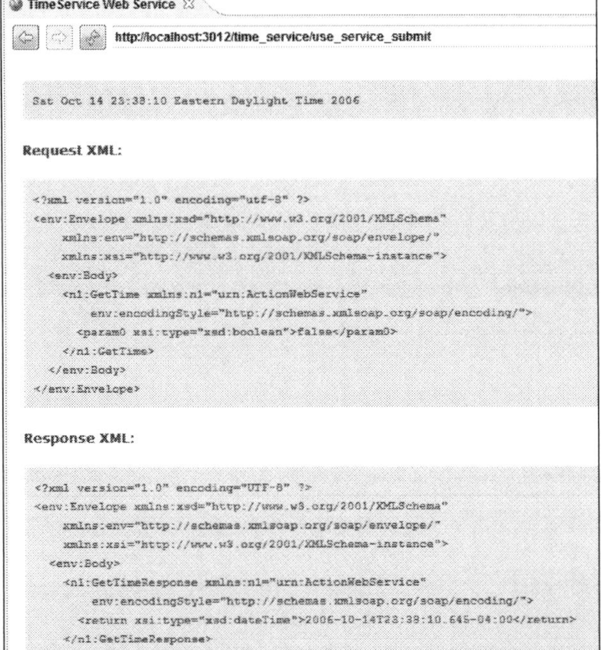

TimeService Web Service
http://localhost:3012/time_service/use_service_submit
Sat Oct 14 23:38:10 Eastern Daylight Time 2006
Request XML:
<?xml version="1.0" encoding="utf-8" ?>
<env:Envelope xmlns:xsd="http://www.w3.org/2001/XMLSchema"
xmlns:env="http://schemas.xmlsoap.org/soap/envelope/"
xmlns:xsi="http://www.w3.org/2001/XMLSchema-instance">
<env:Body>
<n1:GetTime xmlns:n1="urn:ActionWebService"
env:encodingStyle="http://schemas.xmlsoap.org/soap/encoding/">
<param0 xsi:type="xsd:boolean">false</param0>
</n1:GetTime>
</env:Body>
</env:Envelope>
Response XML:
<?xml version="1.0" encoding="UTF-8" ?>
<env:Envelope xmlns:xsd="http://www.w3.org/2001/XMLSchema"
xmlns:env="http://schemas.xmlsoap.org/soap/envelope/"
xmlns:xsi="http://www.w3.org/2001/XMLSchema-instance">
<env:Body>
<n1:GetTimeResponse xmlns:n1="urn:ActionWebService"
env:encodingStyle="http://schemas.xmlsoap.org/soap/encoding/">
<return xsi:type="xsd:dateTime">2006-10-14T23:38:10.645-04:00</return>
</n1:GetTimeResponse>

Figure 13-10: Now you know what time it is.

Part IV

The Part of Tens

"Once I told Mona that Access was an 'argument' based program, she seemed to warm up to it."

In this part . . .

Roughly 5,000 years ago, the people known as the Sumerians used a sexagesimal numbering system. Instead of using our familiar base 10 system, the Sumerian notation had 60 as its base.

It was a hard life. The Sumerian equivalents of David Letterman's writers wrote dozens of jokes for each night's Top 60 List. And imagine watching Charlton Heston play the hero Gilgamesh in a 20-hour movie entitled *The Sixty Commandments*!

Keep all this in mind as you read the next few chapters, and be glad the Sumerians aren't still around.

Chapter 14

Ten (Times Two) Great Web Sites

In This Chapter

- Finding documentation and other resources
- Getting sample code
- Reading the latest Ruby on Rails news
- Taking part in the ongoing discussion

Ten Web sites? Twenty Web sites? What's the difference?

This chapter lists a bunch of useful Web sites. Each Web site has resources to help you use Ruby on Rails more effectively. And as far as I know, none of these sites use adware, pop-ups, or other grotesque things.

Ten Ruby Sites

I divide this chapter into two sections — a Ruby section and a Rails section. I put the Ruby section first because "Ruby" comes first alphabetically. (. . . Or maybe "Ruby" doesn't come first. Whatever!)

Documentation

`www.ruby-doc.org`

When I describe the Ruby language, the phrase "plentiful documentation" doesn't come rushing out of my mouth. But this Web site does a good job documenting Ruby's standard libraries. In addition, the site's frame-based Web interface is easy to use.

Open source Ruby projects

`http://rubyforge.org`

Developers add their open source projects to this vast repository. If you want some Ruby code and you don't feel like reinventing the wheel, check this Web site first.

Starting points for Ruby resources

`www.rubycentral.com`

`www.ruby-lang.org`

`www.rubygarden.org`

These sites have links to all things Ruby. Visit these sites for FAQs, wikis, downloads, articles, and more. (Sure, this paragraph describes three Web sites. Not one. But who's counting?)

Discussing Ruby

`www.ruby-forum.com`

If you have an opinion, need an opinion, want help, have an announcement, or just want to read what other people write about Ruby, visit this site.

A weekly challenge

`www.rubyquiz.com`

Enthusiasts from around the world visit this site for a weekly infusion of Ruby code. Each week's problem uses Ruby's features to the max. If you're a Ruby newbie, you don't have to submit solutions. You learn a lot just by watching.

Add-ons for Ruby

www.rubygems.org

A gem is a Ruby add-on, and RubyGems is the packaging system for gem add-ons. This Web site describes the RubyGems packaging system — what the system does and how to use it effectively.

Meet people

www.rubyholic.com

I love to attend user group meetings. I go to two or three of them each month. They're lively and informative. To find a user group in your area, visit this Web site.

Write Ruby code on a desert island

http://tryruby.hobix.com

Your airplane crashed on a remote desert island. You're Lost. You're stuck in an underground hatch with an old computer running an obsolete operating system. You can't install Ruby but you manage to install a Web browser. While visiting the *Try Ruby!* Web site, you realize that you don't need to install Ruby after all! By typing code in this Web site's work area, you create a Ruby program that solves all of the island's mysteries. Nice going! But can you wrestle a polar bear?

How to be multilingual

www.jruby.org

JRuby is an implementation of Ruby written completely in Java. Using JRuby, you have Java's mammoth power and stability along with Ruby's incredible flexibility.

Agile development

www.agilealliance.com

www.agilemanifesto.org

Learn more about agile development. Browse the Agile Alliance Web site. Then visit the home of the original Agile Manifesto signatories. Yes, you can even sign the Agile Manifesto (online, of course).

Ten Rails Sites

Some Ruby sites contain lots of Ruby on Rails information. But if you want a site that focuses primarily on Rails, visit any of the sites in this section.

Straight from the source's mouth

www.rubyonrails.org

This is the official Ruby on Rails Web site. Start here for the most authoritative Rails information. And while you visit, don't miss this site's http://api.rubyonrails.org pages. These pages document each of the classes and methods in Ruby on Rails.

Find a Web host

www.hostingrails.com

www.railshosting.org

www.rubyonrailswebhost.com

As Web technologies go, Rails is very new. Many Web hosting companies don't yet support Rails. But to make your pages public, you need a compatible host. To start shopping for a host, visit these three sites. (But please think of the three sites as one big site. I'm trying to keep my promise about listing exactly ten items in this section.)

Get hooked on RadRails

`www.radrails.org`

Ruby on Rails has several integrated development environments. But in my opinion, RadRails is the best. This Web site is the official home for RadRails. Pay this site a visit to read more about RadRails and to download the latest and greatest RadRails updates.

Documentation

`http://railsmanual.com`

This site documents many versions of Rails, starting with version 1.0.0 and ending with the most up-to-date Rails release.

Discuss Ruby on Rails

`http://rails.techno-weenie.net`

Ask questions; answer questions. That's what this Web site is all about. If you're stuck on a point, this site's participants can probably help you past the hurdle.

A Rails-friendly operating system

`http://railslivecd.org`

A previous reference in this chapter explains how you can run Ruby on a computer while you're trapped on a desert island. If the computer on the island has a CD-ROM reader, you can also run Rails. The Rails Live CD is a self-contained operating system — a system that you don't bother installing on your hard drive. How cool is that?

Read the latest news

`www.feeddigest.com/digests/ruby-on-rails.html`

In the world of Rails, things change constantly. New developments occur daily. You work hard to keep up with all the gossip. Visiting this Web site can help you stay current. Better yet, subscribe to this site's RSS feed. Have the headlines delivered directly to your desktop.

Steal some code

`www.hotscripts.com/Ruby_on_Rails/Scripts_and_Programs`

Hotscripts features useful pieces of code for many languages and frameworks. The Ruby on Rails page contains some particularly nice goodies — scripts that you might want to incorporate into your own applications.

Brush up on SQL

`http://dev.mysql.com/doc`

Rails is all about databases, and the universal language of databases is SQL. You can issue SQL commands in MySQL Administrator or from the command line by typing **mysql**. So check out the official documentation and give SQL a whirl.

The seminal Ajax document

`www.adaptivepath.com/publications/essays/archives/000385.php`

Jesse James Garrett didn't rob banks or marry Sandra Bullock. But he coined the term *Ajax* — a name for one of the hottest technologies on the Web today. Chapter 13 of this book touches on Ajax, but you might want to read more. For a look at the way Ajax started, visit this Adaptive Path Web site.

Chapter 15

Ten Features That Set Ruby Apart

In This Chapter

- Exploring Ruby's oddities
- Using mixins, unit testing, and other stuff
- Quacking like a duck

This chapter highlights some of Ruby's unique features. I list the features in no particular order. I cover many of these features in Chapters 5 and 6, but a few of this chapter's features blaze new Ruby territory.

Hashes

A *hash* is a collection of key/value pairs. Use curly braces {} to define a hash; use brackets [] to refer to a particular hash value.

```
price_of =
  {'Book' => 20.00, 'Shirt' => 15.05, 'Cup' => 10.20}
price_of['Car'] = 23999.99

puts price_of['Car']
```

The output of this brief program is `23999.99`.

For more info, see Chapter 5.

Open Classes

You can add definitions to a class at any point in the code. For example, in the following program, the definition of `MyClass` ends before the creation of `my_object`. Then the `MyClass` definition resumes after the creation of `my_object`.

```
class MyClass
  def my_method
    10
  end
end

my_object = MyClass.new
print my_object.my_method, " "

class MyClass
  def another_method
    22
  end
end

print my_object.another_method
```

The output of this program is `10 22`.

For more on open classes, see Chapter 6.

Duck Typing

If it walks like a duck and it quacks like a duck, then it's a duck. Consider the following program. At first, the `value` variable walks and quacks like an integer. At that point in the code, `value` is an integer. So `value.times` is legal but `value.each` is illegal. (If you uncomment the first `value.each` line and try to run the program, Ruby displays an error message.)

```
value = 3
value.times do
  print "Hello", " "
end
# value.each { |x| print x }

value = "Goodbye"
# value.times do
#   print "Hello", " "
# end
value.each { |x| print x }
```

Later in the same program, `value` walks and quacks like a string. So in the second half of the program, `value.times` is illegal and `value.each` is legal.

The program's output is `Hello Hello Hello Goodbye`.

Modifiers

A *modifier* is a quick and easy control flow construct.

```
print "one equals zero; " if 1 == 0
print "one equals zero; " unless 1 != 0
print "zero equals zero; " if 0 == 0
i = 0
print i += 1 while i < 5
```

This program's output is `zero equals zero; 12345`.

To read more about modifiers, see Chapter 5.

Blocks

A *block* is a collection of statements accompanying a method call. When the method's body executes a `yield`, Ruby executes the statement (or statements) inside the block.

The following code illustrates Ruby's `each` method. When applied to an array, the `each` method executes `yield` once for every array element.

```
puts __FILE__

class Stooge
  @@note = 'A'

  def sing_hello
    @@note.succ!.succ!
    print "Hello... ", @@note, "  "
  end

 end

stooges = [Stooge.new, Stooge.new, Stooge.new]

stooges.each { |stooge| stooge.sing_hello }
```

This program's output is

```
C:/Users/bburd/user/PartOfTensExamples/blockheads.rb
Hello... C  Hello... E  Hello... G
```

This program illustrates a few additional Ruby tricks:

- The keyword `__FILE__` stands for the name of the file containing the code.
- A variable that begins with `@@` is a *class variable.* No matter how many (or how few) instances you create, a class has only one copy of a particular class variable.
- The successor (`succ!`) method adds 1 to a string. The strange thing about `succ!` is that the method does circular addition with carrying, working from right to left. So `'ACE'.succ!` is `'ACF'`, and `'ACZ'.succ!` is `'ADA'`.

For more about blocks, see Chapter 5.

Everything Is an Object

Well, almost everything is an object. At least, things that aren't objects in many other languages are objects in Ruby. A number (such as `42`) is an object, and a class is an object. (In fact, the `new` method belongs to each class.) Methods, and even arrays of methods, are objects.

To make things even more bizarre, every object has a `class` method. Calling the `class` method gives you the class of which that object is an instance. For example, the output of the following program is `Fixnum Class MyClass NilClass Array`.

```
class MyClass
  def my_method
  end
end

a_class = MyClass
an_object = MyClass.new
a_method = an_object.my_method

print 42.class, " "
print a_class.class, " "
print an_object.class, " "
print a_method.class, " "
print a_method.methods.class
```

For more about numbers' being objects, see Chapter 6.

Objects Might Have Their Own Methods

In the following program, both `first_object` and `second_object` have `speak` methods (because both are instances of `MyClass`), but only `first_object` has a `sing` method.

```
class MyClass
  def speak
    puts "Ruff, ruff!"
  end
end

first_object = MyClass.new
second_object = MyClass.new

def first_object.sing
  puts "Give My Regards to Broadway"
end

first_object.speak
second_object.speak
first_object.sing
second_object.sing
```

The output of this program is

```
Ruff, ruff!
Ruff, ruff!
Give My Regards to Broadway
C:/Users/bburd/user/PartOfTensExamples/more.rb:17:
undefined method 'sing' for #<MyClass:0x3932748>
(NoMethodError)
```

Mixins

A *mixin* is a module whose code you include inside another module or a class. The output of the following program is `May cause sneezing, Meat, Meow`.

```
module Allergen
  def show
    "May cause sneezing"
  end
```

```
end

class Pet
  def food
    "Meat"
  end
end

class Cat < Pet
  include Allergen
  def sound
    "Meow"
  end
end

cat = Cat.new
print cat.show, ', ', cat.food, ', ', cat.sound
```

Built-In Unit Testing

A *unit test* is code that tests a single class. The experts recommend that you write unit tests before you write the classes themselves. That way, you don't fudge the tests so that your classes pass each of the tests.

Ruby includes a unit-testing framework that's similar to other languages' frameworks. For example, the following program tests two hypotheses about Ruby's `reverse` method. If you reverse the array `[1, [2, 3], 4]`, do you get `[4, [2, 3], 1]` or `[4, [3, 2], 1]`?

```
require 'test/unit'

class TestReverse < Test::Unit::TestCase
  def setup
    @a = [1, [2, 3], 4]
    @b = @a.reverse
  end

  def test_reverse
    assert_equal([4, [2, 3], 1], @b)
    assert_equal([4, [3, 2], 1], @b)
  end

  def teardown
    puts "Done!"
  end
end
```

When you run this code, Ruby's unit-testing framework starts by calling the setup method. Then the framework calls any test methods (such as test_reverse). Finally, the framework calls teardown (to clean up after itself). The resulting output is

```
Started
FDone!

Finished in 0.02 seconds.

  1) Failure:
test_reverse(TestReverse)
[C:/Users/bburd/user/PartOfTensExamples/
test_reverse.rb:11]:
<[4, [3, 2], 1]> expected but was
<[4, [2, 3], 1]>.

1 tests, 2 assertions, 1 failures, 0 errors
```

The failure indicates that the second assert_equal call expected the value [4, [3, 2], 1]. But instead, the value of @b was [4, [2, 3], 1].

Built-In Reflection

You can easily turn a string of characters into a Ruby name or turn a Ruby name into a string of characters. One way to turn a string of characters into a method name is to use Ruby's send method.

```
my_string = "times"

3.send(my_string) { print "Hello " }
```

The output of this program is Hello Hello Hello.

For more info about reflection (and the send method in particular), see Chapters 1 and 9.

Chapter 16

Ten Pivotal Ruby on Rails Concepts

In This Chapter

- What's so good about Ruby on Rails
- What Ruby on Rails contributes to database applications
- What makes Ruby on Rails an effective tool

If you wake me up at three in the morning and ask me for the ten most important Ruby on Rails concepts, I'll probably start with Don't Repeat Yourself and Convention over Configuration. Then I'll have to think a bit. After a few minutes, I'll remember four more concepts, recite them to you, and look around to make sure the cat hasn't gotten out, the basement isn't flooded, and that no one left the freezer door open overnight.

With those concerns out of the way, I'll think of two more concepts. And eventually (after reviewing tomorrow's tasks in my mind) I'll recite two more, for a total of ten.

I'll go back to sleep mumbling one question to myself. "Why don't I write all ten of those concepts in one place? If I do, the reader doesn't have to wake me at three in the morning."

So I'll add one item to the list of things I plan to do tomorrow.

Don't Repeat Yourself (DRY)

Any particular piece of information about an application should be housed in only one place. The information should not be replicated throughout the application. Duplication of information is inefficient and error-prone. With a piece of information in one part of an application, all other parts of the application should consult that one, authoritative part of the code.

For more of my DRY humor, see Chapters 1, 8, and 9.

Convention over Configuration

A developer doesn't need total flexibility in naming all parts of an application. Sure, it's fun to name a controller `DonaldTrump` and name the model `CindyCrawford`. But if you stick with some simple naming conventions, everyone's life is easy. Name the controller `ThingsController`, and name the model `Thing`. Then you don't need a configuration file — a file in which you associate the controller name `DonaldTrump` with the model name `CindyCrawford`.

For more of my nagging about convention over configuration, see Chapters 1 and 8.

Model/View/Controller (MVC)

Separate the code that processes data from the code that displays the data. Why should you separate these two parts of the code? You separate them because the processing of data and the display of data are completely different kinds of problems. One problem has little to do with the other. Thinking about both problems at once gets you tangled in unnecessary complexities.

Also, if you separate the two problems, you can easily change the solution to one problem without upsetting the solution to the other problem. Do you want to switch from a desktop browser to a mobile phone's browser? If so, you can do it. You can modify the view without changing the model's code.

For an intimate look at the Model/View/Controller structure, see Chapter 8.

Agile Development

The worth of a software project isn't measured by the thickness of the project's planning documents. Emphasize results, not formalities. Plan frequent milestones in the development lifecycle. Build prototypes and test them often. Consult users regularly during the development process. Embrace change.

To read other inspiring sentences about agile development, see Chapter 1.

Dynamic Discovery of a Database's Characteristics

A database speaks for itself. You don't need a separate piece of code describing the database. Let an application dig into the database and automatically discover the names and types of the database table's columns. Have the application determine the database's characteristics at runtime. If you do, you can modify the database between runs of the application.

In Ruby on Rails, the name for this dynamic discovery trick is *Active Record.* You can read more about Active Record in Chapter 9.

Object-Relational Mapping (ORM)

The ORM concept isn't unique to Ruby on Rails. Many software frameworks use object-relational mapping in one form or another.

Here's how ORM works: On one side, you have a database table's row. On the other side, you have a piece of code (Ruby code, Java code, or whatever). The code instantiates an object — an object with variables that have values. The essence of object-relational mapping is to have the object's values correspond to the values in the database table's row. If a row has columns `name`, `address`, and `phone`, the code has variables `@name`, `@address`, and `@phone`. To top it all off, some standard, one-size-fits-all piece of code keeps the database columns and the object's values synchronized. The programmer doesn't worry about the boring, repetitive synchronization task.

A database row's values are an application's reason for being. And an object within the computer program can perform *business logic* (can do what needs to be done with the row's values). Using ORM, the programmer thinks only about the business logic. The ORM strategy effectively separates business logic from the mechanics of synchronizing the object and the database.

For more about object-relational mapping, see Chapter 9.

Using Generators

Do you need a controller? If so, don't write the controller code from scratch. Instead, run a generator that creates the code automatically.

What about a database table? Do you want a new table? Then generate some migration code. And while you generate things, create a scaffold.

A generated model and a scaffold form a simple but complete application. Naturally, you want to customize the application. But the generated code makes a great prototype.

For the first word on generators, see Chapters 3 and 4.

Create, Read, Update, and Delete (CRUD)

Someone who was in a very bad mood decided on the name CRUD for the four fundamental database operations. Every database application implements these four operations. Other operations (searching, for example) are combinations of the CRUD operations. Still other operations (such as credit card processing) are exotic combinations of combinations of combinations of CRUD operations.

With its cool scaffolding, Rails elevates CRUD to new heights. For more CRUD, see Chapters 3 and 9.

Using Migrations

Migrations have advantages and disadvantages. On the good side, you can use the same migration code with different kinds of databases. If you change from a MySQL database to a Postgres database, you can reuse the migration code. Migrations also provide a decent versioning system.

But versioning can be tricky, and migrations don't do enough to enforce good versioning practices. You can easily clash with another person doing a migration. (Nothing prevents you from giving your migration the same version number as another person's migration.) And rolling back a migration can make trouble for your Rails code.

Of course, you can ignore the pros and cons and focus on the mechanics of migrations in Chapters 9 and 11.

Using Partials

A Web page for editing an item looks very much like a page for creating a new item. Both pages have fields for supplying the item's values. The Edit page shows you the existing values, and the New page doesn't. But that's the only difference. In other ways, the Edit and New pages are alike.

So why bother to reinvent the wheel by coding two different Web pages? Instead, create a reusable piece of `rhtml` code (a partial page). Then render this *partial* on both the Edit page and the New page.

Rails provides nice support for partials. The story is in Chapter 8.

Chapter 17

Ten Ways to Override Rails Defaults

In This Chapter

- Circumventing the Rails naming conventions
- Using alternative page layouts
- Moving away from the development environment

The phrase "legacy database" is a euphemism for "an old database that's difficult to connect to modern software," and for "a database that someone forces you to use."

Consider the following scenario. You have a database that someone created several years ago, before Rails was invented. Table names, primary keys, and many other aspects of the old database don't follow the Rails standard naming conventions. What can you do about it? Here are some alternatives:

- **Modify the old database so that the database uses Rails conventions.**

  This alternative involves another euphemism. The phrase "modifying an old database" actually means "asking for trouble."

- **Forget about Rails. Instead, use legacy software to access the legacy database.**

  Sure. And ten years from now, you think about replacing the Commodore 64 that you bought in 1982. No! Wait! Maybe someone still writes software updates for the Commodore 64.

- **Use Rails and override some Rails conventions so that Rails accesses the legacy database.**

  That's a good choice.

Strangely enough, I need to establish some of my own conventions for this chapter's examples.

- **In each example, I assume that you start with a new Rails project.**

  You can combine two or more of this chapter's tricks into one project. But if you're not careful about combining tricks, you can easily become confused. So start with a fresh project for each of this chapter's examples.

  For details on creating a Rails project, see Chapter 3.

- **If you have a model, I assume that the model's name is `Thing`.**

  See Chapter 3 for specifics on creating models.

- **If an example requires you to create a database table, you can create a one-column database table.**

  Just delete the pound sign in the Rails-generated migration file. You get a column whose name is `name` and whose type is `string`. (Actually, you get two columns — an `id` column and a `name` column. But the `name` column is the only content column. See Chapter 9.)

  For info about migrations and creating database tables, see Chapter 3.

Overriding the Database Name

To use an alternative database name, change the `development: . . . database:` name in the project's `config\database.yml` file. More specifically, do the following:

1. **Create a new Rails project as in Chapter 3.**
2. **Double-click the `database.yml` file on your project's `config` branch in the Rails Navigator view.**

   The `database.yml` file opens in a RadRails editor. The file's content is divided into three sections. The sections' names are `development`, `test`, and `production`. Each section has lines labeled `adapter`, `database`, `username`, `password`, and `host`. (See Figure 17-1.)
3. **In the `database.yml` file's development section, replace the name in the `database` entry (*`blah_blah`*`_development`, or whatever) with your database's actual name.**

   Again, see Figure 17-1.

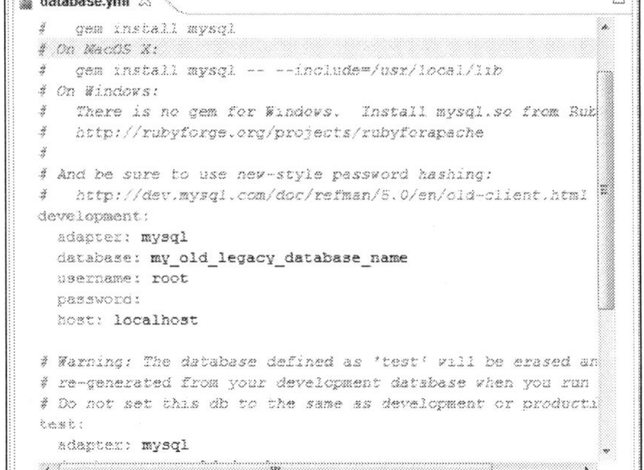

database.yml
gem install mysql
On MacOS X:
gem install mysql -- --include=/usr/local/lib
On Windows:
There is no gem for Windows. Install mysql.so from Rub
http://rubyforge.org/projects/rubyforapache
#
And be sure to use new-style password hashing:
http://dev.mysql.com/doc/refman/5.0/en/old-client.html
development:
  adapter: mysql
  database: my_old_legacy_database_name
  username: root
  password:
  host: localhost
Warning: The database defined as 'test' will be erased an
re-generated from your development database when you run
Do not set this db to the same as development or producti
test:
  adapter: mysql

Figure 17-1: Overriding the Rails database naming convention.

The steps in this section change what Rails expects to find on your system. But the steps don't change an existing database's name. You must have a database with the alternative name on your system (on a hard drive, a network drive, or somewhere else that's accessible by Rails). When you experiment with this section's steps, you can use MySQL Administrator to create a database with a particular name. But to use a legacy database, you must copy the database to a place where Rails can access it.

In the filename `database.yml`, the letters `yml` stand for *YAML,* which in turn stands for either "Yet Another Markup Language" or "YAML Ain't Markup Language" (depending on whom you ask). One way or another, YAML is a language for storing small amounts of data. In this example, the `database.yml` file stores some configuration information. For more information on YAML, visit `www.yaml.org`.

Overriding a Database Table Name

To override a table name, add a call to method `set_table_name` in the model. The details follow:

1. **Double-click the `thing.rb` file on your project's `app\models` branch in the Rails Navigator view.**

   Remember, in many of this chapter's examples, I assume that your project has a model named `Thing`.

   The `thing.rb` file opens in a RadRails editor.

2. **In the RadRails editor, add one line to the `Thing` class (the bold line in Listing 17-1).**

Listing 17-1: Setting a Table Name

```
class Thing < ActiveRecord::Base
  set_table_name 'your_different_name'
end
```

3. **Double-click the `001_create_things.rb` migration file on your project's `db\migrate` branch in the Rails Navigator view.**

   The `001_create_things.rb` file opens in a RadRails editor.

4. **In the RadRails editor, change the table names. (See Listing 17-2.)**

Listing 17-2: Changing the Table Name in the Migration File

```
class CreateThings < ActiveRecord::Migration
  def self.up
    create_table :your_different_name do |t|
      t.column :name, :string
    end
  end

  def self.down
    drop_table :your_different_name
  end
end
```

5. **In the Rake Tasks view, run `db:migrate`.**

   For details, see Chapter 3.

6. **In the Generators view, generate a `Thing` controller.**

   For details on generating a controller, jump to Chapter 4. Do not pass Go. Do not collect $200.

7. **Double-click the `thing_controller.rb` file on your project's `app\controllers` branch in the Rails Navigator view.**

   The `thing_controller.rb` file opens in a RadRails editor.

8. **In the RadRails editor, add a line of code to the controller. (Add the bold line in Listing 17-3.)**

Listing 17-3: Using a Method Call to Create a Scaffold

```
class ThingController < ApplicationController
  scaffold :thing
end
```

In this example, you don't use the Rails Generators view to create a scaffold. Instead, you add a call to the Rails `scaffold` method inside the controller's code.

9. **Visit `http://localhost:300x/thing`.**

   For details, see Chapters 4 and 8.

When you create a scaffold by using the technique in Step 8, the word that you add to the `localhost:300x` URL is singular. In Step 9, you visit `http://localhost:300x/thing`, and not `http://localhost:300x/things`.

The Rails migration library has a `rename_table` method. Check it out!

Overriding a Controller Name

Overriding a controller name isn't complicated. Do all the stuff you normally do to create a full-blown Rails project. (See Chapter 3.) However, make two small changes:

1. **When you create a scaffold by using the Generators view, type two words in the text field on the right. Type the name of the model followed by the name of the controller. (See Figure 17-2.)**

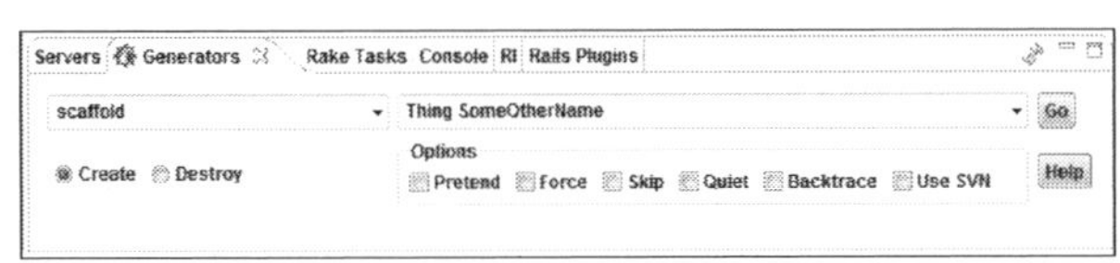

Figure 17-2: Creating a scaffold with an unconventional controller name.

When you click the Generator view's Go button, RadRails creates the usual scaffold code. RadRails also creates a controller file named *some_other_name*`_controller.rb`. This new controller file defines the *SomeOtherName*`Controller` class.

2. **When you open your Web browser, visit `http://localhost:300x/`*`some_other_name`*.**

Overriding the Name of a Table's Primary Key

You want a database table with a primary key whose name isn't `id` (the Rails default). To make this happen, do what you normally do to create a Rails project (as in Chapter 3), but modify the migration file. Also, tell your Rails model about the primary key's name. Here's how:

1. **In a RadRails editor, add a `primary_key` option to the project's migration file. (See Listing 17-4.)**

Listing 17-4: Explicitly Naming the Primary Key

```
class CreateThings < ActiveRecord::Migration
  def self.up
    create_table :things,
        :primary_key => 'legacy_key_name' do |t|
      t.column :name, :string
    end
  end

  def self.down
    drop_table :things
  end
end
```

For details on migration files, see Chapter 3.

2. **Open the model file (`app\models\thing.rb`, for example) in a RadRails editor. In the editor, add a `set_primary_key` call to the model. (See Listing 17-5.)**

Listing 17-5: Informing the Model about the Primary Key's Name

```
class Thing < ActiveRecord::Base
  set_primary_key 'legacy_key_name'

  def legacy_key_name_before_type_cast
  end
end
```

Listing 17-5 sets the primary key's name and defines a method named `legacy_key_name_before_type_cast`. The method's body contains no statements. But if you don't define the method, you get a big, fat error message when you try to visit the application's New Thing page.

When you visit this application's New Thing page, you see a text field that you don't normally see. In particular, Figure 17-3 has a text field for the Legacy Key Name (the database table's primary key).

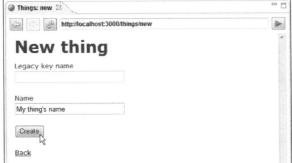

Figure 17-3: Adding a new row to the database table.

By default, the database auto-increments the primary key's value. So, the first time you visit the New Thing page and click the Create button, the database puts 1 in the new row's `legacy_key_name` column. The second time around, the database puts 2 in the new row's `legacy_key_name` column. And so on. This auto-increment operation overrides any value that you type in the Legacy Key Name field in Figure 17-3.

You can rid yourself of the useless Legacy Key Name field in Figure 17-3. To do so, open the project's `app\views\things\_form.rhtml` file in a RadRails editor. Then delete two lines in this file — the line that creates a `legacy_key_name` label, and the line that creates a `legacy_key_name` text field.

Using Singular Nouns

If you've worked through some of this book's examples, you might have noticed a Disable Table Pluralization option in the New Rails Project wizard. (On the other hand, if you're as oblivious to infrequently used features as I am, you haven't noticed this option.) One way or another, look at Figure 17-4.

When you select the Disable Table Pluralization option, RadRails adds a line of code to your project's `config\environment.rb` file.

```
ActiveRecord::Base.pluralize_table_names = false
```

This line forces table names to be the same as model names (with the usual differences in capitalization). Later, when you create a migration within this project, the generated file contains a singular table name. (See Listing 17-6.)

Listing 17-6: Changing the Table Name in the Migration File

```
class CreateThings < ActiveRecord::Migration
  def self.up
    create_table :thing do |t|
      t.column :name, :string
    end
  end

  def self.down
    drop_table :thing
  end
end
```

From that point on, your work on the project looks exactly like the work in Chapter 3. (. . . Well, your work looks *almost exactly* like the work in Chapter 3. Because the database table's name is `thing` [singular], you must visit `http://localhost:300x/thing` [singular] to use this project's Web pages.)

Figure 17-4: The New Rails Project wizard.

Creating Irregular Plurals

When it comes to creating plural nouns, Rails is pretty smart. If you create a model named `Person`, Rails creates a table named `people`. If you create a model named `Sheep`, Rails creates a table named `sheep`. (I guess the plural of *sheep* comes up often in database programming. Maybe a large number of Rails developers are sheep farmers!)

Alas, if you create a model named `Foot`, Rails gets the plural wrong with a table named `foots`. (So few Rails developers are podiatrists.) To prevent this *foots* problem, do the following:

1. **Start creating a new Rails project (as in Chapter 3). Stop before you create a model.**
2. **Use MySQL to create a database for your project.**

   Again, see Chapter 3.
3. **Double-click the `environment.rb` file on your project's `config` branch in the Rails Navigator view.**

   The `environment.rb` file opens in a RadRails editor. The file contains many commented lines (lines starting with pound signs).
4. **In the RadRails editor, uncomment the line `Inflector.inflections do |inflect|` and the corresponding `end` line. Then type an `inflect.irregular` line, as shown in Listing 17-7.**

Listing 17-7: Educating Rails about Plural Nouns

```
Inflector.inflections do |inflect|
#   inflect.plural /^(ox)$/i, '\1en'
#   inflect.singular /^(ox)en/i, '\1'
#   inflect.irregular 'person', 'people'
    inflect.irregular 'foot', 'feet'
#   inflect.uncountable %w( fish sheep )
 end
```

5. **Using the RadRails Generators view, create a model named `Foot`. (For details, see Chapter 3.)**

   Rails generates a migration file named `001_create_feet.rb` to create a table named `feet`.
6. **Proceed as in Chapter 3 to migrate the `feet` table, generate a `Foot` scaffold, and do all that other good stuff.**

   To visit this project's Web site, type **http://localhost:300*x*/feet** in the Web browser's Address field.

This section's trick doesn't always get you off the hook. For example, I added the following line to a project's `config\environment.rb` file:

```
inflect.irregular 'mother_in_law', 'mothers_in_law'
```

When I generated a `Mother_in_law` model, Rails created a file named `001_create_mothers_in_law.rb` (good). The file's `self.up` method used the correct pluralization `create_table :mothers_in_law` (also good). But the migration file started with the words `class CreateMotherInLaws` (bad). When I tried to run the migration, Rails gave me an error message. "Uninitialized constant `CreateMothersInLaw`," said old Mr. Rake. So I manually edited the first line of the `001_create_mothers_in_law.rb` file. I changed the start of the line to `class CreateMothersInLaw`. Thereafter, everything went smoothly. (P.S. To visit the project's Web site, I typed **http://localhost:300x/mothers_in_law** in the Web browser's Address field.)

Overriding a Default Layout

Chapter 8 describes the use of layouts in Ruby on Rails. By default, a layout's name is the same as the model's pluralized name. For example, a layout for the `Thing` scaffold is named `things.rhtml`.

But you can use a different layout, and you don't have to rename `things.rhtml`. (You can use the `things.rhtml` layout for testing with Internet Explorer, and use another layout, `alternative.rhtml`, for testing with Mozilla Firefox. Or use one layout for desktop browsers and another for mobile phone browsers.)

Here's how you tell Rails to use a layout with a nonstandard name:

1. **Create a Rails project, as in Chapter 3.**
2. **Right-click your project's `app\views\layouts` branch in the Rails Navigator view. In the resulting contextual menu, choose New⇨File.**

   A New File dialog box appears.
3. **In the File Name field of the New File dialog box, type** alternative.rhtml **(or** *some_other_name*.rhtml**). Then press Enter.**

   A blank editor opens in the center of the RadRails workbench.
4. **In the RadRails editor, type the code for your alternative layout.**

   If you want to try this section's steps, but you don't know what to type, try typing the code in Listing 17-8.

Listing 17-8: A Simple Layout

```
<h3>Look! I created an alternative layout!</h3>

<%= yield  %>

<p>&copy; 2006 My Company
```

In Listing 17-8, the `yield` statement does what it does in any Ruby program — it executes a block associated with the sending code. (If you don't understand this gobbledygook about sending code, have a look at Chapter 5.)

5. **Double-click the `things_controller.rb` file on your project's `app\controllers` branch.**

   The `things_controller.rb` file opens in a RadRails editor.

6. **Near the top of the `things_controller.rb` file, add a call to the Rails `layout` method. (See Listing 17-9.)**

Listing 17-9: Telling Rails to Use an Alternative Layout

```
class ThingsController < ApplicationController
  layout "alternative"

  # Etc. ...
```

7. **Run the application the way you run other Rails applications.**

   Each page of the application uses your alternative layout. (Figure 17-5 shows the application's New Thing page.)

You can create as many different layout files as you need. To switch from one layout to another, change the second line in Listing 17-9.

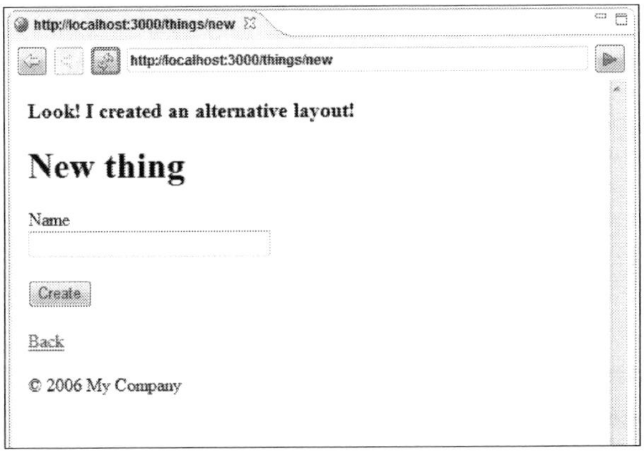

Figure 17-5: The New Thing page uses your alternative layout.

Creating Additional Web Pages

The familiar Rails Welcome page is stored in the `index.html` file in your application's `public` directory. You can modify this file, but you can also create a different Welcome page for each model in your project. Here's how you create a Welcome page for a model named `Thing`:

1. **Right-click your project's `app\views\things` branch in the Rails Navigator view. In the resulting contextual menu, choose New⇨File.**

   A New File dialog box appears.

2. **In the File Name field of the New File dialog box, type** index.rhtml. **Then press Enter.**

   A blank editor opens in the center of the RadRails workbench.

3. **In the RadRails editor, type the code for your new Welcome page.**

   Your Web browser can display just about anything you type in the new Welcome page. But if you're a compulsive person and you want the browser to display something reasonable, try typing the code in Listing 17-10.

Listing 17-10: A Simple Welcome Page

```
<h1>Main Menu</h1>

<%= link_to 'List', :action => 'list' %> |
<%= link_to 'New', :action => 'new' %>
```

4. **Visit `http://localhost:300x/things`.**

   When you do, your Web browser displays a page like the one in Figure 17-6.

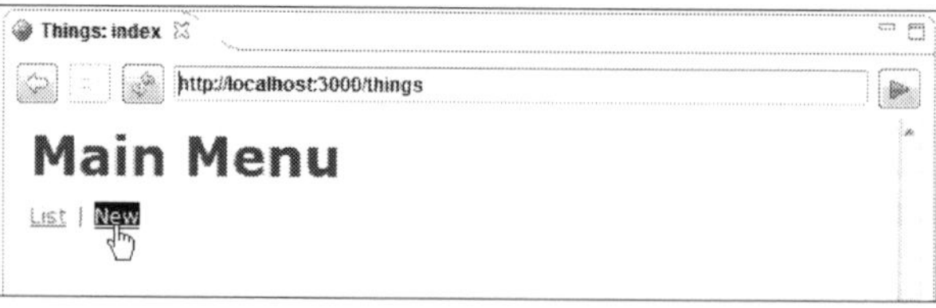

Figure 17-6: Visiting your alternative Welcome page.

Life doesn't have to stop after you create an `index` page. You can add several pages for a particular model. For example, to create a Help page, add a `help.rhtml` file to your project's `app\views\things` directory. Then, to see the Help page in your browser, visit `http://localhost:300x/things/help`.

Modifying the Meanings of URLs

Normally, you type **http://localhost:300*x*/things** to visit an application's Listing Things page. But in some cases, you might want to change the Listing Things page's URL (or the URL for some other page). Here's how you can do it:

1. **Double-click the `routes.rb` file on the project's `config` branch in the Rails Navigator view.**

   The `routes.rb` file opens in a RadRails editor.

2. **In the RadRails editor, add a call to the Rails `connect` method (the bold code in Listing 17-11).**

Listing 17-11: Specifying a Default Page

```
ActionController::Routing::Routes.draw do |map|
  map.connect 'things', :controller => 'things',
                        :action => 'new'

  # Etc. ...
```

   This call to `connect` tells the server to respond with the `things` controller's `new` page when a visitor types `http://localhost:300x/things` in the browser's Address field.

You can do all kinds of neat tricks with the Rails `connect` method. For example, you might be tired of typing the word `things` in `http://localhost:300x/things`. (Life's tough, isn't it?) To avoid typing the extra word `things`, add another call to the Rails `connect` method (the bold code in Listing 17-12).

Listing 17-12: Specifying a Default Controller

```
ActionController::Routing::Routes.draw do |map|
  map.connect '', :controller => 'things'

  # Etc. ...
```

Then, when you visit `http://localhost:300x` (without the extra word `things`), the server responds with the Listing Things page.

Changing the Server Environment

The typical software lifecycle has three phases — development, testing, and production.

- In the **development phase,** you create code.
- In the **testing phase,** you test the code. (Then you return to the development phase because testing highlights the code's deficiencies.)
- In the **production phase,** you run the code. People visit your Web site, buy things, add comments, share photos, or whatever.

You perform different tasks during each phase of the lifecycle. For example, in the testing phase, you might run special programs called *unit tests.* (For a word or two about unit tests, see Chapter 15.) One way or another, you use different databases during each phase.

- In development, you use a small "toy" database.
- In testing, you try to challenge your software's correctness using a larger database. But you don't use live data. (You don't want to change a real customer's account balance while you check your application's correctness.)
- In production, you use a real database containing live data.

By default, a new Rails project runs in development mode. The application server does the kinds of things a server does in development mode, and Rails uses a database named `whatever_development`. You can change to a different mode with the following steps:

1. **Start creating a new Rails project and a model (as in Chapter 3). Stop before you create a database.**
2. **Using MySQL Administrator, create a database named `something_production`.**

   For example, if your project is named `album`, the database name is `album_production`. For details on creating a database with MySQL Administrator, see Chapter 3.
3. **In the RadRails Servers view, select the server belonging to the project you created in Step 1. Then click the Servers view's Edit button, as shown in Figure 17-7.**

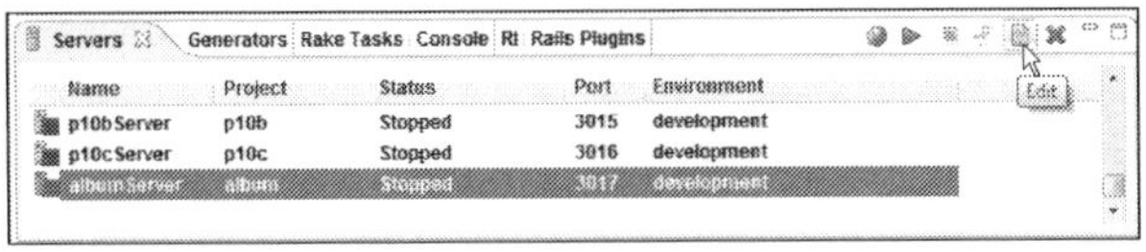

Figure 17-7: Finding the Servers view's Edit button.

When you click the Edit button, RadRails displays a small Server Properties dialog box.

4. **In the dialog box's Environment drop-down list, select Production. Then click OK.**

   See Figure 17-8.

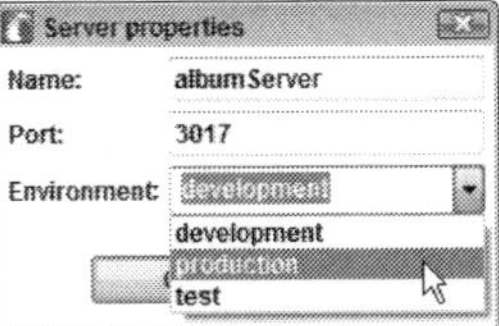

Figure 17-8: Selecting the server's production mode.

5. **Perform a database migration, as in Chapter 3. But in this example, type** RAILS_ENV=production **in the text field on the right side of the Rake Tasks view. (See Figure 17-9.)**

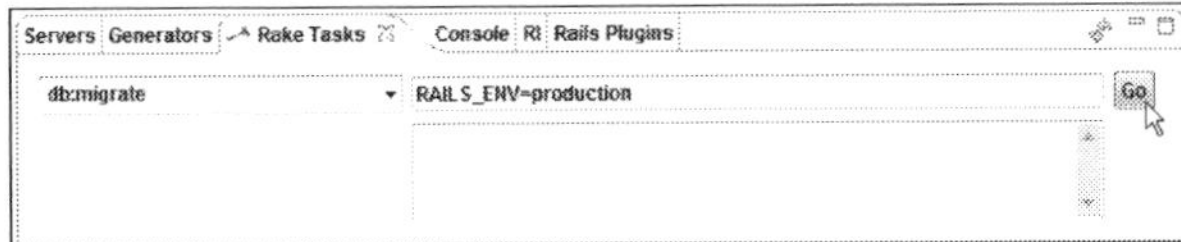

Figure 17-9: Migrating the production database.

6. **In the RadRails Generators view, generate a `Thing` controller.**

   For details, see Chapter 4.

   From this point onward, you break from standard practice. Rails aficionados discourage the use of scaffolds in the production environment. But to move this example forward, you can create a scaffold (just this once).

7. **Double-click the `thing_controller.rb` file on your project's `app\controllers` branch in the Rails Navigator view.**

   The `thing_controller.rb` file opens in a RadRails editor.

8. **In the RadRails editor, add a line of code to the controller. (Add the bold line you can see back in Listing 17-3.)**

9. **Visit `http://localhost:300x/thing`. (That's `thing`, singular; not `things`, plural.)**

   Once again, your application runs like a charm.

Index

• Symbols •

• A •

• D •

• E •

• F •

• N •

• O •

• P •

• Q •

• R •

• S •

• T •

• U •

• W •

BUSINESS, CAREERS & PERSONAL FINANCE

0-7645-9847-3

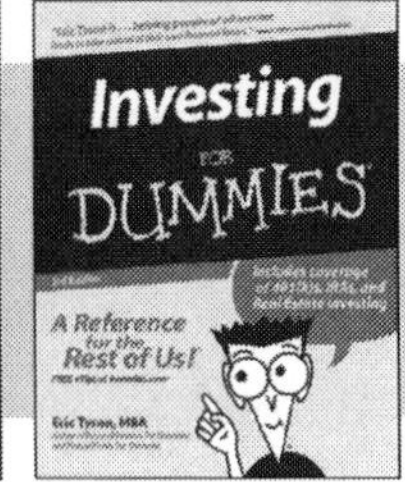

0-7645-2431-3

Also available:

- Business Plans Kit For Dummies 0-7645-9794-9
- Economics For Dummies 0-7645-5726-2
- Grant Writing For Dummies 0-7645-8416-2
- Home Buying For Dummies 0-7645-5331-3
- Managing For Dummies 0-7645-1771-6
- Marketing For Dummies 0-7645-5600-2
- Personal Finance For Dummies 0-7645-2590-5*
- Resumes For Dummies 0-7645-5471-9
- Selling For Dummies 0-7645-5363-1
- Six Sigma For Dummies 0-7645-6798-5
- Small Business Kit For Dummies 0-7645-5984-2
- Starting an eBay Business For Dummies 0-7645-6924-4
- Your Dream Career For Dummies 0-7645-9795-7

HOME & BUSINESS COMPUTER BASICS

0-470-05432-8

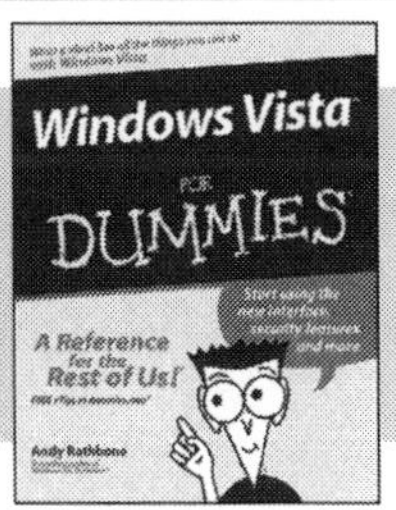

0-471-75421-8

Also available:

- Cleaning Windows Vista For Dummies 0-471-78293-9
- Excel 2007 For Dummies 0-470-03737-7
- Mac OS X Tiger For Dummies 0-7645-7675-5
- MacBook For Dummies 0-470-04859-X
- Macs For Dummies 0-470-04849-2
- Office 2007 For Dummies 0-470-00923-3
- Outlook 2007 For Dummies 0-470-03830-6
- PCs For Dummies 0-7645-8958-X
- Salesforce.com For Dummies 0-470-04893-X
- Upgrading & Fixing Laptops For Dummies 0-7645-8959-8
- Word 2007 For Dummies 0-470-03658-3
- Quicken 2007 For Dummies 0-470-04600-7

FOOD, HOME, GARDEN, HOBBIES, MUSIC & PETS

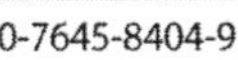

0-7645-8404-9

0-7645-9904-6

Also available:

- Candy Making For Dummies 0-7645-9734-5
- Card Games For Dummies 0-7645-9910-0
- Crocheting For Dummies 0-7645-4151-X
- Dog Training For Dummies 0-7645-8418-9
- Healthy Carb Cookbook For Dummies 0-7645-8476-6
- Home Maintenance For Dummies 0-7645-5215-5
- Horses For Dummies 0-7645-9797-3
- Jewelry Making & Beading For Dummies 0-7645-2571-9
- Orchids For Dummies 0-7645-6759-4
- Puppies For Dummies 0-7645-5255-4
- Rock Guitar For Dummies 0-7645-5356-9
- Sewing For Dummies 0-7645-6847-7
- Singing For Dummies 0-7645-2475-5

INTERNET & DIGITAL MEDIA

0-470-04529-9

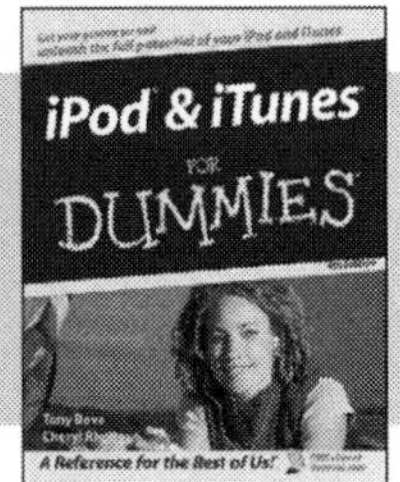

0-470-04894-8

Also available:

- Blogging For Dummies 0-471-77084-1
- Digital Photography For Dummies 0-7645-9802-3
- Digital Photography All-in-One Desk Reference For Dummies 0-470-03743-1
- Digital SLR Cameras and Photography For Dummies 0-7645-9803-1
- eBay Business All-in-One Desk Reference For Dummies 0-7645-8438-3
- HDTV For Dummies 0-470-09673-X
- Home Entertainment PCs For Dummies 0-470-05523-5
- MySpace For Dummies 0-470-09529-6
- Search Engine Optimization For Dummies 0-471-97998-8
- Skype For Dummies 0-470-04891-3
- The Internet For Dummies 0-7645-8996-2
- Wiring Your Digital Home For Dummies 0-471-91830-X

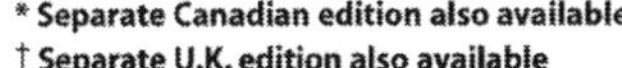

*** Separate Canadian edition also available**
† Separate U.K. edition also available

Available wherever books are sold. For more information or to order direct: U.S. customers visit www.dummies.com or call 1-877-762-2974. U.K. customers visit www.wileyeurope.com or call 0800 243407. Canadian customers visit www.wiley.ca or call 1-800-567-4797.

SPORTS, FITNESS, PARENTING, RELIGION & SPIRITUALITY

0-471-76871-5

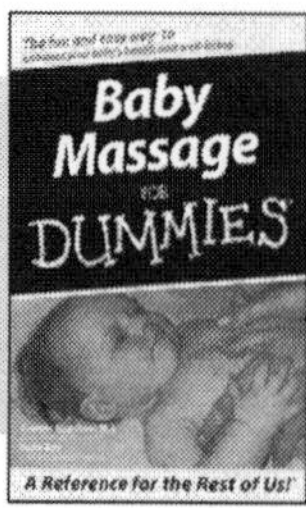

0-7645-7841-3

Also available:

- Catholicism For Dummies 0-7645-5391-7
- Exercise Balls For Dummies 0-7645-5623-1
- Fitness For Dummies 0-7645-7851-0
- Football For Dummies 0-7645-3936-1
- Judaism For Dummies 0-7645-5299-6
- Potty Training For Dummies 0-7645-5417-4
- Buddhism For Dummies 0-7645-5359-3
- Pregnancy For Dummies 0-7645-4483-7 †
- Ten Minute Tone-Ups For Dummies 0-7645-7207-5
- NASCAR For Dummies 0-7645-7681-X
- Religion For Dummies 0-7645-5264-3
- Soccer For Dummies 0-7645-5229-5
- Women in the Bible For Dummies 0-7645-8475-8

TRAVEL

0-7645-7749-2

0-7645-6945-7

Also available:

- Alaska For Dummies 0-7645-7746-8
- Cruise Vacations For Dummies 0-7645-6941-4
- England For Dummies 0-7645-4276-1
- Europe For Dummies 0-7645-7529-5
- Germany For Dummies 0-7645-7823-5
- Hawaii For Dummies 0-7645-7402-7
- Italy For Dummies 0-7645-7386-1
- Las Vegas For Dummies 0-7645-7382-9
- London For Dummies 0-7645-4277-X
- Paris For Dummies 0-7645-7630-5
- RV Vacations For Dummies 0-7645-4442-X
- Walt Disney World & Orlando For Dummies 0-7645-9660-8

GRAPHICS, DESIGN & WEB DEVELOPMENT

0-7645-8815-X

0-7645-9571-7

Also available:

- 3D Game Animation For Dummies 0-7645-8789-7
- AutoCAD 2006 For Dummies 0-7645-8925-3
- Building a Web Site For Dummies 0-7645-7144-3
- Creating Web Pages For Dummies 0-470-08030-2
- Creating Web Pages All-in-One Desk Reference For Dummies 0-7645-4345-8
- Dreamweaver 8 For Dummies 0-7645-9649-7
- InDesign CS2 For Dummies 0-7645-9572-5
- Macromedia Flash 8 For Dummies 0-7645-9691-8
- Photoshop CS2 and Digital Photography For Dummies 0-7645-9580-6
- Photoshop Elements 4 For Dummies 0-471-77483-9
- Syndicating Web Sites with RSS Feeds For Dummies 0-7645-8848-6
- Yahoo! SiteBuilder For Dummies 0-7645-9800-7

NETWORKING, SECURITY, PROGRAMMING & DATABASES

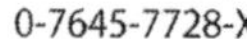

0-7645-7728-X

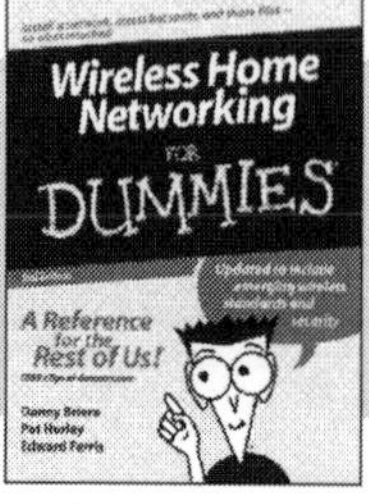

0-471-74940-0

Also available:

- Access 2007 For Dummies 0-470-04612-0
- ASP.NET 2 For Dummies 0-7645-7907-X
- C# 2005 For Dummies 0-7645-9704-3
- Hacking For Dummies 0-470-05235-X
- Hacking Wireless Networks For Dummies 0-7645-9730-2
- Java For Dummies 0-470-08716-1
- Microsoft SQL Server 2005 For Dummies 0-7645-7755-7
- Networking All-in-One Desk Reference For Dummies 0-7645-9939-9
- Preventing Identity Theft For Dummies 0-7645-7336-5
- Telecom For Dummies 0-471-77085-X
- Visual Studio 2005 All-in-One Desk Reference For Dummies 0-7645-9775-2
- XML For Dummies 0-7645-8845-1

HEALTH & SELF-HELP

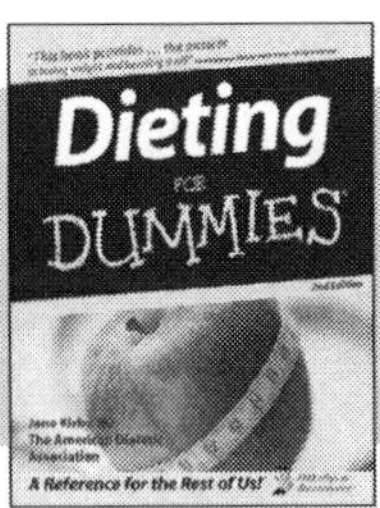

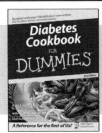

0-7645-8450-2 0-7645-4149-8

Also available:

- Bipolar Disorder For Dummies 0-7645-8451-0
- Chemotherapy and Radiation For Dummies 0-7645-7832-4
- Controlling Cholesterol For Dummies 0-7645-5440-9
- Diabetes For Dummies 0-7645-6820-5* †
- Divorce For Dummies 0-7645-8417-0 †
- Fibromyalgia For Dummies 0-7645-5441-7
- Low-Calorie Dieting For Dummies 0-7645-9905-4
- Meditation For Dummies 0-471-77774-9
- Osteoporosis For Dummies 0-7645-7621-6
- Overcoming Anxiety For Dummies 0-7645-5447-6
- Reiki For Dummies 0-7645-9907-0
- Stress Management For Dummies 0-7645-5144-2

EDUCATION, HISTORY, REFERENCE & TEST PREPARATION

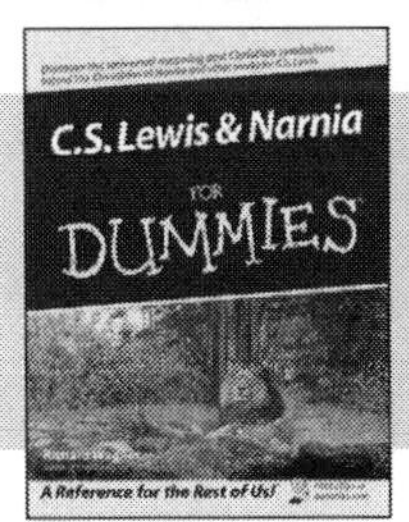

0-7645-8381-6 0-7645-9554-7

Also available:

- The ACT For Dummies 0-7645-9652-7
- Algebra For Dummies 0-7645-5325-9
- Algebra Workbook For Dummies 0-7645-8467-7
- Astronomy For Dummies 0-7645-8465-0
- Calculus For Dummies 0-7645-2498-4
- Chemistry For Dummies 0-7645-5430-1
- Forensics For Dummies 0-7645-5580-4
- Freemasons For Dummies 0-7645-9796-5
- French For Dummies 0-7645-5193-0
- Geometry For Dummies 0-7645-5324-0
- Organic Chemistry I For Dummies 0-7645-6902-3
- The SAT I For Dummies 0-7645-7193-1
- Spanish For Dummies 0-7645-5194-9
- Statistics For Dummies 0-7645-5423-9

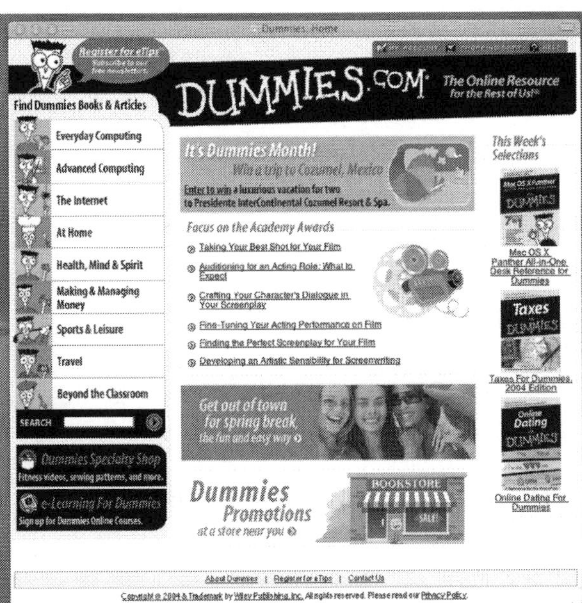

*** Separate Canadian edition also available**
† Separate U.K. edition also available

Available wherever books are sold. For more information or to order direct: U.S. customers visit www.dummies.com or call 1-877-762-2974. U.K. customers visit www.wileyeurope.com or call 0800 243407. Canadian customers visit www.wiley.ca or call 1-800-567-4797.

Notes

Notes

Notes

Notes

Notes

Notes

Notes

Notes

Printed in Great Britain
by Amazon